1930

# Nevada Youths Make First Auto Jaunt to Nicaragua

## Are First to Drive From U. S. to Central America; Cover 4562 Miles in 26 Days' Driving Time

Nev. State Journal

June 2 - 1930

Two young Nevadans, Arthur and Joseph Lyons of Winnemucca, yesterday completed what is believed to be the first automobile trip from New York to Managua, Nicaragua, using a light roadster to travel the 4562 miles in 26 days of actual driving time.

Associated Press dispatches from the Central American city, carrying the story of the Lyons brothers' fete, state that they left New York City on March 23, camping out every night, 'traveling unarmed and experiencing no trouble on the road through Mexico, Salvador, Honduras and Nicaragua."

The youths carried only the usual tourist papers and passports, and commended the hospitality of officials in the countries through which they passed, the dispatch continues.

Their small roadster made the trip on the same set of five tires, with only two punctures. The car was in good condition when they arrived, but they sold it in Managua, and will return to the United States by steamer.

The boys, 25 and 21 years of age respectively, are the sons of Assemblyman and Mrs. J. M. Lyons of Winnemucca. Arthur, who was prominent in Winnemucca 20-30 club activities, is said to have been largely responsible for Winnemucca's national publicity in sending its high school basketball team to the national tournament at Chicago in 1929, garbed in wild west attire. Both boys attended the University of Nevada. Elmer Lyons, student body president at the university in 1928-29, is their brother.

An Associated Press release about the Lyon brothers' pioneering road trip from Manhattan to Managua quickly made its way to the *Nevada State Journal* in Reno on June 2, 1930.

# 1930

Manhattan to Managua,
North America's First Transnational
Automobile Trip

by Arthur Lyon

edited and introduced by Larry Lyon
with annotations by Denis Wood
and a conclusion by Sally Denton

George F. Thompson Publishing
in association with the
American Land Publishing Project

All along the route these agencies furnished us gas free also all repair work and one time it amounted to $60.00. Ford man in New York had given us the addresses of all these agencies.

Note: This caption and all others that come from the original (1985) manuscript were written by Arthur Lyon. Unlike the main text, his captions are presented as written; that is, they are unedited, except for presenting new information in brackets (as shown on page 6) and concluding each caption with a period. Captions to new illustrations (as listed on page 31) are written by Larry Lyon.

# Contents

Joe and night watchman at Tierra Blanca [Mexico].

# Original Preface

This transcript was written by my brother, Arthur Lyon, in response to a request by Mr. E. W. James of the Bureau of Public Roads for a report on our trip to Nicaragua by automobile.[*]

There was some question originally as to who was the first to drive so far south. There were two expeditions in the 1928–1930 era. Jose Mario Barone claimed to have driven his Studebaker from Argentina to the United States, and the brothers Adam and Andrew Stroessel claim to have driven their Chevrolet over the same route. Admittedly, both shipped their cars by steamer from Columbia to Panama, and the information we got along the way indicated that they also shipped by rail where roads were non-existent.

Fifty-five years later, I am convinced that we, in our 1929 Model A Ford Roadster, were the first to traverse the whole distance under our own power. This was possible, of course, only because we were lucky enough to travel 509 miles through southern Mexico on steel rails and with steel tires.

We did suffer the ignominy of being hauled the last forty-two miles into Managua, Nicaragua, on a railroad flatcar.

The last few pages, starting on page [199], is an unedited transcript of Arthur's hand-written diary covering his hitchhiking trip on down to the Panama Canal after we parted at Managua.[†]

Joe Lyon, Jr.
April 10, 1985

---

[*] The title of the original (1985) manuscript was *Central America through a Windshield: 1930.* Edwin W. James (1877–1967) was a pioneer and mainstay at the U.S. Bureau of Public Roads (USBPR), beginning in 1910 as a fully trained road engineer. He later became General Inspector of the Office of Public Roads and Rural Engineering as well as Chief of the Division of Highway Transport for the USBPR. See "E. W. James on developing the Federal-aid system and developing the U.S. numbered highway plan," a two-part letter to Frederick W. Cron (February 21 and March 1, 1967); available online at www.fhwa.dot.gov/infrastructure/ewjames.

[†] The page number has been changed [in brackets] to reflect the current pagination.

*Lyon residence, National, Nevada*

Home of JM (Joseph McClurg) Lyon, Sr., and family in National, Nevada, 1913.
Photographer unknown.

Arthur and Joe were born in the mining camp of Pearl, Idaho, in 1904 and 1909 respectively.

In 1911, the family moved to the mining camp of National, Nevada, near McDermitt in northern Humboldt County, Nevada.

In the twenties and thirties, they were engaged in the trucking business based at McDermitt and Winnemucca, Nevada.

In 1935, they pioneered the Boise-Winnemucca Bus Line, which they operated until 1946.

—from the original manuscript (1985)

Children of JM and Inga Johnson Lyon: (left to right) Joe Jr, Eloise, Arthur, Glenn, and Kelley. Photographer, year, and location unknown.

# Introduction

*by Larry Lyon*

Soon after the death of my oldest paternal uncle, Arthur Lyon, I was asked by his former wife, my Aunt Bertha, to help her make copies of a 308-page typewritten and illustrated "transcript" that Arthur had written decades earlier. *Central America through a Windshield* was Arthur's account of the amazing journey he and his younger brother, Joe, had taken in 1930 from Manhattan to Managua in their 1929 Model A Ford Roadster. The original purpose for chronicling the trip, as my Uncle Joe wrote in his preface to the 1985 homemade manuscript, was " . . . in response to a request by Mr. E. W. James of the Bureau of Public Roads for a report on our trip to Nicaragua by automobile."

When Bertha sought my assistance in making additional copies of the book-length manuscript, several were already in existence, but she wanted a wider distribution among family and friends.* After making and distributing thirty new copies, our recognition of the richness and historical importance of the material grew, as did our idea of having the work formally published. The project met with many delays and roadblocks, including the resolution of copyright issues and demands on time. Thanks to a chance conversation with Sally Denton, my writer friend and fellow Nevadan, she encouraged me to pursue publication of the work and helped me navigate the publishing world, so that this dramatic story can finally be shared.

In order to provide a context for my two uncles' extraordinary automobile trip from Manhattan to Managua, I offer a biographical sketch of their lives. I also include some earlier family history that will not only set the stage in its time and place, but provide insight into the characters of these two adventuresome, ingenious, and enterprising men.

---

* The original (1985) typescript is in my possession. All photographs and illustrations (except for the three maps by Morgan Pfaelzer) come from the family collections of either JM and Inga Lyon or sons Arthur and Joe Jr.

My brother, Dave, and his wife, Jackie, have conducted extensive genealogical research in recent years, retrieving previously unknown and fascinating details about the family's history. Among the nuggets they found is the revelation that, in 1862, Joseph Price Lyons, the brothers' great-grandfather, and another man had been shot and killed by bushwhackers while sitting under a tree in southern Missouri, where the family was living. Irvan Lyons, Joseph Price Lyons's son and the brothers' grandfather, witnessed this killing and the killing of his older brother a few years later. Joseph McClurg "JM" Lyon, the brothers' father, had dictated to their mother, Inga Johnson Lyon, an account of the family's move west in 1889, which also mentioned that JM's maternal grandfather, William Stafford, had a business escorting wagon trains to Oregon. JM also recounted how his father, Irvan Lyons, raised cotton in Texas for two seasons during the early 1880s before returning to Missouri to run the Lyons grist mill. In 1889, when Irvan moved the family west, JM, at fourteen, was the oldest of six children. Another child was born while the family was living in Oregon.*

In JM's narrative of the trip west by covered wagon, he recalled that he had nearly died of typhoid fever. His youngest brother at the time, Lewis, succumbed to spinal meningitis. The family spent the winter of 1889–1890 in Grant's Pass, Oregon, where Irvan had a contract hauling wood for the railroad. During the next several years, the family relocated a number of times around southern Oregon and northern California. Irvan eventually moved his family to Parma, Idaho, where they camped by a river; JM initially stayed behind. After the death of Irvan's wife, he moved the family to Pearl, Idaho, a mining town north of Boise. In JM's recollections of the family's move west and events that occurred in the next few years, he mentioned that he was " . . . called back [from California] to Idaho and went to work for Lot Feltham, the lawyer, to pay back what we owed him." When Dave and Jackie questioned Uncle Arthur about the reference to his father's return to Idaho to repay the attorney, Arthur refused to elaborate. But, in the archives of the local newspapers, Dave found articles revealing that Irvan had been convicted of murdering a man who had made improper advances toward his twelve-year-old daughter and spent nearly ten years in the Idaho State Prison. Feltham had represented Irvan, who was eventually pardoned.

Clippings from the local newspaper suggested that the court would likely be merciful, considering that Irvan hailed from the South, where violence was perceived to be common. Other family members, it appeared, had also met violent ends. Court documents later retrieved by Dave showed that Irvan may have killed

---

*It is unknown as to when the family surname Lyons was shortened to Lyon, but it happened by the time that JM was born.

JM and Inga Lyon and four of their children, ca. 1912, National, Nevada.
Front row: Glenn (on JM's lap), JM, Inga, and Joe Jr. Back row: Kelly and Arthur.
Eloise is not yet born.

the wrong man, since he had shot from a distance at a man who had traded hats with the alleged perpetrator. Letters to the Board of Pardons from numerous individuals who knew Irvan and the family supported his eventual pardon. C. S. Perriu, a former warden, described Irvan as a model prisoner whom he had appointed as a trustee during his tenure at the penitentiary.

In Boise, JM met and married Inga Amelie Johnson, a native of Black River Falls, Wisconsin. The couple and their young family resided in Pearl for a number of years, where their first three children—Arthur, Kelly (my father), and Joe Jr.—were born. Their youngest son, Glenn, was born in the mining town of National, Nevada, and the only daughter, Eloise, was born in Boise. Inga's relatives, including her brothers, Otto and Timan, stayed in close contact with the family and were involved in business ventures with JM, according to family accounts. In 1910, JM and Inga moved the family to the mining town of National, where JM worked as a barber and postmaster and also became involved in gold mining. Inga served as the town's librarian, lending out issues of *National Geographic* magazine and other publications.

The National Mine was known as one of the richest, if not *the* richest, gold strike in Nevada. One version of the story of the National Mine appeared in the

November-December 1962 edition of the magazine *True West*.[*] William Whelchel reported a story he claimed that JM had told him and his brother about a Paiute Indian named "Charlie" discovering a piece of high-grade gold ore in 1906 or 1907. When Charlie showed the ore to a pair of white men, they staked claims on the site where the ore had been found and then leased small blocks of the area to others, cheating Charlie out of any profits from the discovery. The resulting mining operations produced millions of dollars' worth of rich ore. The *True West* story alleges that three men employed in the mining operations had been sent to find a source of water for the project and accidentally discovered the "Mother Lode," in the form of ". . . massive chunks of gold-saturated quartz . . ."[†] These men allegedly hid their find by dynamiting the tunnel, hoping later to return and mine the area when the main company eased restrictions on further leases.

The leader of the group, Billy Daniely, reportedly moved to Quincy, California, where he remained for the rest of his life. According to this article, JM was initially involved in some small mining leases but squabbled with some of the owners and relinquished his share. JM had been told by Daniely about his alleged bonanza. He then shared the information with Frank Stall, one of the brothers who owned a major lease in the area. Based on the information given him by JM, Stall explored the area and found what he thought was the rich vein discovered earlier by Daniely and his partners. But when winter storms suddenly set in, Stall returned to his home in California, hoping to return in the spring and mine the bonanza. Stall then died in a hunting accident. Though Daniely wrote to JM about returning to National and reclaiming his find, communication broke down, and Daniely never returned. By that time, JM had moved the family to McDermitt, Nevada, and turned his attention to other business ventures.

Numerous accounts of the National Mine exist. Roy E. Gayer, who was involved in the mining operations, told a story to Inga Lyon around 1930. Though less dramatic than the article in *True West*, Gayer's account detailed the legal and business wrangling that took place among the various individuals and companies claiming ownership of the gold-bearing veins. Many of the disputes concerned the legality of following a vein and mining it, if the vein ran in a particular direction with regard to a neighboring claim. Chicago capitalists brought a series of lawsuits, attempting to wrest control from the company formed by some of the original stakeholders. During one of the injunctions that occurred during the litigation, the company blew up the

---

[*] William E. Whelchel, "The Lost Bonanza of the Santa Rosas," *True West* (November-December 1962): 6–10 and 54.

[†] Ibid., 9.

Bird's-eye-view of National, Nevada, ca. 1914. Photographer unknown.

Winter fun in National, Nevada, ca. 1915. JM and Inga Lyon (far left) lead the long improvised sled with runners. Photographer unknown.

tunnel. The mine eventually belonged to the Chicago "bunch," as Gayer described them, and was, at the time, thought to be the second-richest gold mine in the world, with production at one point being reported as $19,000,000.

In 1915, Waldemar Lindgren prepared a bulletin for the U.S. Geological Survey that provided geographic details regarding the area around the National Mine. Lindgren's account included the history of the original prospecting and the ensuing changes in ownership, complete with lawsuits and injunctions. "The camp has had a checkered history," Lindgren wrote. "When the rich ore shoot was discovered adventurers and gamblers of all kinds flocked to National, with the usual consequences," including both pilfering and large-scale stealing of high-grade ore. Gayer also admitted to some unauthorized removal of high grade in his account. Lindgren noted that, by 1911, the production was said to have reached $4,000,000, with work then still in progress.[*]

After my uncle, Joe Lyon Jr., died in 1990, I received several inquiries from an individual who wanted to know whether I had any maps or photographs of the town of National. At that time, I had several boxes of photos and other records from Uncle Joe's home in Salt Lake City. But I had neither the time nor inclination to retrieve and examine the boxes, so I denied knowing whether or not I possessed any such items. Later, I discovered that I did indeed possess such records. I have often wondered whether the individual who contacted me, and whose name I do not recall, was hoping to gain some clues about the location of the "Lost Bonanza."

In the summer of 1918, after the mining camp died, JM and Inga moved the family from National to nearby McDermitt on the Oregon/Nevada border. Joe Jr wrote his recollections of the family's early days in McDermitt in a three-page document entitled "McDermitt Diary." Joe found the move to McDermitt to be an adventure. He wrote that, prior to the move, he had heard his father and his uncle talking about the financial opportunities available at McDermitt due to the success of the Basque sheepmen selling wool at a high wartime price and the cattlemen profiting as well. JM took over the McDermitt Garage, and the family temporarily occupied a tent-house home that the former owner had fixed up behind the garage. They soon moved into more suitable housing, and JM and his brother-in-law, Otto Johnson, built the family a home out of materials salvaged from the mercantile store in National. All the nails were saved from the store building, and Joe and his older brother, Kelly (my father), straightened the nails to be used in building the new house. According to Joe, the house, finished in 1919, was " . . . as nice a home as there was in McDermitt."

* Waldemar Lindgren, *Geology and Mining Deposits of the National Mining District, Nevada*, U.S. Department of the Interior, U.S. Geological Survey Bulletin 601 (Washington, DC: Government Printing Office, 1915), 20.

Before the national Volstead Act set prohibition in motion, Oregon, Idaho, and Washington were already "dry" states. In Joe's words from his "McDermitt Diary," the town "being on Nevada's north border, became a principal supply point for bootleggers servicing the Northwest." One result of this business was a huge pile of Old Crow bourbon boxes, which had been discarded by the bootleggers in favor of gunny sacks for ease of transporting the liquor in their cars. Several of the local boys, including Joe, stacked the boxes to form a club room. For a while, the older boys smoked and played poker in the makeshift club room, but eventually the adults decided that the empty boxes made too much of an advertisement for the illegal alcohol trade, so the boxes were soon turned into kindling. The bootleggers were good for JM's growing auto-repair business, however, as they all had cars and the money to repair them.

JM's garage business grew and eventually was named the "Lyon Super Service Station." Joe later recalled that he frequently held the light for his father in the pit below the vehicles, as JM worked on them. At night, while lying in bed waiting to go to sleep, Joe would envision the mechanical assemblies he had seen in the garage and learned how the parts fit together. JM also formed the Lyon Truck Lines, transporting cargo of all kinds. Joe and his brothers learned to drive when they were very young, occasionally driving for the Lyon Truck Lines. Over the years, they all took part in the family business, which provided financial support for their education and business ventures. They were also spending time in Boise along the way.

In his later years, Joe shared with me one experience that he believed had solidified his interest in automotive engineering and which led to his primary occupation. A local rancher sent a ranchhand to fetch JM to his home to bring back to life a car that had been sitting on blocks for some years. Over the ranchhand's objections, JM insisted that his son, Joe, who was only about twelve or so, could do the job. But, before Joe left with the hand, he was reminded of the important steps to take in preparing the car to run again. Once Joe had gotten the car ready to start, a crowd, including the rancher's family and the ranchhands, gathered around to observe the event. There was a difference of opinion between Joe and the rancher regarding the position of the spark advance/retard lever that was necessary for the car to start, due to the fact that the lettering was worn off the lever. For the first attempt, the rancher's advice was followed, and the car failed to start when a hand turned the crank. For the next attempt, the lever was in the position Joe recommended, and the motor started immediately. Onlookers cheered and threw their hats into the air.

Arthur, Joe, and their two brothers had first attended school in one-room schoolhouses in National and McDermitt. Arthur was kicked out of Elko High School

Top: Lyon Super Service Station in McDermitt, Nevada, ca.1925. Photographer unknown. The couple standing on the far left are JM and Inga Lyon; Joe Lyon, Jr. is third from the right. Others in the photograph are difficult to identify with certainty.

Bottom: Lyon Truck Line, ca.1925. Photographer and location unknown.

National, Nevada: Downtown (top) in 1911 and a one-room schoolhouse (bottom) ca. 1911. Photographers unknown.

for constructing a still in the chemistry lab, according to Bertha. He then graduated from Reno High School, thanks to the sympathy of the principal, who granted him all possible credits. He attended the University of Nevada for one year, where he practiced his writing skills and entertained his classmates in an English class by composing "hobo stories," based largely on his own adventures, and reading them to the class. In my interview of Bertha that occurred about twenty-five years ago, she commented that Arthur was a "natural accountant in his own way" and recalled that Arthur prepared his father's first income-tax return at age nineteen. Later, when he arrived in New York City, he was able to find an accounting job at a company that made airplanes (the name of which she could not recall). Joe graduated from high school in Winnemucca and then attended the University of Nevada from 1927 to 1929. He was a member of the Alpha Tau Omega fraternity and later was a member of the Society of Automotive Engineers. He would later be noted in *Who's Who in the West* from 1954 to 1956.

During the years that Arthur and Joe were growing up in National and McDermitt, Arthur's future wife, Bertha Blattner, was being raised on her father's ranch in Paradise Valley, Nevada, which lay on the other side of the mountain range from National. Bertha graduated from Humboldt County High School in Winnemucca. She then attended the University of Nevada in Reno, where she received her degree in education. She taught for two years in remote ranching areas in Nevada and at Humboldt High School in Winnemucca. In my tape-recorded interview of Bertha toward the end of her life described earlier, she said she was concerned that, if she stayed in Winnemucca, she would marry an eligible man (Arthur Lyon), which she decided against, so she instead decided to attend graduate school at Columbia University. She later met Arthur on a vacation to Chicago in the spring of 1929, and, though Arthur was ambivalent about marriage, they were married in New York City on December 3, 1929. Thus, the couple had only been married for a few months when Arthur and Joe decided to travel from Manhattan to Managua.

After the trans-continental journey was concluded and the brothers returned to McDermitt, they ran the Lyon Super Service and the Lyon Truck Lines for a period of time. Along the way, JM expanded his business ventures into oil prospects at Dry Mesa, Colorado. Arthur and Bertha then left their apartment in Greenwich Village in 1931 and headed back west. Bertha returned to Winnemucca, where she tutored Arthur and Joe's sister, Eloise, who would spend a year at Principia College. Arthur went to Dry Mesa to help with the oil-exploration project

Bertha B. Lyon with artwork by Benjamin Cunningham, a friend of Arthur and Bertha. Photographer, location, and date unknown.

and then returned to McDermitt. Together, Arthur and Bertha drove to Dry Mesa in 1934, camping along the way. This was their first time alone since being married and served as their honeymoon.

The next major project of Arthur, Joe, and Bertha was to found a transportation company that would become known as the Boise-Winnemucca Stages. In 1935, the company was called the Idaho-Nevada Stages and ran a tri-weekly service using Ford V-8 DeLuxe sedans over the I.O.N. (Idaho, Oregon, and Nevada) highway. In the early days, Arthur, Bertha, and Joe performed all of the operations of the company, including ticket sales, loading luggage, and driving. Arthur rented office space in the Boise Hotel, and Bertha, who was Vice-President of the company, remained in Winnemucca. By 1938, the company was named the Boise-Winnemucca Stages. In 1940, the company began using sixteen-passenger Crown Super Coaches, which were designed down to the last detail by Joe. The company grew and profited during World War II, providing transportation for troops traveling to and from the war. The Boise-Winnemucca Stages was then purchased in 1945 by the Achabal family, which still runs it as a charter operation.

In my interview with Bertha, two of her memories most impressed me—both related to the spirit of equality and fairness that was a hallmark of the Lyon family. During the 1940s, Arthur and Bertha owned a nice ranch-style home in Boise. One weekend, Louis Armstrong, the famed African-American musician, came to town with his band. When the word got out that the black musicians would be unable to stay in any local hotels, Arthur and Bertha volunteered their home to house the group, and, of course, they enjoyed a jam session for the rest of the night. Another brave, independent, and conscientious move by the two was to house a Japanese-American family, who would otherwise have been interned at the relocation camp located in Minidoka, Idaho, during World War II. Naturally, some members of the community criticized the couple, but Bertha's response was that it was "just that way!"

Once the Boise-Winnemucca Stages was well established, Joe turned his attention to other engineering projects. After he joined the U.S. Army in 1944, he designed a tank retriever, which was the Army's largest land vehicle in use during the war. He also served as a cartographer with the 655th Topographic Battalion of the U.S. Army Corps of Engineers.

After selling the Boise-Winnemucca Stages in 1945, Arthur and Bertha moved to Las Vegas, where Arthur took up flying. He flew to the Four Corners area of the Southwest, where he invested in gas and oil exploration during the post-war boom

Top: Idaho Nevada Stages, ca. 1935. Photographer and location unknown.
Joe Lyon, Jr. is on the far right.

Bottom: Boise-Winnemucca Stages, with their distinctive design, ca. 1940.
Photographer and location unknown.

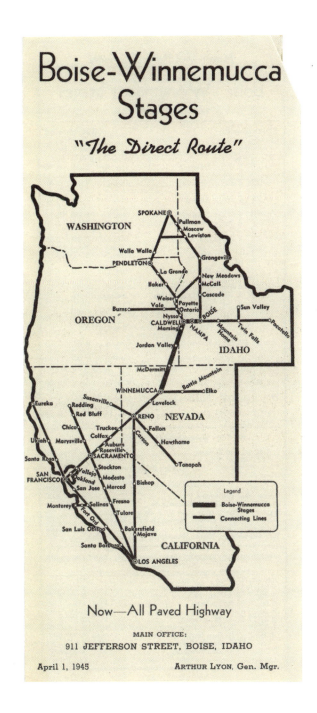

Route map of Boise-Winnemucca Stages, April 1,1945. Cartographer unknown.

Joe Lyon, Jr. (left) in front of a tank retriever, of which he was the chief draftsman, ca. 1942. Photographer and location in Europe unknown.

years of the industry in that area. Joe lived in Southern California for several years. He also took up flying and partnered with Arthur in oil and gas exploration. Their ventures in oil and gas investment resulted in royalties that provided much of their income throughout the rest of their lives. Both brothers also invested in uranium exploration. Arthur continued throughout his life to be involved in business ventures and spent time in Europe on several occasions. According to Bertha, Arthur's opinion was that traveling around was not good enough, that it was important to live there and meet the people. Much of his time in Europe was spent in Paris. During the final years of his life, Arthur lived in Boise, where he helped a protégé establish and run a custom wood-products company. Arthur died in Boise on February 24, 1993.

Bertha and Arthur were married for thirty years before divorcing. Still, they remained lifelong friends and business partners. The artist, Benjamin Cunningham, was among their many friends from the early years in Nevada. Some of his work has recently been exhibited at the Guggenheim Museum in New York City. Bertha had a keen interest in art and literature, and, while living in Albuquerque at one point, she became interested in American Indian art and culture. She amassed a collection of fine American Indian art and pottery, and, when I was about twelve years old, she took my sister, my cousin, and me to sacred dances at the Hopi reservation. We were among a very few white members of the audience.

Joe married Amanda (Mandy) Barr, who was his third wife, on February 22, 1947. Mandy was born in New Zealand, the daughter of Captain Alexander Barr, who was the master of a three-masted barkentine that was one of the last sailing ships to engage in commercial trade with the countries of the Far East. Captain Barr brought Mandy from New Zealand in 1921 on his last voyage. In 1956, Joe and Mandy moved to Salt Lake City, where they bought a home near the Utah State Capital. The home, which was in disrepair when Joe bought it, had walls of foot-thick concrete and had been built by a cement contractor to look like a castle, complete with turrets. Joe restored the home, without turrets, and it was called "The Castle" by family, friends, and business associates. Joe lived in that home until his death on December 22, 1990. The house's large garage became the extensive shop that Joe used to design and build many items. For a number of years, he designed and built working models of plastic containers for a company that sold the containers used to dispense various products such as pills.

As I conclude this introduction as a preview to my two uncles' historic adventure, I recall with great pleasure my own recollections of them over the years I had the good fortune to know them. Both enriched my life and that of my family in

Mandy and Joe, ca. late 1950s, likely in Salt Lake City, Utah.
Photographer and airfield unknown.

many ways. Along with helping to provide for our material needs, they visited frequently, shared their homes with us, took us on trips, and showered us with interest and encouragement.

I feel honored to share with readers the exciting journey that formed the centerpiece of my uncles' lives and which has taken so many years to find its way to a larger audience through the publication of this book. Arthur and Joe Jr. leave behind a legacy of pioneering, adventure, creativity, and generosity. I am especially grateful for the encouragement and support of my extraordinary aunt, Bertha Blattner Lyon, who was a partner with Arthur and Joe—and the Lyon family—every step of the way. The publication of this book is as much a tribute to her as to Uncle Arthur and Uncle Joe. That the book will be officially published on March 23, 2020, on the ninetieth anniversary of my uncles' departure for Managua from Manhattan, seems providential.

The parents of Arthur and Joe Jr.: JM (top) and Inga (bottom), ca. 1930.
Photographe(s) and location(s) unknown.

# The Editorial Method

In the spirit of documentary histories, the story of Arthur and Joe Lyon that follows is presented as close to a facsimile of the original (1985) manuscript as possible, although obvious errors and occasional inconsistencies in spelling, spacing, punctuation, italicization, and capitalization have been corrected in the text to facilitate reading. No changes, however, were made to the original captions or the Appendix, which are unedited and presented as written. Occasional clarifications and the rare missing word appear [in brackets] within the text and captions.

The new editorial annotations by Denis Wood appear as footnotes, rather than endnotes, to provide convenient contextual reading. Spanish words are now presented in *italics* and with accents. For those unfamiliar with Spanish, translations of all Spanish words and phrases (no matter how common) are provided upon first mention. All population figures and monetary conversions are accurate as of October 10, 2019.

All illustrations originally presented in the 1985 typescript, beginning with Chapter I, are integrated in the text where they first appeared. The illustrations that appear on pages 8, 10, 13, 15, 16, 19, 20 (top and bottom), 22, 24, 26, 28, 30, 46, 74 (top), 103 (bottom), 216, and 218 are new to the original (1985) manuscript, as are the maps by Morgan Pfaelzer on pages 34, 62, and 96. All illustrations (except for the maps) come from the family collections of either JM and Inga Lyon or sons Arthur and Joe Jr.

George F. Thompson, the publisher, served as a de facto co-editor. He oversaw the entire process by which the original typescript was edited, annotated, and illustrated. Early in his career when George was an acquisitions editor at the Johns Hopkins University Press (1984–1989), he served as the Press's principal liaison with the Papers of Frederick Law Olmsted, George C. Marshall, The First Federal Congress of the United States of America, Dwight David Eisenhower, and Thomas A. Edison. For this book, he relied heavily on that extensive hands-on experience.

1930

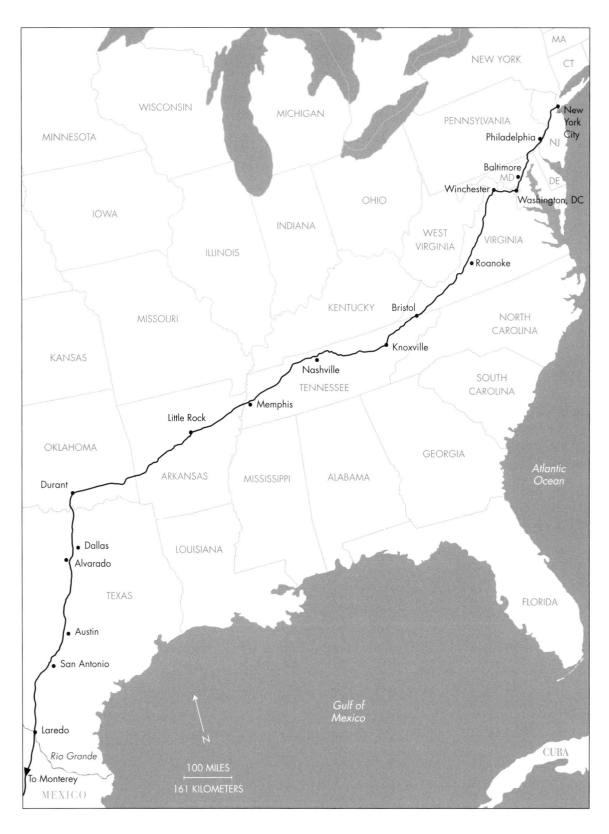

The brothers' journey from Manhattan to Laredo, Texas, where they crossed into Mexico.
Map by Morgan Pfaelzer. © 2020 Center for the Study of Place.

Chapter I

# Getting Started*

Successfully crossing Sixth and Seventh Avenues at Fifty-first Street, we headed our Ford down Broadway for a last look at Times Square, then pushed on to the Holland Tunnel, emerging at sharp noon into Northern Jersey's Sunday confusion.** We did not dream that two months later we would be offering this same car as an even trade for an oxcart (with power attached) to a startled Nicaraguan native sixty-eight kilometers [42.25 miles] north of Managua, Nicaragua, nor could we imagine—but wait, on with the story—or, rather, back to the beginning.

It is a cold, bleak March day in New York—and it *can* be both cold and bleak in New York, even in the fifties.† We are four, enjoying a late Saturday luncheon in my apartment and have reached the coffee-and-cigarettes stage, while outside a few unreasonable snow flurries swirl down out of the blue-specked and wind-swept upper atmosphere.

"That," said I, "is a hell-of-a-way for Saturday weather to treat us five-day-and-a-half-week wage slaves"—and, furthermore (with rising inflection still profane), "It's a hell of a weak-kneed, jelly-backboned, wage-slave who'll stand for it."

---

* Chapter I in the original (1985) typescript was untitled. The publisher suggested "Getting Started."

** The date is March 23, 1930, though, at the end of this opening paragraph, the narrative drops back a few weeks to the story's actual beginning. The automobile is a 1929 Model A Ford Roadster. The Model A replaced the venerable eighteen-year-old Model T in late 1927. The cost of a Roadster in 1930 was around $385 (around $5,625 in 2019). No wonder the car was a sensational success.

† Though Arthur doesn't say so, it is 1930, so four or so months have passed since the Black Tuesday crash of the U.S. stock market in late October 1929. Arthur, then twenty-five-years old, narrates the book. Born in Idaho in 1904 and raised in Idaho, Washington, and Nevada, he attended the University of Nevada for one year before heading east to work as an accountant in New York City. See Larry Lyon's introduction to learn about the family's history.

Brother Joe, just twenty-one, still fresh to New York and burdened with nothing worse than good health, good nature, and the reputation of being the fastest automobile driver in Humboldt County, Nevada, answered provocatively, with a grin—"Yes, you're right, he is that—and how!'"

Buck laughed, a little loudly I thought, and Bert stirred her coffee.[†]

"Joe," I mused, "if you weren't planning M.I.T. next fall, and if my big-hearted boss hadn't given me a two-fifty raise last week, and if (among a few other things) Bert here hadn't the undeniable right to the companionship of her quite worthless husband (meaning myself, of course), I would venture to say that we might crank up the Ford and let it lead us out of this dismal life, which Mammon, money, and 'thinking of my landlord's last untimely and insistent visit' have forced into downright hard-hearted materialism. Let it carry us away for a while, at least, from this beastly weather and, as an afterthought, from the almost certain deleterious aftereffects of the recent disastrous Wall Street crash."[‡] I could believe anything now. The stimulation of this new-born idea so gripped my imagination that I could almost see myself out of a job, perhaps forced to join that restless mob which swarms in and out of tawdry Sixth Avenue employment agencies. Against this I could see the sweep of an open road and hear the sing of six-ply rubber slipping over gray concrete and the miles piling up and falling down over themselves on the dashboard.

"And, Joe, we'll go south, we'll go further south than anybody ever went before in an automobile." A map of the North American continent flashed into my mind. "We'll drive that car down through Mexico and Central America, and we won't stop till we draw up head on against the Panama Canal—way down in the heart of the tropics—What say, Brother?"

This monologue rather surprised them. It was all right to be dissatisfied with one's job, quite all right to rail against the weather, it *was* just beastly right now, but to launch full-fledged a project to motor down to Panama, how many thousand miles one could only guess, was a bit far-fetched, and its accomplishment, to say the least, would be a large and somewhat doubtful undertaking. I could see these and other thoughts rising in the minds of my little audience—but one.

---

* Younger brother, Joe Jr., was born in 1909, also in Idaho, and he, too, attended the University of Nevada for a few years before heading to New York City to join his brother.

† Buck is lost to the shades of history, but Bert is Arthur's wife, Bertha Blattner (see page 22), the daughter of a rancher in Paradise Valley, Nevada. They married in 1929.

‡ These deleterious after-effects have become known as the Great Depression.

Across the table Joe had listened casually at first but with rising interest, and by the time I had mentioned "Central America" and the "tropics" his eyes had begun to sparkle with excitement, as eyes of twenty-one can sparkle, and as I finished he leaned forward to exclaim—"That's an idea—think of it (he leaped three thousand miles)—we'll roll down the Valley of Mexico with Cortez (he covered fifteen hundred more of swamp and jungle)—and swap yarns with the Marines in Nicaragua—and—"

"Swim the Canal with Halliburton, I suppose" interposed Bert, with just a shade of hauteur. We brushed that aside and went on.[*]

"As far as M.I.T. is concerned, I need a year of EXPERIENCE more than I do college right now. Your recent raise (he looked me straight in the eye and didn't smile)—was totally insufficient. You are underpaid exactly ten times that amount now." With a toss of his curly hair, he dismissed my marital obligations. "No woman (he said sternly)—can keep a man from exploring the still undiscovered wastes of this earth, in the interest of—of—(he floundered momentarily but concluded triumphantly)—in the interest of science!"

It grew, it rolled down hill, this idea tumbled on top of us so unexpectedly, had, by its utter simplicity—just motoring—and its intriguing appeal of travel in close at hand but little-known countries, so captivated us that its plausibility became less doubtful every minute. We brewed more coffee and let it stand cold in the cups while we smashed cigarette after cigarette and planned a fresh conquest of the American tropics after the manner of 1930 in (of all things) a Ford.[†]

We scurried away from this portentous luncheon to gather maps, data on roads, and other information on the countries to be traversed. Joe made a raid on the New York Public Library and returned with half an armful of travel books on Central America and Mexico, while I visited several map companies and spent the better part of a week's salary on the best available maps.[‡]

There was a singular uniformity about them—charted railroads (actual and projected) [and] airways in all stages of operation and organization, but in the matter of roads they were almost totally lacking in information. Here and there would appear a

---

[*] Started in 1919 when Erle P. Halliburton began the new Method Oil Well Cementing Company in Oklahoma, Halliburton remains one of the world's largest oil-field services company. Even in 1930 it was a famous business enterprise.

[†] What else? Actually, there were plenty of options at the time, including equally low-priced Chevies and Plymouths. In 1930, in fact, Chevies outsold Fords.

[‡] Though, in 1930, there was more of this kind available than had ever been the case before, there still wasn't much of it. It was nothing like today.

tenuous wavering line running from nowhere in particular to its complement somewhere else, and the map legend would tell us that this was a *camino cartero* (cart road) or perhaps El Camino Real (The King's Highway), but due to the fact that they were located in such improbable places and often ran between such unimportant towns, we concluded (and rightly too) that they were often the product of the draftsman's imagination or, more probably, of his inaccurate sources of information.* But most of our charts simply left the matter of roads entirely to the imagination, filling up the blank spaces with projected railroads, projected canals, or projected airways.† The travel books too were nearly unanimously silent on the subject of automobile travel. Occasionally a short bit of road would be mentioned, with the interesting information appended that it was sometimes passable in the dry season but only if the rivers had reached a low enough stage to be forded.

We soon realized that we were getting nowhere and learning very little that we wished to know from all our books and charts—that is, we were learning little about the roads—[though] we were learning about the countries we planned to visit. Before, they had been no more than names vaguely remembered and seldom heard. Now was being unfolded to us the strange story of the North American tropics, tiny Republics governed by impossible presidents who held office through military force, who lost office as soon as control of the army slipped from their hands, or, as more often was the case, as soon as the opposition organized a better army. Of course, we were more or less familiar with our southern neighbor, Mexico, but of the six republics further south—Guatemala, El Salvador, Honduras, Nicaragua, Costa Rica, and Panama—we had all to learn. The descriptive adjectives applied most often to them seemed to be "romantic" and "tropical." Inescapable then—the romantic tropics, the dauntless we are going to motor through the "romantic tropics!"—enough to get some excited about, don't you think? Shades of O. Henry, Richard Harding Davis, and the U.S. Marines—what names! Enough to make our pulse quicken as it has other men's since the golden days of the Spanish Main.‡

"But wait a minute, Brother, how about a road, just a little trace of a road say, perhaps a hundred miles of highway or so out of every thousand miles, something to

---

* Or both, the absence of information fueling the draftsman's imagination.

† Unlike the fabled beasts with which mapmakers used to fill up their empty spaces. It is hard to realize but, in 1930, the numbered U.S. highway system was only five years old. The American Association of State Highway Officials was responsible for this system which, in 1930, essentially consisted of hardly a dozen east-west routes with a pair that paralleled the Pacific and Atlantic coasts. No route or collection of routes was paved from New York City to the border at Laredo, Texas.

‡ O. Henry, of course, is the pen name for the famous author whose real name was William Sydney Porter (1862–1910); Richard Harding Davis (1864–1916) was a war-correspondent and writer equally famous at the time; and the Marines, then occupying Nicaragua, were constantly in the news.

rest up on and relax on after we have carried, ferried, and pushed that bus for weeks through the 'impenetrable jungle' and over the 'mountain fastnesses.'" "Right! We *are* pretty good, but a road would be a big help—Let us find a road."

Then followed a week or so of further investigation. We called on the consul of each country. Each gave us as much information as he could. It was not very encouraging. Yes, there were roads. "We have just completed a fine highway from the capital down to the seacoast, as fine a highway as there is in all Central America." "North and South roads?" "Oh no, this highway runs East and West—In a few years . . ."

But bit by bit we managed to piece together a fairly continuous road down the backbone of the Continent, ending in the untracked jungles of northern Costa Rica. That was not Panama, by any means, but still, as Costa Rica borders Panama on the north, it was somewhat near our objective. There were important gaps to be sure. In fact, no country but Honduras had anything remotely resembling a road stretching from border to border. Southern Mexico was a gap of several hundred miles. But this in itself was a challenge. We would be not only tourists, but if you please explorers, tracking out new paths in the wilderness. Our enthusiasm for this project grew every day and the skeptical attitude of most everyone we interviewed only served to heighten it.

We soon heard that an Italian Count had driven a car up to the United States from the Argentine.* As he was at this time in New York [City], we tried to interview that worthy. He consistently refused to see us, however, and after a little investigation the reasons became apparent. For that he certainly could not be blamed, but it was rather unsportsmanlike to claim to have driven through certain sections when the facts were that he conveniently placed his automobile on a flat car or a boat and detoured around them. One outraged railway official in southern Mexico offered us an affidavit to the effect that he shipped it (after reading in the Mexico City and American papers that Count Barone had driven his car completely across Mexico) some five hundred miles as cargo on his railroad. We declined, but the facts remain.

But Joe epitomized our thoughts one day. "Every day we learn more about the impossibility of making this trip and we get no closer to where the bad roads begin. I say let's get going and have a look at them. When we reach the point where the

* The count was José Mario Barone (dates of birth and death are unknown). The brothers included an account of that trip as an attached appendix in their original typescript: José Mario Barone, *Pan-American Trail Blazer: From Rio de Janeiro to New York City by Motor Car* (Washington, DC: Pan-American Confederation for Highway Education, 1929), 16 pages. They also included, as a second appendix, a newspaper account of the two-year journey (April 19, 1928 to April 8, 1930) by the brothers Adam and Andrew Stroessel (ages thirty-three and twenty-three, respectively), whose route was similar to Barone's of 1928–1929: "Adventurous Brothers Drive from Argentina: Reach New York after Journey of 19,000 Miles Through Jungles and Across Mountains—Two Years on the Way" (the newspaper, date, and page numbers are unknown).

next hundred yards can't humanly be negotiated, we'll trade the 'tin can' off for two burros and continue a la mode." "OK," I replied. "We *can* drive to Texas. We'll start worrying in Mexico. Set the date." "Sunday," said he. That was Wednesday. I bade my boss a fond farewell. His sorrow at my resignation was no doubt tempered by the fact that my last two weeks in the office were more or less a total loss to the company.[*] I couldn't balance a ledger in less than twice the allotted time, and on their blue lined pages would form strange vistas of palm-lined beaches or snow-capped volcanoes sending wings of smoke up to blue, blue skies. Even the patter of typewriters would fade away, and in through the window would come the sweet tinkle of a guitar from far off Mexico. Oh, I was steeped in idyllic dreams those days! I cursed silently each unbalanced ledger that came my way and looked ahead impatiently to an early release. Nor when it came was I sorry. As I slammed my desk shut that last day, it was with a feeling of immense relief, and as I stepped out on to Fifty-seventh Street to run the taxi handicap down to Fifty-first, I was as far up in clouds as only a dreamer can be. Who, pray tell, would putter with profits and losses, and debits and credits, when Alvarado himself—that reckless but amazingly brave lieutenant of Cortez fresh from the conquest of Mexico—is waiting to lead us on to Guatemala and to new frontiers to the South?[†]

So on Sunday, March 23, 1930, we dragged out the sock, found in it the sum of $324, which same we deposited in our jeans, trundled our Ford over from its modest garage in Queens, piled the rumble seat high with five large suit-cases, one duffle bag, a bed roll, and many nondescript packages of various sizes and kinds, and just as the sun was getting well across the equator on its annual journey northward, we passed under the Hudson River on our way south to meet it.[‡]

[*] The company was Standard and Poors, where Arthur worked in accounting.

[†] Pedro de Alvarado (1485–1542) had been the second-in-command to Hernán Cortés during the conquest of Mexico and was deputed by Hernán Cortés (1485–1547) to subjugate Guatemala, Honduras, and El Salvador. Alvarado is best remembered for his unspeakable cruelty to the indigenous population.

[‡] In 2019, $324 would amount to around $4,733. The brothers passed under the Hudson River by way of the Holland Tunnel, which had only been completed in 1924. The George Washington Bridge was being built when the brothers left, but it would not open until 1931.

Chapter II

# Bucking the Traffic Problem

Bowling along with the Sunday crowd down New Jersey's highways, I had ample time to reflect that this was probably the poorest equipped expedition that ever left New York bound for Central America.* The first and largest deficiency was, of course, our financial limitations. $324 dollars could be divided up into various parts, of course, but each form of budgeting invariably brought me to the same conclusion—that we would find ourselves somewhere in the vicinity of Mexico City with a worn-out car on our hands and faced with the alternative of walking back to New York (not a pleasant prospect) or going to work at the local wage scale of some fifty cents a day (even less pleasant). Still, I reflected, there could be alternatives. We might even run into a well-financed Mexican revolution and sell our services to the highest bidder. The warring parties, of course, would be delighted at the chance to bid for the services of two "gringoes" and their automobile.†

Our second serious limitation was the fact that we could speak little Spanish, I not having any, and Joe's command of it being gauged by a two years' casual study in high school. He expressed confidence to master enough of it in a short time, though, to ask for anything we wanted, or had money enough to pay for, so we proceeded hopefully on that rather unwarranted assumption.

Starting to enumerate the things we didn't have which any self-respecting expedition should have, I find I have reversed myself and merely completed the bit

* Seeing that U.S. 1 was paved through New Jersey, they probably were "bowling along."

† *Gringoes* is also spelled *gringos*. *Gringo* and *gringa* have many meanings, depending on context, but here the translation might be "two white guys from America or another foreign country." The first known use was 1849, but its origins are with *griego* (Greek) and its association with anyone who spoke an unintelligible language.

of things we had—a little money, a little Spanish, a little car.* Oh yes, and a rifle and five suit-cases of clothing, for a trip into the tropics!

But after all, why sacrifice the florous NOW on the altar of the unknown FUTURE? Besides, we may as well apply the same philosophy to our other limitations, as we have to the Central American roads which we resolved to tackle, when, if, and as we encountered them, not before. And in regard to the roads, as Joe says, "No roads can be as bad as they say those are. If by any chance though they are as bad as that, we'll probably take one look at them and immediately commit suicide, thus ending our troubles. And if they aren't that bad, we'll proceed to travel them. Either way we have nothing to worry about, except—Can we get a passport in Washington without our birth certificates?" Faultless logic! Drive on, big boy, here comes Philadelphia.

We didn't see much of America's third largest city but its traffic problem.† That was bad and it took us nearly as long to go through the city as it had to drive from New York.‡ O Congress! How about a few interstate arterial highways for us Americans who are going places?§ Rather clumsy arrangement whereby we have to buck the red and greens for two hours to get back to the road to Washington.

Stepping into line again beyond Philadelphia, we rolled along the winding, hilly Baltimore Pike to that city, so justly famed throughout America for its oysters, its "B&O" and its Mencken or perhaps the last should come first.¶ Baltimore and Boston—how closely related they seem to us from the West who have never visited either. Boston has Harvard, but Baltimore has her Johns Hopkins. Boston's fame rests, somewhat vaguely, on Boston beans, and Baltimore is no less intimately associated with that delicious and profitable bivalve which generates her largest

---

* As a reminder, this was a 1929 Model A Ford Roadster or, as a newspaper describing the trip put it, "a light roadster of popular make." As mentioned in note * on page 35, it probably set the brothers back $385. The L-head four-cylinder engine was water-cooled, had a displacement of 201 cubic inches, and provided forty horsepower. The top speed on a good surface was about sixty-five miles per hour. It had a 103.5-inch wheelbase, a conventional three-speed sliding gear, manual, unsynchronized transmission with a single-speed reverse, and four-wheel mechanical drum brakes. It had a soft top.

† Philadelphia had a population just under 2,000,000 in 1930, putting it between Chicago and Detroit. It is fifth largest today, with 1,500,000 people in the city and between 5,000,000 and 6,000,000 in the metro area.

‡ U.S. 1 was also paved across Pennsylvania.

§ America's Interstate Highway System was only inaugurated in 1956 with the initial construction of I–70 west of St. Louis, Missouri. Today, the brothers could take their entire trip to Laredo on interstates.

¶ "B&O" refers to the Baltimore and Ohio Railroad. H. L. Mencken (1880–1956), the "Sage of Baltimore," was at the height of his fame during the late 1920s, having published *The American Language* in 1919 and having covered the Scopes Monkey Trial in 1925 and the trial of the evangelist, Aimee Semple McPherson (1890–1944), in 1926. Again, U.S. 1 was paved across Baltimore.

industry.* Both too old to die, they go right on living in spite of prohibition, competition, [and] the devastating attacks of Upton Sinclair and Haywood Broun.† Baltimore, seventh, and Boston, eighth in population (or did Los Angeles pass them twice instead of once in the recent census count?), seem destined to continue exerting an erudite force on American civilization out of all proportion to their mere size and commercial importance.‡

We civilized thoroughly two dozen of Baltimore's best [its oysters] in a roadside cafe before continuing on. Hardly more than started on the second dozen, a loud crash from the street in the general direction of our parked car drew us out of the cafe on a high lope, with a napkin in one hand and part of the establishment's silver service in the other. There before our astonished eyes was an upturned sedan apparently using our inoffensive roadster for a lounging place after a bounding ricochet off the side of a street car. I say apparently because after a hasty, closer examination it showed that it hadn't yet decided just where to lounge but was rocking unsteadily on its side with the two upper wheels spinning merrily in exactly the place where our top would have been were it not folded down. We quietly switched on the parking lights and pushed our beloved out of harm's way just as a motor cop and the conductor went into a huddle to decide who was to blame for the accident—the driver of the sedan or—the driver of the sedan.

After letting the rest of the oysters join their little brothers, we drove on down [south] to Washington—and learned how to make a left turn.§

It appears that Washington too has a traffic problem and some genius on the traffic commission had figured out that it was all due to the faulty left turn they were then using. In those unenlightened days when one wanted to turn left, he simply signaled for it, got out in the center of the street, and then as expeditiously as possible crossed the opposite stream of traffic and fled on his way, leaving nothing behind worse than the screams of the brakes on the cars which avoided hitting him. Now, thanks to our hero, we understand all that is changed. When wishing to make a left

* The oyster, of course.

† Upton Sinclair (1878–1968) is the well-known and prolific novelist, but Heywood Broun, Jr. (1888–1939) was a crusading journalist and member of the celebrated Algonquin Round Table who founded the Newspaper Guild in 1933. Both writers believed that they—and all writers—could help alleviate social ills through their work.

‡ In fact, Baltimore was eighth and Boston ninth in 1930, while Los Angeles was already fifth. Neither East Coast city makes the top ten anymore, although, if you take into account their metro areas, Boston is tenth and Baltimore twentieth.

§ They are still on a paved U.S. 1.

turn, you signal left, as in days of old (we are not quite sure of this point, as subsequent events will show it is a most illogical thing to do, but for lack of more definite information we did it and seemed to get away with it)—and then, of all things, you turned right instead, and after successfully passing the curb line you pull hard over to port and describe a semi-circle in the center of the street (the street into which you are trying to get). This maneuver successfully completed, you should find yourself hard up against the curb on the right-hand side of the street and headed in the general direction you wish to go, only waiting for the green light to be on your way.[*] That is where you should find yourself, but the odds are better than ever you will be in some other position less advantageously situated. Our usual predicament was to come to rest with the right front wheel up on the sidewalk, headed in no particular direction unless it was up the Capitol steps, and blocking the pedestrians effectively off the cross street (which was of no particular moment except for the dirty looks) and in no position to see the traffic lights when they flashed green, unless we happened to catch a glimpse of them by chance in the rear view mirror.

All in all, it is very complicated and I would suggest to any one that they pick up a guide on the outskirts of the city, or avoid left turns altogether. One could turn right and go down to the Lincoln Memorial and spend a pleasant day by the Potomac. When returning one could continue turning right, going out by way of Rock Creek Park and avoiding any left turn until well over into Maryland.[†] Of course, if one had to turn left to the Capitol or the Senate Office Building, I would earnestly recommend the guide.

Washington Monument was our early morning objective.[‡] We spent a brief half-hour admiring our National shrine from its peaked summit, then rushed on to the important business deal of getting clearance papers from these United States of ours and incidentally a few letters of introduction which were in the weeks ahead to smooth out many a little wrinkle in our dealings with various Central American officials.

Our senator from Nevada, Tasker L. Oddie, gave us assistance far out of proportion to the political prestige to which two inconsequential votes might entitle us, and for that we owe and hereby give him a hearty vote of thanks.[§] He steered us to places and people

---

[*] This used to be known as "a farmer's turn," due to the large turning radius required by a horse and wagon. Early cars usually had large turning radii as well.

[†] Rock Creek Park, the heart and soul of Washington, D.C., is twice the size of Central Park in Manhattan.

[‡] This is March 24, the second day.

[§] Tasker Oddie (1870–1950) was a silver miner and, as an elected Republican, the twelfth Governor of Nevada (1911–1915) and a U.S. Senator (1921–1933) from Nevada. As governor, he signed the city charter that officially created Las Vegas on March 17, 1911.

where we greatly augmented the information we already had on Central American roads and made it possible for us to get a letter of introduction explaining our mission from no less a power in Latin American affairs than the Pan American Union.*

Senate gallery seats held us for a time while we listened to some Southern Senatorial prophet flay in a shockingly frank and candid manner the current edition of the Hawley-Smoot Tariff Bill.† From there we wandered into the House gallery, where the incredibly correct Speaker, Hon. Nicholas Longworth, was debating on the floor a bill providing funds for sending some previous administration's blundering deliverance into private hands of lands important to the scheme of beautifying Washington.‡ Rather a striking contrast did his carefully groomed figure and well-modulated voice present to the rank and file of his colleagues. We were rather surprised at the general appearance and rather informal air of what is *still* called the Lower House of Congress.

Passports were issued to us in the astonishingly short time of one hour, after Joe had sworn that he had known me for twenty-one years and had every reason to believe that I was "Made in America" and I had done the same for him. Feeling quite important with these attractive documents embellished with our picture and the Great Seal of the U.S.A. in our possession, we made a late start out of Washington and drove over the Potomac into Virginia and on through a rainstorm to Winchester.§ This is a most attractive little town with most of the aura of the old South still clinging to it. Old and immaculately kept Colonial houses vied with each other for a share of the Northern tourist's dollars, some with a discreet sign near the gate "Tourist Accommodation" or with the more openly solicitous "Fine Rooms with Bath and Garage." We were tempted, but finally chose the more democratic tourist camp.

---

* Formed in 1890 to promote cooperation among the countries of Latin America and the U.S., the Pan-American Union was renamed the Union of American Republics in 1910 and reconstituted as the Organization of American States in 1948. Nonetheless, many at the time of the brothers' journey still called it the Pan-American Union.

† The Hawley-Smoot tariff (the Tariff Act of 1930) raised tariffs on imports to their highest level in a century. Hawley and Smoot were Republicans from Oregon and Utah. Four years later, Democrats lowered tariffs with their Reciprocal Trade Agreements Act.

‡ Nicolas Longworth III (1869–1931) was a Republican from Cincinnati. Serving as Speaker of the House from 1925 to 1931, he restored to the position the power he had earlier helped reduce and ran the House of Representatives as autocratically as any Speaker ever had.

§ At this point, the brothers have left U.S. 1 and are very likely taking U.S. 50 west to Winchester, Virginia, and its intersection there with U.S. 11. Winchester remains a small but important town stuffed with historic sites, notable buildings, a thriving downtown, an endowed high school, the amazing Museum of the Shenandoah Valley, an excellent hospital, and a growing Shenandoah University. Following 9/11 and, specifically, the attack on the Pentagon in Arlington, Virginia, numerous federal agencies and archives formerly located in and near Washington, D.C., became based here.

These are the passports that Uncle Arthur (top) and Uncle Joe (bottom) used on thier journey.

Winchester was proud, in a subdued Southern way, of the exploits of its most famous native son—Admiral Byrd—but one felt that they really thought more of him as a "Byrd" than as the conqueror of the Poles and the actual discoverer of more land than perhaps any other human being.[*]

From Winchester our route lay through the charming, smiling Shenandoah Valley, past Civil War battlefields innumerable.[†] It was with reluctance that we sped at fifty miles per hour past markers telling us in realistic fashion a great deal of the history of that tragic conflict, but we had set Knoxville, Tennessee, as our sleeping place, and that was 468 miles away.

In the mountains beyond Roanoke, we ran into a blustering snowstorm driven by a gale that at times retarded us much as if the brakes were thrown on. Our delusions about the sunny South were being unpleasantly dispelled, but, of course, this weather was "unusual." But, then, so was the weather in New York unusually cold when we left. What we were looking for was a place where the weather wasn't "unusual" most of the time (and I hasten to say we eventually found it).

The famed Natural Bridge of Virginia was on our route, too.[‡] We came to a section of the highway where the scenery was effectively hidden from the road by a high board fence and a sign announced that this was the Natural Bridge. In our indignation at finding this natural wonder capitalized and so completely barred from the public view, we drove on without venturing to ask what the price of admission might be. I have since wondered if perhaps we were not just a little hasty in our decision that it cost money to have a look. For all I know, the entrance fee may not have existed and the fence may have been built just to keep the cattle off the road—but I doubt it.

---

[*] Rear Admiral Richard E. Byrd, Jr. (1888–1957) was a pioneering pilot who undertook world-famous polar expeditions by sea and air in 1928–1931, 1934, 1939–1940, 1946–1947, and 1955–1956. He received uncountable awards and medals, including the Medal of Honor, the highest honor for valor given by the United States.

[†] On this, their third day, March 25, the brothers headed south through the legendary Shenandoah Valley on U.S. 11, historically known as the Valley Road and Valley Turnpike (or Pike).

[‡] Natural Bridge is actually around forty miles north of Roanoke (2019 population around 100,000) on U.S. 11 and is at the southern terminus of the Shenandoah Valley. Carved through limestone by Cedar Creek, Natural Bridge—a natural arch 215 feet high with a span of ninety feet—was long a sacred site of native peoples that became one of the most famous attractions for tourists and artists in the U.S. during the eighteenth, nineteenth, and early-twentieth centuries. Thomas Jefferson owned the property from 1777 to his death in 1826. In 1997, it was listed on the National Register of Historic Place and became a National Historic Landmark in 1998. In 2014, it was deeded to the Commonwealth of Virginia and, in 2016, was designated a state park.

West [south] of Bristol, Tennessee, we began to encounter a traffic hazard in the form of negroes walking along the roadside after dark.* Dressed in their dark clothing, they blended perfectly with the night and it was often necessary to wait till you saw the whites of their eyes before careening wildly out of the way. It was startling, to say the least, to be slipping along at forty-five or fifty and see a big, black-clad negro loom up out of the night, as if from nowhere, apparently completely unconcerned as to his fate if this hustling ton of steel didn't swerve far enough to miss him.

We made good our promise and at eleven were dead to the world in a tourist camp on the outskirts of Knoxville.† Away to an early start in the morning, we got more ambitious and planned to end our day in Little Rock, some 600 miles westward.‡

The road conditions were with us as we sailed down Tennessee's fine concrete highway at a great pace, covering incredible distance. The miles had veritably begun to pile up and fall over themselves on the dash, and it took a little calculation to figure just which hundred we were in.

These mountain fastnesses of the Old South held their share of surprises and delights. Innumerable mule teams, loaded with hardwood logs, were sharing with us this concrete ribbon which Tennessee so hopefully calls the "Broadway of America."§ Automobiles were not so plentiful and we slowly came to the realization that this was indeed the Old South, almost unchanged since the Civil War, and peopled with that strange race, the Tennessee mountaineers. Never having seen one in his native state, we slowed up a little and glanced more than casually at these hardy mountain men with their guns and dogs and offspring trailing along the road for all the world as if they were on the way to clash with the neighbor clan in settlement of an ancient feud. More probably, they were goin'-a-huntin', but there was no law against attributing more romantic motives to their picturesque prowling.

---

* Bristol is still a small city, perhaps best known as the "birthplace of Country Music." Half of Bristol lies in Virginia (2019 population around 17,000) and the other half in Tennessee (2019 population around 27,000). The brothers are still on U.S. 11. At that time, "Negro" (also negro) was the commonplace term used to describe African Americans. The origin of the word is *niger* (Latin), meaning "black."

† Knoxville (2019 population around 187,000) is sort of a big deal, being the state's third-largest city after Memphis and Nashville and home to the main campus of the University of Tennessee and headquarters of the Tennessee Valley Authority (TVA). Oak Ridge, about twenty-five miles to the west, is also home to one of America's two large nuclear-research laboratories, the other being Los Alamos, New Mexico. Arthur and Joe Jr. spend their eight hours in Knoxville mostly in the dark.

‡ This begins the brothers' fourth day, March 26.

§ The brothers are sailing along what is more or less U.S. 70 today. Its "Broadway" moniker comes from its importance as an east-west route prior to the initial construction of the Interstate Highway System in 1956.

We stopped and asked one how far it was to Nashville.[*]

"Dunno," said he—"Ain't never been to Nashville."

"About a hundred miles?" I ventured, knowing it was about that.

"Dunno, mebbe more'n a hundred, mebbe less'n a hundred," and delightfully true to form he hitched his trousers and stalked off.

"I thought," opined Joe, "that the South, what with going Republican and having rayon mills and all that, had stepped up to the automobile and radio age, but that (indicating the retreating mountaineer) proves just how little I knew about it."[†]

Nashville was hot, and that was fine.[‡] We peeled off layer after layer of heavy woolen clothing until the seat between us was piled high with discarded coats and sweaters. We folded the top down and reveled in glorious Tennessee sunshine while the unceasing miles fled by in reckless haste. Forty-five, fifty, fifty-five, sixty—we held that prancing roadster to a cool sixty for one solid hour. A big Studebaker challenged us for a while, but we slipped away around a stream of traffic and held undisputed control after that with not even a motor cop to spoil the fun.

Memphis at sundown was just an incident, [and] crossing the Mississippi on a narrow toll bridge with the languorous misty river flowing beneath was a thrill.[§] The lights of river boats and the retreating city reflected through the warm evening held a half-spoken promise of romance to be had for the asking along Memphis['s] waterfront. But we couldn't tarry now—our twenty-five cent toll was paid, and we regretfully bade good-bye to "Ole Man River" with the mental note taken that this was another place to be visited again, when time and money were more plentiful.[¶]

[*] Had the brothers asked when in Knoxville, it would have been 180 miles. It's less here.

[†] There was at the time significant sentiment against the presidency of Franklin D. Roosevelt (FDR) and the federal-government programs of the New Deal in this part of the South. Eastern ("East") Tennessee remains staunchly Republican.

[‡] Nashville (2019 population around 675,000) is the capital of and most populous city in Tennessee. Located on the Cumberland River, it is one of the nation's fastest-growing cities and metropolitan areas.

[§] Memphis (2019 population around 650,000) is the largest city along the Mississippi River and, with its fifteen square miles, one of the most expansive cities in the U.S.

[¶] "Ole Man River" (composer: Jerome Kern; lyricist: Oscar Hammerstein II) is the most famous song from the musical *Show Boat* in which the Mississippi River is contrasted with the hardships of African Americans. Paul Robeson (1898–1976) recorded the song in 1928 with his unforgettably soulful rendition.

In the meantime, a hundred mile detour through the canebrakes of Arkansas lay ahead.* That state hadn't started to build highways until "Smack-over" oil was discovered, so she still lagged behind and was even now just completing her main east and west arterial.† We successfully solved the maze of dirt and gravel roads crossing each other at right angles and slipped into Little Rock before midnight to turn in a day's run of 602 miles, a little too much for comfort, but—boy, howdy, we were leaving these United States behind us!‡

A cursory examination of Little Rock by day proved it to be a most uninteresting place, so we hurried on to Texas.§ I couldn't help wondering how Senator Joe Robinson had emerged from the utterly common-place of the so-called "Bible Belt" to become a leader in the Democracy.¶

* Canebrake refers to cane (*Arundinaria gigantean*), a member of the grass family and the only bamboo native to the U.S. Its habitat has regional associations, especially in Arkansas, Louisiana, and Mississippi. Much of that once-dominant landscape is now endangered.

† The Smackover Field—Smackover derives from an anglicization of the French for "covered in sumac"— was discovered in 1922 and reached its peak production in 1925, though it was pumping plenty of oil in 1930. It remained productive into the mid-1940s. Needless to say, it's once again of interest.

‡ U.S. 70, though graded and mostly paved to Memphis, wasn't a whole lot of either west of the Mississippi.

§ This is day five, March 27. It doesn't look like the brothers spent half a day in Little Rock—the capital of Arkansas and in 2019 a city of around 200,000. The William J. Clinton Presidential Library and Park along the Arkansas River at Little Rock was dedicated in 2004.

¶ Interesting thought! Joseph Taylor Robinson (1870–1937) represented Arkansas as its U.S. Senator from 1913 until his death in 1937. As the running mate of Alfred E. Smith (1873–1944), he was a vice-presidential candidate in 1928. For the last four years of his life, he was the U.S. Senate's majority leader. But, then, we've had some mighty "common-place" leaders.

Chapter III

# Skyscrapers and Cactus

Ferrying across the Red River, we discovered that it was in truth red with the silt of Arkansas and Oklahoma.* Nothing like a little travel to brush up on one's geography.

Out of the hills of Arkansas we rushed across the plains of Texas to its northeastern metropolis, Dallas.† And here, my friends, is a city. Just out of its swaddling clothes, it is rushing pell-mell into the manhood of skyscrapers and big business—with a vicious traffic problem thrown in for good measure. Handicapped with very narrow streets, a heritage of the Spanish era, she is bragging and boosting, and building herself into a modern city with all the accoutrements. Right now she was girding herself for the big 1930 census handicap to be run off in April against several other Texas cities, Fort Worth, San Antonio, Houston, and El Paso, for the coveted prize of being the biggest, in a state where any other superlative lacks conviction. (I learn that Dallas came into the tape by a nose, more power to her. New Orleans had better look to her laurels as the biggest city in the South.)‡

We spent three days in Dallas trying to collect a hundred twenty dollars owed to us by a young man who was trying to buck the current economic depression, via the soap game.§ We suggested that he give up that hopeless task and join us in a trip to

---

* Rising in east-central New Mexico and the Texas Panhandle, the Red River flows 1,360 miles to its confluence with the Achafalaya and Mississippi Rivers in Louisiana. The Red is a significant tributary to both rivers.

† Impressive even in 1930, Dallas-Fort Worth in 2019 had a metropolitan population of more than 7,500,000. The brothers likely reached Dallas on U.S. 75, which intersected with U.S. 70 in Durant, Oklahoma.

‡ Indeed, while Dallas-Fort Worth in 2019 was the fifth-largest city in the U.S., slightly behind Houston, New Orleans was ranked fiftieth. The race Arthur had his eye on was more than handily won by Dallas.

§ These would be days six, seven, and eight: March 28, 29, and 30. The "soap game" of the 1930s and 40s was a "confidence trick" that involved the wrapping of bars of soap in $20 bills, which were then sold to "victims."

that land where depression was not a chronic evil, and who cared anyhow as long as the bananas held out. But he was loath to give up his debts and sundry other troubles for so Elysian a promise, and showed up two days later with twenty-five dollars and two cases of soap to help us on our way.

During the interim, we purchased a tent, two cots, and a large tin grub box at Dallas'[s] large mail-order store. At Woolworth's we stocked up with a good supply of cooking and eating utensils, and for the surprisingly small sum of $32.40 we got together a fairly respectable camp outfit topped by a rainproof umbrella tent which was all that could be desired for our purpose.*

While I was away one afternoon, Joe mounted a fifty-five-gallon oil drum in the fore part of the rumble seat and connected it with a copper tube and shut-off valve to the carburetor.†

"There, now," he declared triumphantly when I returned just as he was finishing tightening the last connection, "there'll be none of that fifty-cent-a-gallon gasoline we've been hearing about. With both tanks full we shall have sixty-five gallons aboard and that ought to carry us a thousand miles over any kind of roads."

And so it would! A master stroke eliminating at once the high price of gasoline and the absence thereof! I had visions of driving to Panama on three tanks of gas with just a couple of changes of oil thrown in for good measure.

"Boy! You'll be the success of this expedition yet," I enthused. "In my dim wit I never conceived of such a scheme for cheating the high cost of touring in Latin America. Now for a gas war!"

And we found one in the outskirts of Dallas. We drew up to a dingy service station where a large sign announced that gasoline was "twelve cents with oil." I waited till the proprietor had obsequiously filled the radiator and polished off the windshield before I announced, "Five quarts of oil and sixty gallons of gas!"

"W—h—a—a—t?" His mouth hung open.

"We want the oil changed and sixty gallons of gasoline," I repeated pointing up to the sign.

"Sure," he nodded, "but where are you goin' to put it?"

"Right here," I said, indicating the oil drum.

He became almost unruly, but after we convinced him that we didn't run a rival service station and were only poor tourists headed for Mexico he calmed down and

* Founded in 1878, Woolworth's pioneered the dime-store concept to become the world's most successful. It went out of business in 1997. The brothers spent between $360 and $450 at today's rates.

† The boys' father, Joseph M. ("JM") Lyon, operated the Lyon Super Service Station in McDermitt, Nevada, on the Oregon state line during the late 1920s and early 1930s. Joe came by his skill with cars naturally.

began to pump out the sixty gallons, complaining meanwhile that he was losing a penny every time the indicator clicked, making his profit, if any, on the oil.

Our poor little roadster, with its sixty-five gallons of gas, five suitcases, cots, tent, camp equipment, two cases of soap, two passengers, bed roll, and what not else, was beginning to slump down like a tired pack animal at the end of a hard day, and I began to have doubts about the springs, axles and tires and so forth standing the strain. Joe reassured me, though, by saying that this was the identical chassis that Ford used under his three-quarter ton truck, but nevertheless I noticed a surprising tendency on the part of the car to settle down on one side and stay there until a bump in the road shifted the load and it settled down just as convincingly on the other.

So, under a full Texas moon, we left Dallas bound south, all too anxious to get across the border into a foreign land where adventure, surely, would be waiting to embrace us with outstretched arms.[*]

Our foreign travel had been limited, quite. Joe's to a single venture into the tourist-baiting halls of chance—and infamy—of Tia Juana, and mine to a Pullman ride on the North Shore Limited through a small section of Canada, on the way from Chicago to New York.[†] We anticipated keenly, then, the prospect of wandering, unfettered and free (particularly free from money) through the unspoiled, unexploited, and untourist-infested Republic of Mexico. Just what else we expected to find in that Silver Republic south of Texas I cannot quite recall.[‡] I am very sure, though, that we both secretly hoped that a revolution would flame up, with perhaps a silver mine to be found and a fleeing senorita or two to be rescued, to give us the excitement and adventure we craved. These, and other hopes and visions too fantastic to be recorded, flitted through our minds as we rolled away to Romance down toward the Rio Grande.

Toward three in the morning we slipped off the road down near Austin and prepared to take a little rest.[§] Rain was beginning to come down so out came the

---

[*] It is uncertain from the text on which road the brothers left Dallas, but one expects they picked up U.S. 65, which intersected with the Meridian Highway (old State Highway 2, today's U.S. 81) at Alvarado. From there they would have followed that unpaved but graded road all the way south to Austin, San Antonio, and Laredo.

[†] There were many ways to spell Tijuana, which is how the city is spelled today. The name comes from the Kumeyaay—the language spoken by the indigenous inhabitants of southern San Diego and Imperial counties—word "Tiwan," meaning "by-the-sea." (The derivation from the Spanish for "Aunt Jane" is mythical.) The North Shore Limited ran 230 miles through Canada between Detroit and Buffalo. It competed with the 20th Century Limited, which ran along the southern shores of the Great Lakes.

[‡] Silver was the most important product Spain hauled out of Mexico. The metal fueled a great trans-Pacific trade between China, through Manila, and Acapulco beginning in the mid-sixteenth century, which underwrote Spain's ascendance as a world power. Mexico remains the world's largest producer of silver.

[§] And with this the brothers dismiss the capital of Texas, site of the University of Texas and, in 2019, the eleventh-largest city in the U.S. and the self-proclaimed "Live Music Capital of the World."

tent, and we began to struggle with its intricacies in a rising windstorm. Dismayed, we found no ropes. I insisted a tent should have ropes, but Joe hopefully suggested that perhaps umbrella tents didn't have them and began methodically staking down every part in sight, which looked as though it should be attached to the ground. In the excitement I tore a gap in the mosquito netting, which according to the salesman was one of its most desirable features, and Joe severely reprimanded me for that. I reminded him of his inexpert handling of the car somewhere back in Tennessee, so we got to reminding each other of various things in true brotherly fashion, ending by his reminding me that this trip was my misguided idea in the first place. So, confronted with the truth, I had to shut up and try to sleep while our tent bellied and flapped and threatened momentarily to take off for a long distance balloon race to California.

I have a hearty respect that no mere figures could engender for the bigness of the Lone Star State. After clicking off the miles for two solid days, there was still, to borrow a fitting phrase, "Texas to the right of us, Texas to the left of us, Texas ahead of us." And such a big, flat Texas it was, with no mountains or other earthly configuration to gauge distance by, so that we seemed to be just crawling along at a dilatory pace which belied the realistic "50" which faced us on the speedometer. But fifty miles an hour inevitably brings results, and San Antonio's pretentious towers soon loomed up out of Texas flatness to mark another milestone on our Panama trail.[†]

The lady secretary in the San Antonio Chamber of Commerce retreated into a corner when I poked my unshaven face past the door which bore the legend "Touring Information" to ask about the road to Mexico City.

"The road is very bad. We don't advise making the trip."

I tried patiently to explain to her that we had turned down a lot of good advice already and were prepared to disregard more if necessary, but that we were interested in learning the actual condition of the road if possible.

"We don't advise it," was her only comment on that and in vain I tried to ferret out some estimate of the time required—whether a week, a month, or perhaps (sarcastically) a year would suffice, but she had her orders and when we left she was still repeating, "We don't advise it."

---

* It's hard to understand what Arthur means here. It seems he's referring back to their crossing the Red River from Arkansas and including this drive to San Antonio, which is a mere 275 miles from Dallas. This is confirmed later when he mentions the five day's driving time it takes them to get to Laredo from New York.

† San Antonio, the seventh-largest city in the U.S. in 2019, had 250,000 residents in 1930, so it was already quite entitled to its towers.

Joe tried to excuse her by reflecting that she was probably bothered to death by tourists who considered the trip to the Mexican capital an ideal week-end jaunt and, if not discouraged, would go across in droves, only to wind up out of gas or water on the Mexican desert to curse the San Antonio Chamber of Commerce.

"She had no way of knowing that this is an *expedition* and not just a couple of half-baked tourists trying to get lost in the wilds of Mexico. Furthermore," and he looked accusingly at my salt-and-pepper hirsute adornment, which had sprung up in the last few days while I reveled in the luxury of no morning shave, and no afternoon shave either, "I don't blame her for backing up from a mug like that. You'd better see a barber before we start across the border, or they'll refuse us entrance as suspicious characters. It is a form of moral turpitude to take no more pride in your personal appearance than that."

But I still felt hurt and observed that the brown *señoritas* [unmarried young women] who thronged San Antonio's narrow sidewalks felt no such reluctance to associate with me; in fact, some of the smiles suggested just the opposite. I was dragged away from what promised to be a quick romance with a flashing little beauty about twelve hands high and perfumed with all that Woolworth['s] could offer, by my ever-practical brother.

"Lay off these brown babies," hissed the villain, "they knife you at night when you wish they were white."

"Why anybody should wish that is beyond me," I retorted, but suffered myself to be led away to safety and the Ford. We stowed away in the bulging interior and started threading through the narrow streets of town.

San Antonio, too, has its skyscrapers and a traffic problem. They, the 'scrapers, grow to unusual heights and the San Antonians have adopted color in profusion in the decorating of them, thereby stealing a march on the rest of the United States, which is just awakening to the fact that form plus color in a large building is more attractive than form alone.

I was surprised to find Spanish in quite as common use as English here.[*] In fact, a great many of the smaller businesses are run by Mexicans and the brown out-number the whites on the streets by a good margin. The architecture, too, is all very much Spanish in complexion and the town has an international air rarely attained by an American city. It seemed a shame to sacrifice it also to the goddess of mileage, but our rapidly diminishing funds whipped us into a realization that speed was

* Even today, the population is more than half Hispanic, and the city is completely bilingual.

the best economy. So speed it was, and still more speed until the lights of Laredo twinkled in the distance and we bore down on the last American town between us and Mexico.

After we left San Antonio, the country began to take on a different appearance and hinted at the scenery which lay ahead.* There still remained the baked red earth and the interminable flatness which was characteristic of all southeastern Texas, but the increasing frequency of cactus growth and the dense thickets of chaparral bespoke a closer acquaintance with those two desert plants in days to come.† Mexican peons with enormous hats, astride, or plodding alongside diminutive burros, were numerous, too, apparently as indigenous to the country as they would be to Mexican territory further south. A few grazing Texas long-horns were peering out of chaparral or racing across the road ahead of us with much snorting and flinging of tails. As we neared Laredo the pavement ended and we bounced over a graded dirt road with the realization that our fifty-mile-per-hours were numbered.

After circling the truly Mexican plaza which is the center of Laredo, we drew up at a restaurant and ordered our first meal from a Spanish menu with a waiter in attendance who spoke only that language, while still on American soil.‡ Between Joe's questionable Castilian and much pointing, we managed to order a 100 per cent American beefsteak with hard fried potatoes and indigestible apple pie. After that gastronomic conquest, we retired to the plaza to smoke and contemplate a Mexican exclusion law when conditions had reached the sad state wherein one had to speak a foreign tongue while still under the Stars and Stripes.

Mexico, in the form of Nuevo Laredo, State of Tamaulipas, was not a sight to quicken the pulse or materialize the imagery with which we had surrounded the Silver Republic, as it lay sprawled along the sluggish Rio Grande, which is grand in name only, being a small, sluggish stream wandering aimlessly between high banks down

* In fact, the brothers are leaving the grasslands and woodlands of the Edwards Plateau for the scrublands of the Rio Grande Plain.

† While not in the Chihuahuan Desert, Laredo isn't far from it. It's definitely on the dry side of the 98th parallel; in fact, it's almost at the 100th. West of that, rainfall is less than twenty inches per year, and, if you were farther north, you'd be in bison country. The Laredo area is generally regarded as sub-tropical steppe or semi-arid brush land.

‡ Laredo (2019 population around 275,000) has long been essentially Mexican. Even today, the city is ninety-five percent Hispanic, so its "truly Mexican plaza" should have been no surprise..

toward the Gulf of Mexico.* But somewhere out near the middle of that muddy river lay the International Boundary, and it marked the end of the first stage of our journey. We had driven the 2,335 miles from New York in five days' driving time with the enviable record of no punctures, no arrests for speeding, and no automobile trouble of any kind.† Our tires had gone more than eleven thousand miles when we started on the expedition, now had more than thirteen thousand to their credit, and four of them contained original Detroit air—Joe having picked up one nail in Wyoming last winter when he drove back to New York from Nevada. Such a trouble-free record speaks well for American automotive manufacturers and their product. I guess they will still be exporting cars and tires long after the rest of the world has howled itself hoarse over our tariff laws and has erected a twice-as-high barrier against us in protest.‡ You can't beat quality like that with mere mathematics, and who, I wonder, is going to suffer more than the foreign nations themselves, if forced to buy an inferior product at higher prices. (Gosh! I sound just like a good old 100 per center who is always raving about his country, right or wrong, and then drinking her health in some potent fluid which suggests she sometimes might be wrong.)

To go from tariff in the abstract to tariff in the concrete—we found that we either had to pay a duty of $80 on our automobile, which was out of the question, or get it bonded for re-export.§ This latter we proceeded to do.

Mr. Mumm, of the Laredo Chamber of Commerce, very kindly recommended us to the bonding company, which handled such matters, and also gave us the much-sought-after information on the Mexico City road. It was not, he assured us, as bad as we had been led to believe, and with good luck could be made in a week. This was reassuring news, to be sure, and we immediately resolved to cut off a few days from that good time which had been made recently by a man from the San Antonio Chamber of Commerce. (Can you beat it! I wanted more than ever to wring the lady secretary's handsome neck.) Mr. Mumm forewarned us of the

---

* Nuevo Laredo is just barely in Tamaulipas, lying at the northernmost tip of a salient of the state running as a sliver 143 miles north along the Rio Grande. The Rio Grande, at 1,896 miles, is one of the principal rivers of the American Southwest and northern Mexico and serves as the international border from El Paso and Ciudad Juárez to South Padre Island, Texas. Most of Tamaulipas lies along the Gulf of Mexico. It's a big place, with well over 500,000 people, but bigger cities in the state are Reynosa and Matamoros.

† So, a day to get from Manhattan to Washington, D.C., another to get to Knoxville, another to Little Rock, a fourth to Dallas, and a fifth to Laredo. Altogether this is day nine, April 1.

‡ This is a reference to the Hawley-Smoot Tariff Act they heard being reviled in the U.S. Senate in Chapter II.

§ In 2019, $80 was around $1,169.

formalities prerequisite to entering Mexico, so I started off to unroll the red tape while Joe rolled the Ford into a garage to strengthen the rear spring and have a mechanic touch up the valves.

After a visit to the Mexican consul, I went back and hauled Joe out from under the car to have another picture taken for the Mexican tourist passports. He was a little sulky at being taken away from his work and absolutely refused to clean up for the event, so I sat him down, grease and all, and had the photographer snap him for a photo, to go down in history as the worst ever presented with an application for a Mexican passport—the consul himself said so.

In the meantime, I had ascertained that it was to be something of a task to get our rifle into Mexican territory. The Mexican government, it seemed, looked with suspicion on gringos entering the country with firearms and were as like as not to confiscate the gun. I gathered, though, that the Mexican Commandant in Nuevo Laredo (a general, of course!) would, if convinced in the proper manner, and not in need of a gun for his latest recruits, grant the *permiso* [permission].[*] Only, of course, with the understanding that under no circumstances would the gun be fired. No one except the governor himself down in Victoria, three hundred miles away, could grant that privilege, and even then it would be valid only in the one state. It began to appear that we weren't going to do much promiscuous discharging of firearms in Mexico. Humorous in the extreme was the picture which came to mind of two Mexican bandit chiefs approaching each other and gravely asking to see each other's permission to carry and discharge firearms before beginning hostilities.[†]

I carried these tidings back to Joe, hard at work on the car. We decided we might as well do what everyone else did, smuggle the gun across. The gun was a long-barreled Winchester, though, and we could find no place about the car to conceal it, so perforce we became honest men and not smugglers (except for two cartons of cigarettes I had bought back at Macy's for eighty-nine cents each) and resolved to get the *permiso*.

That evening we met two young fellows from Decatur, Illinois, just back from a round trip to Mexico in a Ford coupe. They were highly enthusiastic about their trip, and after looking our outfit over, with the fifty-five-gallon auxiliary tank and

---

[*] It has been long been against the law, period, to take guns or ammunition into Mexico without a permit. Those who try face jail time and stiff fines.

[†] We will encounter the image of the Mexican bandit again and again. By this time, the bandit narrative that had emerged during the nineteenth century in struggle over class and nation had become a defining aspect of the national image. President Donald J. Trump, of course, repeatedly resurrected ominous views of Mexican people (as well as Muslims, immigrants, and people of color) during the Republican primary, the 2016 presidential campaign, and his presidency.

all, decided our only trouble would be keeping on the road. Outside of running out of gas, that had been their main difficulty. Their sage advice was to ask everyone in sight, no matter how many we saw, "*Es esta camino para México*" (Is this the road to Mexico)? and then take a majority vote. If most of them answered, "*Si, señor* [Yes, sir]," then it probably would be the road, but if the majority, or even a substantial minority, answered, "No, señor," then it was high time to look for someone who could speak English and find out where we were.

They were, in fact, so enthusiastic about Mexico that they insisted we join with them immediately and cross the international bridge for a "few beers" together. That sounded reasonable enough and with the all-around stipulation that a "few beers" would remain just that we stepped across into Mexico.

Nuevo Laredo's main industry is catering to thirsty Americans, so we had no trouble finding a bar big enough to lean on comfortably and without crowding.* The bartenders all spoke English, and, as the prices were in American money, we had no trouble in getting quick and expert service. After a round apiece we felt quite at ease but a little tired of standing, so we retired to a table in a room to the rear. Our friendship was growing apace, and we were learning more about Mexico every minute.

"If all the bars we stood up against in Mexico were placed end to end, it would make a fine highway from here to the capital," declared young Duncan.

"Yeah," chimed in Brown, "and prob'ly as far back as San Luis Potosí (Potosí rhymes with Tennessee), which reminds me that the gin fizzes at the Hotel Bar in San Luis are the best in Mexico."

This started an argument. Duncan insisted that a silver fizz at the Regis bar in Mexico City was by far the better drink; in fact, so good that one before luncheon just as the sun crossed its zenith outside and the hot afternoon settled down was well worth the entire trip.

I marveled at such fine discrimination and suggested we try one by way of comparing it with Mexico's best. Although it tasted very good to me, they were unanimous in declaring that the gin was very, very inferior.

At this juncture we discovered we had a friend in common—one Ed, a Decatur boy in New York City.

The chorus of "Well, this *is* a small world after all" welled out to the bar and a waiter was sent in immediately to take our order so we could drink to dear old Ed, which we did with much gusto. That gentleman would no doubt have been

---

* Laredo was already the most important trade border crossing between the U.S. and Mexico, and trade was its primary industry, though doubtless American tourists did feel the city lived on them.

much surprised had he heard how fervently we wished he were with us. With our friendship on such a firm foundation now, Duncan and Brown insisted we celebrate together their last night and our first night in Mexico. We pointed out the difference between a first night and a last night, how far we had to go, and how nearly ended their trip was—but all was in vain. They hauled us away in search of excitement. After prowling around Laredo's narrow, dusty streets for a time we found ourselves ensconced in the seats of honor reserved for cash American customers in what was undoubtedly the largest and best equipped dance hall in Nuevo Laredo. The jazz band blared forth some late Broadway hit in deference to the newly arrived gringos and twenty-seven Latin ladies of doubtful virtue and in scanty attire descended on us en masse. Each expressed willingness, yea, an almost uncontrollable desire to have a drink with us, to dance with us, in fact to do anything for us to make our stay in Nuevo Laredo more enjoyable, and a bevy of waiters appeared and started taking down orders. This looked like a sucker's field day and no fooling. Joe and I exchanged one comprehending glance and passed a quick motion to adjourn, which we did precipitately.

Safely back on the street Joe remarked sadly, "I hated to leave Clyde and Fred in there with that flock of vultures, but I hated worse to see this expedition wind up on the rocks in Nuevo Laredo. By the way, is that hundred-dollar bill still in your wallet?"

It was.

We broke into a trot to reach the bridge before nine, when it closed for the night. That is a clever trick they have for keeping unsuspecting Americans on the Mexican side all night and what they do to them and their bankrolls is not funny, if the reports we heard were true.

The entry in my log for that night is eloquent: "April 1—No mileage but terrific headache."*

___

* And so endeth the ninth day of their trip and the brothers' last night in the United States.

Chapter IV

# The Reach for a Lucky Instead of a Gun

At nine o'clock sharp we presented ourselves to the customs authorities for admittance to the Republic of Mexico.* Four hours later we emerged, tired but triumphant, in possession of full permission to enter not only ourselves, but our car, under bond to be reexported within sixty days, and our rifle, to be re-exported also in sixty days. The latter had to be taken out of Mexico, according to the stipulation, at no other place than Nuevo Laredo. Patiently we explained again and again that we were leaving the country at the Guatemalan border and would not find it convenient to come back to Laredo for the purpose of re-exporting a rifle. No difference, that was the law and we must abide by it. The general who granted us the permission even hinted broadly that the Mexican government was doing us a tremendous favor by allowing the gun to enter at all. After waiting an hour, during which he and all of his assistants, one at a time, came out and examined the gun and us carefully and then retired to the inner office for long consultations, we began to realize how serious a matter this was and were on the point of withdrawing our request when the general himself emerged and shook hands with us in true Latin fashion. He explained, through an interpreter, that he had carefully considered the case and had decided to allow us to bring in the gun. He sent us over to the custom house with an employee of the bonding company to get our permit O.K.'d. For two hours the customs employees stamped, signed, and passed judgment on this *permiso* [permission]. While I waited

---

* This is April 2, day ten.

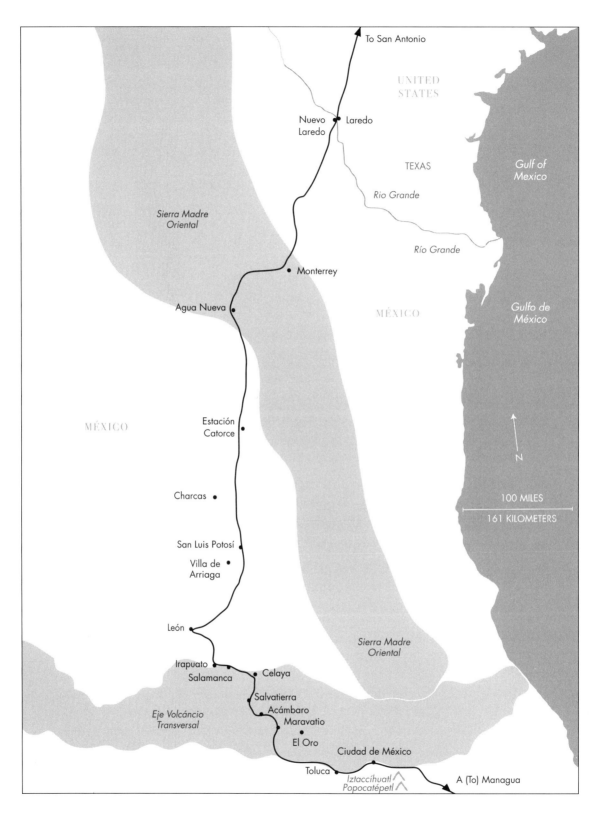

The brothers' journey from Nuevo Laredo to Ciudad de México.
Map by Morgan Pfaelzer. © 2020 Center for the Study of Place.

outside, Joe, as the Spanish-speaking member of the firm, followed it through its tortuous course. He swore that every employee in the building read and signed it at least once. And it was a large, two-story building, too.*

That detail attended to, we visited a money changer and attempted to get seventy-two American dollars changed into Mexican money. Here we found that Mexico had no paper currency, only coin.† We learned, too, that a peso was not a peso, strictly speaking, but fluctuated in value up or down according to the confidence, or lack of it, in the existing government. Today the Mexican government was pegged at about ninety-three percent, and we were given two dollars and fifteen cents Mexican (the peso has a par value of almost exactly fifty cents) for each American dollar. Feeling enormously rich with our sack of one hundred fifty-four silver *pesos*, we lugged it out to the car and debated what to do with it. As it weighed nearly ten pounds it was obviously impractical to carry that much silver in our pockets. We finally deposited it under the seat alongside the tools, just helping ourselves to a generous handful apiece for current expenses. I have never experienced more pleasurable spending than that which we did during the trip to the Mexican capital. Prices were cheap even when measured in that depreciated currency, and whenever the money in our pockets ran low, we just dipped out more handfuls of shining silver to replenish the supply. After a week of dipping and spending, our money sack was still bulging with pesos.‡

I put our reserve, a one-hundred dollar bill, under the rubber floor mat just in case we were held up by bandits, and we started off on our own little conquest of Mexico.

The country south of Laredo is in all respects similar to southern Texas—slightly rolling country with the ever-present cactus and mesquite as the only vegetation.§ The road was a fine, graveled highway, for the most part with an oiled surface. Six miles out we started on the "longest straight piece of highway in the world." For forty miles it continued without deviation to make good that boast.¶

---

* This process is a continuing characteristic of Mexican bureaucracy.

† In fact, the Banco de México had started issuing paper currency in 1925, though with only limited success until it was reorganized in 1931. Thereafter, paper money rapidly became the main medium of payment. There may well have been no paper money in Nuevo Laredo at the time.

‡ It is important to remember that 1930 is only ten years since the conclusion of the Mexican Revolution, which had devastated the country; even during the 1920s, there was turmoil and occasional fighting. Arthur and Joe Jr. are traveling through a poor country, struggling to get on its feet.

§ Most of this was in the state of Nuevo León, the capital of which is Monterrey (2019 population of more than 1,200,000 and growing).

¶ Monterrey's about 150 miles south of Laredo. It was linked with Laredo by rail in 1882 and by Mexico Federal Highway 85, the original route of the Pan-American Highway (also known as the Inter-American Highway) beginning in the 1930s.

As we approached Monterrey a low mountain range appeared to the west, rising higher and higher as we continued south. It is the northern end of the Eastern Sierra—the Sierra Madre Oriental—which with its sister range 300 miles further west—the Sierra Madre Occidental—effectively encloses the high plateau which comprises most of Mexico geographically and nearly all of the civilization, culture, and population.* Except for the ancient Maya race which flourished with such fertility on the Yucatan peninsula, Mexican civilization from the ancient Toltec to the Modern, which is almost sui generis, has risen, flowered, and fallen in this natural cradle.†

These two mountain walls form a wedge in the world, narrowing as the continent narrows toward its southern extremity, until at Mexico City they come almost together, and after one climaxing assault at the heavens in the form of the mountains Popocatépetl, Iztaccíhautl, and Orizaba,‡ they merge and all but disappear at the isthmus of Tehauntepec some 1,500 miles southward. Along the seacoasts and in the *tierra caliente*—hot country—a few cities have sprung up in modern times, but they are a comparatively recent contribution and not the Mexico of history nor even the real Mexico of today which parades itself before the enraptured traveler in such vivid color and high relief, supremely unconscious of the fact that it is North America's greatest show place and, unless I miss my guess, one of the greatest in the world.

Or possibly, instead of a wedge, we should compare this great plateau to a ship with Mexico City occupying the key position of pilot house near the prow. It is easy to think of the Spanish invaders as pirates scaling the sides and swarming over the decks to wrest control of the ship of state by murdering the master, Montezuma, and enslaving his subjects for the crew. To carry the comparison still further, we can picture the revolution which wrested control from Spain as a mutiny of the crew, sweeping down from the north—the stern—and recapturing the wheel only to find

---

* The Sierra Madre Oriental runs 630 miles from the Rio Grande south through Nuevo León, southwest Tamaulipas, San Luis Potosí, Querétaro, and Hidalgo to northern Puebla. There, it joins with the east-west running Eje Volcánico Transversal of central Mexico. We'll be dealing with this later. The Sierra Madre Occidental parallels the Pacific Coast, from just south of the Arizona-Sonora border southeast through eastern Sonora, western Chihuahua, Sinaloa, Durango, Zacatecas, Nayarit, Jalisco, and Aguascalientes to Guanajuato, where it joins with the Sierra Madre del Sur and the Eje Volcánico Transversal. The Central Mexican Plateau they enclose is better than a mile high, and, though not to extent fantasized here, it has indeed been the cradle of much of what we think about as Mexico.

† The Mayans also thrived in the Usumacinta River Valley and the highlands of Chiapas. Arthur also ignores the first major civilization of Mexico, that of the Olmecs, who flourished in the tropical lowlands of Veracruz and Tabasco.

‡ These are all notable peaks in the east-west running Eje Volcánico Transversal. They do disappear at the isthmus, which, with a maximum elevation of 735 feet, was long considered a potential rival to Panama and Nicaragua for the transshipment of goods between the Atlantic and Pacific.

that in three hundred years they had forgotten how to navigate, and could only quarrel among themselves while the ship plunged helplessly on. After a hundred years and more of plunging, during which it came perilously close to the rocks of Imperialism and was never at any time far off the shoals of Exploitation, we find her again under a steady hand and headed straight for the port of Prosperity, which apparently is the modern goal. That is, unless the unexpected happens, which in Mexico is never really unexpected, at most only unforeseen. Read the history of Mexico for four hundred years, and then perhaps you can understand why good government is the only unexpected thing which might arrive—and the country even had a modicum of that under the late, great dictator, Porfirio Díaz.* But, to an Anglo-Saxon, good government under a dictator appears to be a poor substitute for the real thing. However, sometimes I wonder if Latin Americans aren't . . .

But here comes Monterrey to terminate my wondering—and to save me from committing the unpardonable blunder of supposing any people, Latin Americans not excepted, could be better off under the heel of a dictator.

Monterrey is the Pittsburgh of Mexico, if one steel mill can make a Pittsburgh, and sure enough, the smoking stacks of the furnaces were the first object to command our attention.† Slipping naturally off their tops, our gaze rose to the twin mountains beyond.‡ Merged at the base, with the declivity between making a sweeping semicircle, they form a natural saddle which is the background for the city.

We drew up at Kelly's service station, the focus of all things automotive in Monterrey, and registered our car. This is a quaint custom which is nearly universal throughout Mexico and Central America. In most cities, and sometimes in the smallest hamlets, we would be stopped at the city gates by a policeman with upraised hand.

"*Alto!*" (Stop!) "*Que es su nombre?*" (What is your name?)

Then, after taking this down and the number of the car, he would step down from the running board and with a flourish of the hand toward the city, exclaim, "*Adelante!*" [Proceed!] with all the grace of presenting the keys to the city. And, indeed, one felt as if they were doing just that, they were so smiling and affable about it and so sorry to take señor's precious time. We grew to look forward to the

---

* Porfirio Díaz (1830–1915) was a Mexican general and dictator of Mestizo origin who ruled Mexico as its President for thirty years. Many became wealthy under Díaz, but hundreds of thousands were dispossessed and reduced to the most abject poverty. He was overthrown by the Mexican Revolution and died in exile.

† With a metropolitan population in 2019 of more than 4,800,000, greater Monterrey is the third-largest metropolitan area in the country (after Mexico City and Guadalajara). It held that rank in 1930 as well. It remains an industrial city. The brothers are now about 140 miles south of Laredo.

‡ This the Cerro de la Silla (Saddle Hill), 5,970 feet high. Given that Monterrey sits at 1,762 feet, the mountain towers over the city.

little encounters with pleasure and felt almost slighted if not given an opportunity to register our arrival and departure—for the same formality was usually gone through on leaving.

We threaded our way up town through the incredibly narrow streets—so narrow, in fact, that often there was room for only one car and although they were all one-way thoroughfares, it took considerable dexterity to avoid running over the pedestrians who were continually hopping on and off the two-foot sidewalks as they passed each other. To add to the hazard the corners were totally blind, each block presenting a solid, unbroken front of white-washed adobe walls from corner to corner. The Mexican has his yard, the patio, within, so he builds his house flush up against the narrow sidewalk, thereby earning the condemnation of the motorist and, if there be more than one car in town (there weren't in some we visited), creating the need for traffic police.* The continuous din of horns—one sounds the horn when approaching each corner—creates a noise far out of proportion to the traffic, and it was with immense relief that we found a parking place at the plaza and sought out some nourishment before going on to Saltillo.

Leaving Monterrey at dusk, we climbed through a pass which breaks the Sierra Madre here and prowled along through the night toward Saltillo which lies some sixty miles to the southwest.† The moon rose late and revealed us traveling between rather high mountain walls which increased the sense of loneliness that we felt in traveling at night on this, our first night in Mexico.‡ As our headlights swung around corners and over hills I half expected them to reveal the bandits who are supposed to be continually lurking along Mexican roads. None appeared, however, and as the road was degenerating into something resembling a trail, we began to cast about for a camp site.

The headlights of an approaching car swung into view and we hailed it to ask about a camp site. It was a small truck with a road crew looking for a tractor that had left Monterrey that morning. A figure materialized out of the shadows back of the cab. He greeted us in English.

"Where are you going—Saltillo? Oh, beyond. Well, don't stop there. That's a hell of a place. I'm a chiropractor, and when things got quiet up in the States last

---

* This type of home, with rooms arranged around a patio, was exported to Mexico by the Spaniards, where the Romans had brought it, who, in turn, had it via the Greeks from . . . the Egyptians? Its origin is unknown—it's pervasive in the Far East as well—but, in the West, it's thought about as a Mediterranean house type.

† And, in so doing, they crossed into the state of Coahuila, of which Saltillo is the capital.

‡ Of course, the brothers are ascending the Sierra Madre Oriental, which, in these parts, rises to more than 12,000 feet. They are just north of what today is Cumbres de Monterrey National Park (438,355 acres), which was created in 1939 to protect natural flora and fauna from Monterey's growing urbanization. The Cerro de la Silla is actually in the park.

winter I went down there and set up business. I was the only one in town, of course, and I soon saw why. These devils don't understand the first thing about chiropractory. They thought I was some kind of a witch doctor and wouldn't come near me. I had about one patient a week, so after sticking it out for two months, I decided to pull out. The night before I was to leave some *ladrón* (robber) broke into my room and stole everything I had. So here I am, bumming back to the States. Got an American cigarette?"

We had. He was so joyful after the first puff that I, realizing how hard a lot was a chiropractor's in Mexico, gave him the pack.

We ascertained that a camping place could be found a few miles further and pushed on.

"S'long. My name's Waters. See you again someday." And he rode off into the night puffing contentedly on an American cigarette—just a poor, disillusioned chiropractor bound back to the States.

Since leaving Monterrey we had been climbing steadily and the air was noticeably cooler, really cold. We made camp and slept under all the blankets we had, but they were insufficient and toward morning the chill was just at the point which makes it a question of whether to stick it out in bed or get up and start a fire. Being tired, and a little lazy, too, we suffered in bed. The sun finally rose and just as I was getting warmed up to a good sleeping temperature, Joe announced that it was time for all explorers to be up and doing. He answered my noncommittal grunt with a well-placed pair of feet on my back, and I awoke to a glorious Mexican morning—sprawling in the sand.

As we were breaking camp, many cars, all loaded to the limit with happy Mexicans, passed us, headed for Monterrey.[*] In answer to our wave they always chorused "*Buenos dias!*" [Good morning!] and waved in return. I began to like these lighthearted fellows immensely. There was none of the sullen resentment evident which I had come to associate with Mexicans from seeing them in droves at work along the western railroads.

Buzzing through the crisp morning air into Saltillo for breakfast,[†] I became aware that this was the essence of living—a good car under us, ten pounds, more or less, of silver bullion under the seat, a panorama of gray hills strangely like the open

---

[*] It is April 3, their eleventh day of travel.

[†] Saltillo (2019 population of more than 830,000) is the capital of the state of Coahuila, where it's located in the southeastern corner. Founded in 1577, it's the oldest post-Conquest settlement in northern Mexico. Known historically for its tile and serapes, today more than one-third of all cars and nearly two-thirds of all trucks produced in Mexico are assembled here, including those for Chrysler, Ford, and Mercedes-Benz.

country of the West I love so well, unfolding before us and, to top it off, a flood of Mexican sunshine which laved us with a generosity no New York sun ever exhibited.[*]

We had sought the sun. We found it near Saltillo. If it did blaze from a cloudless sky it was still kind, it did not burn—it caressed. The sunshine on the Mexican plateau is misleading. Its intensity is tempered by some unknown quality of that rarified atmosphere which leads the newcomer to underexpose his photographic films, but saves him at the same time from sunburn.

In Saltillo, as always, we drove first to the plaza central to estimate the city. As we drew up, a terrific clanging arose from the cathedral across the park. Two young Mexicans were ringing the two huge bells, which topped that imposing edifice.[†] As if it were great sport they were rolling them over and over, and their competitive spirit was responsible for the tremendous clamor which must surely have caused the wicked to recant and the good to feel rewarded. Or maybe it affected them both alike as an unmitigated nuisance to be endured in silence, as perforce one couldn't talk above that din.

As the noise subsided, we slipped into a little restaurant to have our too-long postponed breakfast. It was quite late, the proprietor told us, but would we be patient for just a short while, and he assured us we would be fed. We waited and still we waited. After a time, in response to our clamorous demand for food, our host appeared and smilingly assured us that breakfast would be served in "*un momento, un momento*" [one moment]. He accompanied his declaration with a gesture in which the thumb and forefinger were poised ever so close together, signifying the smallest, tiniest, space of time imaginable, which in Saltillo resolved itself into a full half hour. We were to learn that "*un momento*" accompanied by this gesture of minuteness means, in Mexico and Central America at least, not "one moment" as it appeared to mean, but was a courteous Latin-American way of saying, "Be patient" or "Keep your shirt on, Rome wasn't built in a day."

While we waited, a pleasant young man with blond hair and blue eyes dropped in to chat with us. He had seen our car with its New York license plates outside and was curious to know how we had happened to stray so far from home. We exchanged formalities and as his name was decidedly German, I ventured a query.

---

[*] Here, he is referring to the arid to semi-arid scrublands of the plateau and to the Madrean pine-oak woodlands of the mountains. These latter are important sites of biological diversity.

[†] In Mexico, church bells are often rung by kids this way. The cathedral, with its Spanish Baroque facade, was built from 1745–1800 and is widely regarded as the best example of colonial religious architecture in northeastern Mexico.

"You are German, aren't you?"

"I am *not*!" Then, proudly, "I am Mexican. My ancestors were German, of course, but I am a native-born Mexican, not pan- nor pro-anything."*

Coffee and rolls arrived and nothing else. Our Mexican friend explained that this was the customary breakfast. We prevailed on him to explain to the owner that we were very hungry and would appreciate something more substantial. That plump, good-natured individual bowed and said he would be pleased to serve us anything we desired would we but suggest it. I suggested eggs, about half a dozen, and Joe suggested bacon, about half a pound. He registered astonishment, but forthwith sent his assistant hurrying out to purchase it. Strange people, these gringos, no end of trouble with their crazy demands for food in such large and unheard-of quantities. He sighed patiently and returned to puttering with his new-fangled oil stove which was the cause of the previous delay.

Our guest was a cartoonist, we learned, and evinced a desire to caricature us then and there. We posed and he turned in a very creditable job, although I think the extra chin which hung from my jowls was more accentuated than even the necessities of caricature called for.

In due time—about two hours after we had entered the restaurant—the bacon and eggs arrived, and ten minutes later we were seeking the city limits.

Out of town we met caravan after caravan of ox-teams loaded with firewood. Plugging along the dusty road at the pace which only an ox—and a Mexican peon— could well maintain, about two miles per hour, they were a never-ending part of the landscape. Led by a Mexican with a pointed stick with which he occasionally gave them a poke, they come closer to slow motion than anything I have ever seen outside a motion picture hall. Each time a ponderous foot is lifted to be deliberately and slowly placed down a short distance ahead, the ox goes through a whole physiological and psychological process. First he decides to lift it, then with a tensing of muscles along his whole mighty frame, he lunges forward and when midway in the lunge, he pulls the hoof out of the creamy, flowing dust and with slow deliberation swings it forward to its new resting place. Then, after the three other limbs have gone through the same process and caught up with the first, he looks around, as far as the binding neck-yoke will permit, to see how far he has moved. The driver arouses him from this contemplative posture with a sharp poke and he lunges forward to take another stride. This pace maintained all day will, if not too much time is taken out

* Germans began migrating to Mexico during the early-nineteenth century, though most arrived during the Porfiriato to take advantage of the opportunities Díaz offered.

for resting—the driver from poking and the oxen from making up their minds to move—will net a good ten miles.*

Between the ox-team caravans were whole trains of burros loaded high with faggots and often as not topped with a little Mexican peon, barefooted, in tight-fitting white cotton trousers, with a poncho drawn tightly around his shoulders and over his nose—to keep out the dust—and between the poncho and the rim of the enormous, unbelievably large hat a pair of gleaming black eyes peering out at the world—and at a Ford roadster with two gringos aboard on the road to Mexico.† Sometimes instead of an *hombre* [man], the beast of burden would be carrying, in addition to the pay load, of course, a smiling *señorita* or a smiling but much heavier *señora* [married woman]. As their steeds went bounding out through the brush on our approach, they laughed gaily and waved to us as we went by. It was all in fun, to be sure, and the holiday spirit so evident in them as they rode along just couldn't be bothered. We soon fell into the spirit of this, the land of eternal sunshine and the radiant philosophy, that the coming of tomorrow was very, very doubtful. If a carelessly roped burro tossed off his burden to stand reflectively gazing at it—he never thought to run away—we stopped and helped pile it on his patient back, exchanging meanwhile effusive salutations and elegant compliments which cleared the way for a borrowed cigarette and a piece of cake—*pan dulce* [sweet bread]—in return.

"Where are the *señores* going?"

"To Mexico!"

"Ah! A *mas grande ciudad*" [largest city]!

"How far?"

"Oh, many, many leagues! How many, *quien sabe* (who knows)? Perhaps *un mil* (one thousand)—perhaps *dos mil* (two thousand)."

"Well, *muchas gracias, señor* [many thanks, sir], and may God go with you."‡ And with a deferential touch of hats they bade us good bye.

Thus, drunk with the charm of Old Mexico and as happy and carefree as our irrepressible, wayside brothers, we swung down to the high plateau toward the haunts of Montezuma.

* As Arthur says, oxen pulling carts do average about two miles an hour. Given feeding, watering, and the like, they can do, as Arthur says, about ten miles a day.

† Sombreros at this time regularly reached two feet across, and scenes like this, with increasingly smaller sombreros, were common in rural Mexico into the 1960s.

‡ The common Spanish phrase is *Vaya con Dios* ("Go with God" or "May God be with you").

## Chapter V

# "Es Esta Camina Para México?"*

**A** short distance out of Saltillo we passed through the pass of Angostura where that doughty old fighter, General Taylor, made American history in February 1847, by turning back Santa Anna and winning the first major battle of the Mexican War.** With five thousand men he effectively blocked the pass against the repeated assaults of the Mexican general at the head of practically the whole Mexican army of some twenty thousand men. General Taylor's forces had been greatly weakened by the withdrawal, against his wishes, of many of his troops to be used by General Scott for the attack on Veracruz and the march to Mexico City.† Thus reduced in number, they fought with such vicious persistency that although outflanked at one time and in grave danger of being routed, they rallied under the personal leadership of Taylor and threw back the Mexican hosts to close the gap, and as it turned out, to win the battle. When the fighting was at its bitterest, General Santa Anna sent word to General Taylor to surrender.

He sent back the reply, later used as a rallying call in his presidential campaign, "General Taylor never surrenders!" Santa Anna, undoubtedly realizing the futility of continuing a battle against a foe who wouldn't be defeated, forthwith withdrew to San Luis Potosí—and thereby helped elect an American President.‡ It is generally

---

* "Is this the road (way) to Mexico?"

**This was the Battle of Buena Vista in the Mexican-American War of 1846–1848. The war resulted in the successful termination of Mexico's effort to reclaim Texas and in the U.S. annexation of Alta California, Arizona, and New Mexico, of the contemporary American Southwest.

† Winfield Scott (1786–1866) is considered by many historians to be one of America's best military commanders during his fifty-three-year career. Veracruz, founded in 1519 by Spanish explorer Hernán Cortés (1485–1547), is a major port on the Gulf of Mexico.

‡ Zachary Taylor's (1784–1850) war-hero status won him election as the twelfth President of the United States (1849–1850). Santa Anna is Antonio López de Santa Anna (1794–1876), a major figure in Mexican military history and politics who, during a forty-year career, served as a general of the army (including a victory at the Alamo in 1836 and eleven non-sequential presidential terms (1833–1855).

admitted that had he continued the battle he must have eventually routed the out-numbered Americans, but of course with great loss to his army, which he needed badly to defend the capital against Scott's tremendous offensive. As we gazed over this time-healed battlefield, I could not help but wonder, with no discredit to the unquestionably brave Taylor, if an American commander had ever been forced into an unavoidable surrender after such a defiant statement—my American history failed to reveal it, but still—I wondered.

Continuing past Agua Nueva, the southernmost American outpost of the Mexican War, we dropped over into another flat valley which continued unbroken for two hundred miles into San Luis Potosí.* We chugged along on the heels of the retreating Santa Anna, filled with wonder that he should have exerted himself to dispute possession of this desolate land which, except for a few desert palms [Joshua trees] and the never-ending cactus, was as devoid of vegetation as an asphalt road.

Occasionally we passed a little village of mud huts, white-washed and clean-looking from a distance, but quite unsanitary appearing—and smelling—from close up. Naked children disputed possession of the dirtiest gutters with scrawny hogs, of the razorback variety, and quite hairless dogs. The children chased the dogs, and the dogs chased the swine, and when we appeared they all joined forces, and with a great shouting and barking and grunting, chased us. I half expected the urchins to follow the dogs' example and bite at the tires, but that evidently was the dividing line; otherwise they acted much the same. The adult population would stand in the doorways and watch the noisy parade evidently enjoying it as much as the children.

Each house had a small, barbed-wire enclosed yard, filled with the spine-covered cactus planted as close together as possible, much as a rural American family would have a vegetable garden. This was the topic for considerable discussion between Joe and me. What earthly use these people could have for this spine-covered, sword-like plant remained considerable of a mystery to us until in one of these yards we found a native drawing off into an evil-smelling pig-skin bag a whitish, almost colorless fluid. He had tapped the huge center stalk of a cactus which had flowered out at a height of ten feet or so.† After considerable questioning, we gathered that this fluid was indeed the nectar of the gods, famous *pulque*, which is to the Mexican peon what

* This was not actually the southernmost American outpost of the war, since not only did Winfield Scott take Veracruz, Mexico City, and Puebla, but Matthew C. Perry (1794–1858), Commodore of the U.S. Navy, also took Villahermosa on the southern Gulf Coast, nearly 600 miles south of Agua Nueva.

† Though a succulent, the agave or maguey is not actually a cactus, which is in a wholly other botanical order. Chiefly Mexican, the agave, or century plant, flowers only once before dying. Its sap can be fermented into pulque, a mild alcoholic beverage. It can also be distilled into a *mezcal*, the best known of which is *tequila*.

Top: Arthur assesses our first stretch of "carreterra", cart-road. 32 miles south of Saltillo, Mexico and about 240 miles from Laredo.

Bottom: Cactus growing on top of rock wall. Probably more effective than barbed wire.

All the 57 varieties of Cacti throve in this region. It seems to be a general rule that when nothing else will grow, you will find one of the varieties of Cacti. This picture was taken 66 miles from Saltillo but it may as well have been 6 or 660 for in both places you would likely find good health Cacti. The Toltecs discovered that Cacti would produce pulque which cause their downfall. Apr. 4, 1930.

"Desert Palms" or Joshua Trees (yucca arborescens) from the right-of-way of the Nat'l Railways of Mexico. Material for "Trees at Night". There is often a patch of somewhat smaller palms than these which resemble an advancing army. This valley was about 25 miles wide and 200 miles long. The Indians in this region were very kind and hospitable, much in contrast to their appearance. Friday, April 4, 1930.

beer is to the German.* From the way our informant smacked his lips and afterward gave a ludicrous exhibition of staggering and whooping, it was apparent that he considered it a fine drink indeed. We refused his generous offer to taste the product and drove on to speculate on the success prohibition might have in a country where every backyard was a small brewery.

"If some ingenious Burbank ever develops that cactus so it will grow in the States, think what a lot of trouble the 'Prohibs' will be in for," Joe mused.†

At Catorce, which means fourteen, and was named for fourteen bad *hombres* who had their headquarters there many years ago, we searched out a restaurant.‡ There were two, so we asked for the better one.

As we went in the door, two pigs bolted by us in a dash for the street. We retreated to the car to think it over. Hunger finally won out and we entered and asked for boiled eggs—*huevos pasados por agu*a—and coffee. Thus began our egg diet which lasted for days. Boiled eggs were at least clean, and obtainable anywhere. We eventually got to be less particular about our food, one had to—or eat eggs—but right now we were not acclimated to such uncleanliness.

An old boy sat in the corner with his poncho wrapped around him while we ate. He was conversationally inclined and told Joe his life history. When a young man— he was sixty-four now—he had heard about the Río Grande del Norte, so resolved to see it for himself. He started out to walk to it. He said that he made it in five days. It was about two hundred miles, and he lived on straight corn while doing it. He had a two-weeks' supply of corn with him, so after looking at the river he turned around and came back. That trip had evidently satisfied his wanderlust, for he hadn't been out of town since. We parted amid eloquent felicitations and the inevitable consignment to the care of God, and he sent his son with us to show us the way out of town.

In spite of the uncleanliness, the Mexican peons have an irresistible appeal for their simple kindliness and naive courtesy. The men never failed to touch their hats in a respectful salute when we passed them along the trail and were always willing to

---

* Indeed, *pulque* was this popular in central Mexico, but today it accounts for less than ten percent of the alcohol consumed in Mexico, beer (*cerveza*) having replaced it.

† Luther Burbank (1849–1926) was an American botanist and horticulturist who developed more than 800 strains and varieties of plants during his fifty-five-year career. Of course, the agave is as native to the southwestern U.S. as the rest of Mexico.

‡ Arthur seems to mean Estación Catorce rather than Real de Catorce. Small towns not ten miles apart, Real de Catorce is usually shortened to Real, and it is distinctly in the mountains. Estación Catorce is on the railroad, which the brothers are next to the following morning.

guide us back to the road if we were lost—which we were a good deal of the time.* There were innumerable cross roads and branches, each looking as well-worn as the other, and the sound advice to inquire about the road from everyone we saw was proving its worth.

We resolved to drive as late that night as we could find the road. About eleven o'clock we came across a car parked by the roadside, the first we had seen since leaving Saltillo. It had a Kansas license, so I chanced a query in English.

"Is this the road to San Luis Potosí?"

A sleepy-eyed face raised up and peered out of the window. "San Luis Potosí? Is that on the road to Mexico [City]?"

"Yes."

"Well, this must be the road, then, because we are heading for Mexico City and the last guy we saw who could speak English said we were right. That was about ten miles back."

Ho! Another tourist! The Pan-American trail wasn't exactly crowded, but it was a pleasure to know there were others on the road.

We thanked them and drove on until we got hopelessly lost in a maze of trails through the cactus, and had to camp.

Dawn was another revelation of pinks and reds and revealed the road a bare hundred yards away.† We had mastered that umbrella tent now and it took us very few minutes to stow it away and fry some bacon and eggs for breakfast. A tattered *gaucho* [cowboy] on a good-looking horse rode up and had a cup of coffee with us. Bandits, he told us, had stolen his cattle last year and reduced him to dire poverty. Would the *señores* give him a coat to replace the tattered jacket which he wore? We found a coat which was crying to be discarded and presented it to him with a couple of bars of soap to boot, of which we still had a plentitude, even after trading off a case and a half at the tourist camp in Laredo. He was as happy as if we had given him a new herd of cattle, to restock his ranch, and rode gaily off waving his sombrero at us until he disappeared into the cactus. I don't doubt that he discarded the soap when out of our sight, for he seemed unacquainted with its use and laughed heartily when I gave a practical demonstration with some water from the canteen.

* It is interesting exactly how the brothers got to San Luis Potosí (also known as San Luis), but, by the time they reached Catorce in the state of San Luis Potosí, they had in all likelihood crossed a corner of the state of Zacatecas.

† This was day twelve, April 4.

Our trail lay along the main line of the Mexican National Railways, first on one side and then on the other.* As our map showed us we were about to cross the Tropic of Cancer, we examined a monument along the right of way, expecting that it might mark the end of the temperate zone and the beginning of the torrid. It proved to be the monument of some Mexican who was killed in some long past revolution— or maybe he just died. The inscription failed to tell the cause of his demise. So we crossed latitude 22 degrees, 30 minutes, north, without offering to the sun-god, which would be fitting and proper as we entered his domain.

We came upon a Ford truck stalled in the road about nine o'clock. It was from Pennsylvania, but the owner, a Mexican gentleman, spoke no English. He managed to convey the idea, though, that he wished us to try and repair the car. We tinkered with it for a while and ascertained that the condenser was burned out and beyond repair. He replied to our offer to send one out by train from San Luis by shaking his head. No, he would wait until someone came along with one! Such sublime faith should be rewarded, but my guess is that he is still waiting.

Not more than one or two cars a day passed by and the chances that one of them would be carrying an extra condenser are considerably less than one in a thousand. He composed himself for rest in the shade of the car and rolled a cigarette while his *señora* unpacked some sweetmeats for the kind *Americanos*. His eight or ten children romped through the brush playing games and altogether it was a happy family group out here in the cactus waiting for a condenser. If patience be a virtue, then these people are certainly the most virtuous in the world.

Charcas on market day: the whole population sitting cross-legged on the streets with every conceivable commodity heaped up before them.† The few purchasers seemed to be buying little and haggling long over the price. But that, apparently, was the sport of the game, enjoyed immensely by the buyer and seller alike, as well as all the bystanders. A particularly noisy or clever bargainer would quickly draw a crowd and if the deal was too quickly consummated, there was a general sigh of disappointment. We drew up to the center of this gay scene and stopped to make a few purchases ourselves. As we drew up a young urchin leaped on each running board with a bucket of lemonade in one hand and a glass in the other. We disclaimed any desire to

---

* "Trail" would definitely seem to be the appropriate word for the road(s) the brothers had been driving since leaving Saltillo.

† Charcas is a municipality in the state of San Luis Potosí known today for its advanced technology and many tourist attractions. Located just south of the Tropic of Cancer, at 6,627 feet elevation, snow is common year-round.

quench our thirst at these traveling soft drink stands, but they followed us hopefully as we walked around, to be on the job if we changed our minds.

As we bought a dozen oranges and a sack of peanuts and some candy that looked clean enough to eat, they seemed disappointed that we didn't haggle about the price, but paid what they tentatively set as the price—which was ridiculously cheap at that, but about twice what they expected to get.

At Charcas are located some of the richest silver mines in the world. Below the town are the vast dumps which attest to the tremendous underground activities which have been carried on since the old Spanish days.[*]

As we crossed the main railroad line again—Charcas is on a branch—we saw a long procession of Indian women with jugs, pails, and five-gallon gasoline cans poised on their heads, marching up to a freight locomotive standing on the tracks. Curiously we watched while the fireman filled each container with water and they marched back into town bearing aloft the *agua* which quenched thirst on the desert. A fine subject for a picture, but as so often happened when a good subject appeared, we were out of films.

As we neared San Luis we entered a large *hacienda*—farm [also a landed estate or ranch]—and traveled for ten miles through the best crop of cactus I have been privileged to see, thousands of acres devoted to the production of *pulque* that San Luis Potosí might not go thirsty.[†] Dozens of men with machetes—long thin knives used in tapping the plants—marching behind trains of burros with pig-skin containers loaded with the day's crop (or should I say the day's run?).

We were still dragging through this endless sea of cactus when I hailed a cathedral spire in the distance as the first sign of San Luis Potosí.[‡] As we bore down on the Silver City, whose praises we had heard sung so loudly and so long, we expected to find a beautiful place where we might linger for a time to refresh ourselves from two long, hard days on the desert—and incidentally to sample the gin fizzes at the Hotel Bar.

The outskirts of the city were not prepossessing, and the suburbs of San Luis looked even dirtier than most towns we had been through. The same naked or half-naked children shouted at us as we drove down the street, and the same mangy-looking curs yelped and snapped at our tires.

---

[*] And which are still being carried on. In fact, a fight was waged recently between a Canadian silver mine and the Huichol Indians not far from Charcas.

[†] Again, the agave is not a cactus, though the attribution is common enough.

[‡] This is about 280 miles south of Laredo, the way they went. San Luis Potosí is the capital of the state of the same name and these days is a thriving city of nearly 800,000.

Market place at Las Comas, Mexico, about 50 miles south of San Luis Potosi.

At the first main street crossing, the policeman gathered his statistics and when we asked the way to the hotel, he climbed aboard and rode with us to direct us. So we proceeded to the plaza central. The policeman blew his whistle to clear the way, we blew the horn to help him, the traffic police at the corners tooted their whistles to clear the way, and amid much noise we officially entered San Luis Potosí with all the ceremony of a Grover Whalen reception (in New York).[*] Two startled Americans, seeing us thus officially escorted up the main street, concluded that here were two gringos in need of help, so they came on a run to ask.

"What's all the shouting about? Are you under arrest?"

"Not at all," I answered. "We just drove in from Laredo and our friend here has given us the keys to the city. Are you on the welcoming committee?"

"Sure, why not?" the tall blond responded. "This being Saturday night, and having plenty of time on my hands, I hereby welcome you to San Luis Potosí and propose a little drink to start the festivities. What do you say, Jim?"

Jim said, "O.K!" so we retired to the nearest bar, which place is never more than twenty steps away in Mexico, and had two drinks on the welcoming committee. We tried to buy the next one, but Jim insisted, "It is the duty, privilege, and prerogative of the committee to furnish the refreshments so hang onto your money. You'll need it before you get to Panama, anyway!"

That was very true, but it was hardly sportsmanlike to let our self-appointed reception committee do all the buying, and I said so.

About this time Joe developed an uncontrollable and still less understandable desire to get out of San Luis. He said later it was caused by catching a glimpse of himself in the bar mirror and realizing that now was the time to leave and not later. So, for better or for worse, we apologized to our genial hosts and slipped away.

As I have said, we anticipated much from this city, famed as the silver capital of the Silver Republic, but it fell far short of our expectations. The streets were thronged with beggars, pitifully crippled in many cases, and everywhere was poverty, filth and disease.[†]

The low price of silver had shut down most of the mines and, as the Mexican seldom saves for the inevitable rainy day, the former miners were added to the

---

[*] Grover Whalen (1886–1962) was a prominent New York City politician, businessman, and public relations guru who, later in his career, was appointed Chairman of the Mayor's Committee on Receptions to Distinguished Guests. He officially welcomed everyone from Charles Lindbergh to Douglas MacArthur and was the master of the ticker-tape parade.

[†] Again, the Mexican Revolution is only ten years behind them, and depressed silver prices had shut down many of the mines. San Luis is actually a beautiful city whose center was declared a UNESCO World Heritage Site in 2010, within the World Heritage Site of the Camino Real de Tierra Adentro, the old Spanish colonial Silver Route to Santa Fe, New Mexico.

poverty-stricken masses. The plaza was a beautiful spot, though. Its tall palms harbored a multitude of birds which sang lustily to cheer the poor Mexican devils who were unfortunate enough to be born in this particular spot in an unjust world.

An attaché of the American consulate hailed us on the street. We asked him the way to the telegraph office and he went along to interpret. The two telegrams cost $7.95, which was more than we had spent in Mexico altogether. He purchased two bottles of gin for the evening, and we drove him out to his home before leaving.

At the city limits was a gate, barred by a heavy chain, which marked the beginning of a toll road. We paid the *peso* demanded and received in return a receipt which had a list of tolls which included burros, five cents; *hombres*, five cents; and carts, twenty-five cents.*

Our trail led us over a mountain road which climbed up and up till the lights of San Luis twinkled far below us in the darkness, all that remained of the visible world except the narrow road ahead which inclined ever upward to the top of the world. San Luis Potosí is more than 6,000 feet above sea level, and we had climbed at least 2,000 feet above it. Soon we leveled off on a high, wind-swept mesa and after driving for an hour, we made a dry camp. A more desolate spot could hardly have been found. As the moon rose it revealed us alone in the center of a vast plateau with nothing in sight except a far-off mountain range to the west. A few coyotes yelped and howled in the distance to intensify the eerie quality of the night. Joe and I cracked a few stale jokes between us to break the everlasting quiet but soon gave up that abortive attempt and relapsed into silence, to fall asleep and dream of bandits and revolutions and other exciting things, amidship in the good barque, "Mexico."

Our third day in Mexico was a repetition of the other two.† We were traveling through a much higher country, but the mountains in sight still rose above us. The aspect was much the same as that on the plateau further north. To all appearance the natives wore the same clothing as their brethren in the lower country, but the ever-present poncho was wrapped a little more tightly to ward off the highland chill. How they could stand a temperature which in the early morning was near freezing, clad in light weight cotton clothes, was a mystery to me. Perhaps they did it with pulque. We noticed the *pulquerías* [bars] filled with roistering crowds this Sunday morning. Age or sex was no deterrent, either, for the women were almost as

---

* The *peso*, of course, is the basic monetary unit of Mexico. Today, travelers in Mexico still have the option of driving on modern toll roads (such as Mexican Federal Highway 87) versus the old roads, which are slow and often congested with all types of vehicles.

† This the thirteenth day of the brothers' trip, April 5.

"High and dry". Camp on a windswept Mesa at about 8000 feet elevation. 18 miles south of San Luis Potosi. Note the beard. We were refused admission to the only decent cafe in Leon the same afternoon after going without breakfast and dinner all day. April 6 (Sunday).

Sunday morning in Old Mexico. Church in Villa de Arriaga. Whatever else they may be, the natives are devout Christians. Americans should blush with shame if statistics on relative "church goin'" in U.S. and Mexico were published. Apr. 6, 1930.

"Hidalgo" Mexican Patriot. This fine bust erected in desolate plaza of Villa de Arriago, Mexico. The poorest villages often have fine monuments and always fine churches. If the money spent in churches in Mexico were spent in schools she could be a world power. Many small villages have churches of which any U.S. town could be proud. Apr. 6, 1930.

The T H Ranch and Fort, north of Leon in central Mexico. We were lost and several miles off our route (it couldn't be called a road) when we stumbled upon this. We made many inquiries about this rancho and finally came to the conclusion that Mexicans like Americans know very little of their own country. Saturday, April 6, 1930.

numerous as the men and children; girls and boys both, were noticeably in attendance at these gaudy drink shops.* Perhaps they drank to gain courage to face the priest or to super-induce a mild state of coma the better to endure the flow of unintelligible Latin, because the churches, too, were filled to overflowing. At Villa de Arriaga I snapped a picture of a church where the devout peons had come to pray in such numbers that a few were forced to kneel outside in the hot sun while the priest inside invoked divine blessings on their bowed heads.† One little fellow had placed comfort above respect, though, for he prayed on unabashed with his hat on the back of his head.

The right road was harder than ever to find. We got hopelessly lost before afternoon and finally stumbled onto a rancho, which was also a serviceable fort for emergencies. There they gave us new directions, and after an hour's traveling over what was little more than a boulder-strewn trail, we landed on a good road which climbed over the mountain into León.

A few miles out of that city we crossed a pass and started down a grade which was nothing more than a series of switchbacks across the face of a great mountain.‡ León itself lay beneath us and all about was a panorama of highly cultivated countryside, as striking a contrast to the desert we had been crossing as suburban Los Angeles is to the Mojave Desert.

For an hour our brakes smoked and our engine raced while we let ourselves down from the clouds to the city at our feet. León ranks in size with San Luis Potosí, but differs from it in that it is the center of a rich agricultural country where irrigation has seduced a bountiful crop of semi-tropical fruits from the arid soil.§ Poverty is not the ever-present background that it is in San Luis, so in our short stop we awarded León the banner over its sister city further north. But even in León that malady is by no means absent.

To the casual eye, beggars seem to outnumber the non-beggars on the streets. One wonders why the richest church in the world does so little for its poverty-stricken communicants.

Maybe the policy of redeeming the soul and allowing the body to starve is best for the immortal man, but it is certainly tough on the mortal one.

---

* *Pulque* can be quite mild and is rich in vitamins C, B complex, D, and E, amino acids, and minerals.

† In Villa de Arriaga, the brothers are in the extreme southwestern corner of the state of San Luis Potosí and about to cross over into the state of Guanajuato. In 2019, the town was home to some 15,000 people.

‡ In Arriaga, the brothers were at 7,100 feet, and the pass would have been higher. León itself is at nearly 6,000 feet elevation.

§ In 2019, with nearly 1,800,000 inhabitants, León was the seventh-largest metropolitan area in Mexico.

With undying devotion to the God of Speed we cut our stay in León to the time required to eat a hearty Spanish dinner and fill the radiator. When we sat down to eat, it was five o'clock and I felt a little weak, but not until Joe called my attention to it did I remember that we had had no breakfast. We had forgotten that detail in the absorbing business of keeping on the road, at least so I thought. But up spoke the Spartan brother.

"No, I never forgot about breakfast, but it was a good chance to economize so I never mentioned it!"

The Plaza Central of Irapuato intruded into our consciousness about nine in the evening, as we rolled off a narrow side street into its noisy glare.[*] For half an hour we watched the beauty and gallantry of this somnolent little Mexican city, as they paraded around the plaza to the jazz tunes brought to life by the local band. "[It] Ain't Gonna Rain No Mo'" was the favorite.[†] They played encores until I began to think it was the only number they knew. The girls and women marched around the plaza in the inner circle, to the right, while the men marched in an outer circle to the left. Occasionally a man would drop away from the rest and join the inner circle with the lady of his choice. Not often, though. True to the Latin tradition that love should be made from a distance they usually walked apart, content to smile and bow at each passing. The advantages of this system were obvious, though. If one hadn't made up his mind conclusively, here was a fine opportunity to review all the eligible face to face.[‡]

Some of the *señoritas* had shoes on and some were fair to the eye. After a bit I made a suggestion.

"Let us join the parade, brother, and get acquainted. This is a fine opportunity to observe the genus Mexicano in the act of mating."

"Nothing doing," said Joe. "You make me tired, with your evasions. What you want to do is to get one of those brunettes on your arm and lead her away from the temptation of music. It is a good thing you have me here to take care of you or you'd be decorating one of these Mexican jails with a suit for breach of promise hanging over your head, or—more likely—papa'd be taking pot shots at the *gringo* who'd besmirched his daughter's reputation by luring her ten feet away from a chaperone."

---

[*] Irapuato (2019 population of more than 575,000) is the center of an important agricultural region, notably strawberries and the raising of cattle and pigs.

[†] The song, recorded in 1923 by singer and instrumentalist Wendell Hall (1896–1969), was a hit in the U.S. and Britain, though it had been widely performed in nineteenth-century minstrel shows.

[‡] Long supposed to be a characteristic of life in Mexico, this ritual had pretty comprehensively disappeared by the 1960s.

Cactus lane on the outskirts of Celaya, Mexico.

With that indictment the Unemotional One stepped on the starter and soon Irapuato the romantic was behind us and we were trying to get directions from a *pulque*-soaked Indian at a crossroad miles away. He pointed every direction including straight up, so we gave up in disgust and found a place to camp.

Salamanca, Celaya, Salvatierra, Acámbaro; just dots on the map and not much more than that to us as we swung along.* At Salamanca we drove through a lane shaded by cactus fully twenty-five feet high. At Celaya we admired the cathedral for which the town is noted. At Salvatierra the streets were paved with enormous lava stones which rocked and racked our car unmercifully. Salvatierra also had another distinction—it was the dirtiest town we had seen, and when I say that I mean it *was* dirty. And at Acámbaro was a handsome stone bridge.†

Now we climb again, higher and higher to Maravatio.‡ From there the road pitches up so steeply that we are just crawling for miles in low gear. Four youngsters hail us as we turn a corner and when we slow down a bit they climb on the running boards. Apparently they are catching a ride home, so we let them stay. [It's] not long before five more run shrieking out of the brush and despite the shoving and pushing of the first four they hang tenaciously on to the spare tire and every other available hand hold. This stops us completely, as the road is steep and this extra five or six hundred pounds is more than we can pull. They don't budge when we shout "*Vamos*" [Let's go], so I get out and start pulling off Mexican kids. They stick like flies, though, and the best I can do is hold three off at a time. Joe sets the brake and climbs out to ask, "What the hell is going on here?" in Spanish.

"Oh, *señor*, the road is steep and we want to help push the car for '*poquito centavos*' [a few cents]," and they refuse to budge.

"So, that's it? The road is steep and they want to push—for *poquito centavos*—nine of them. Well, we'll have to have a little game of ninepins," said Joe.

With that we started tossing *muchachos* [boys] into the brush until we had about half of them off, then Joe jumped in and started off while I roamed the after deck and detached the balance. Thus unloaded, we climbed easily enough and before long crossed the summit at an elevation of more than 9,000 feet.

El Oro, the richest gold camp in Mexico, hung on a mountainside high above us and her many twinkling lights, which were all we could see of her, flashed a cheering

* This is the brothers' fourth day in Mexico, the fourteenth of the trip and April 6.

† Salamanca, Celaya, Salvatierra, and Acámbaro are small towns in southeastern Guanajuato. The brothers are about ready to leave the state.

‡ Maravatio is in the state of Michoacán. It is near the famous sanctuaries for Monarch butterflies.

One of many. This one happens to be in Celaya Mexico. Let's take a ride. Apr. 7, 1930.

message through the darkness.* My mind flashed back to Tonopah, Nevada, the silver camp, seen for the first time as a sparkling desert jewel through twenty miles of crystal clear Nevada night.†

In the bottom of a little *arroyo* [gulch] a car was parked and beside it was a bed with two recumbent figures. The car, a decrepit-looking affair with the fenders off and sundry other non-essentials missing, bore the legend, "Around the World Studebaker" and various oil and gasoline trademark signs.

"Hello, there! Where are you bound?"

A startled man popped up out of the bed, and dragging an automatic from under the pillow had us covered in about the time it takes a Paddock to run a yard.‡

"Put up your hands!"

We did—reached for the stars. Joe cried, "*Amigo, amigo*!" and then tried English again: "Where are you going?"

Our blond friend was fully awake now, and seeing that we were unarmed Americans he returned the gun to the pillow and apologized—in rather broken English—for such a rude reception. He said they were on their way to South America and where were we going?

We confided that we, too, were attempting to follow the Pan-American trail, at least as far as Panama. Thus united in a common cause, we shook hands all around and under the friendly glow of four cigarettes we discussed the roads and peoples and other conditions affecting tourists in the tropics.

As their story unfolded we began to learn about automobile trail blazing from experts.

"Didn't you see the articles in the papers about us? Two Belgian army officers on a tour of the world? No? Well, the papers were full of our stuff wherever we went. They took our pictures with the 'stars' out in Hollywood and we had a big write-up in a movie magazine. We make expenses as we go along, endorsing gasoline and oil and so forth. See those five new tires. The Firestone Company gave 'em to us out in Los Angeles."§

---

* At this point, the brothers have entered the state of Mexico. El Oro's nearly 9,000 feet high. By 1930, the mines had been pretty well played out, and today El Oro is a tiny town, despite the architectural remnants of its grand mining past.

† One wonders when this was. Founded with the discovery of gold in 1900, Tonopah peaked in 1910, and by 1920 Tonopah had less than half the population it had at its height. In 2019, fewer than 2,500 people lived there. Arthur would have been fifteen in 1920.

‡ "Charley" William Paddock (1900–1943), an American athlete, was known as "the fastest man alive," for having run the 100-meter dash in 10.2 seconds, a world record that stood from 1921 to 1956.

§ Despite all efforts, no information can be found on who these Belgians are.

We looked, and sure enough, there were five new tires on the car.

"What about the Studebaker people?"

"Oh, they gave us a complete overhaul job free. Not all they might have done, but better than nothing."

"Do you speak Spanish?" I asked.

"Sure, Spanish, French, German, Belgian, English. I pick up a language in about a month. We traveled all over Europe before we came to the States."

"You fellows getting paid by Ford for this trip?"

"No," we admitted sadly. "We are on our own 'para sport' [for sport]—as the Mexicans say."

"You are foolish," Fritz answered. "Ford ought to pay your expenses at least for the advertising he gets."

I didn't tell them that we had given Ford a chance to participate on any basis he saw fit—with no results. I was a little ashamed of our amateur standing in the face of such successful commercialization.

They examined our outfit and declared it perfect for the job.

"Twice as good as that old bus of ours. But then, publicity is publicity and we got to be satisfied."

(The "Round the World" expedition was out of bread so we gave them half a loaf for breakfast, before we left.)

Ice froze in our canteen that night.

"Why go south?" complained Joe in the morning as he stood shivering over the fire.* "The further we go, the colder it gets. Good thing we didn't drain that anti-freeze out of the radiator. I meant to, yesterday, but didn't have time."

And another thing we didn't have time for was learning the correct, or for that matter, any pronunciation of the names of some of the towns we were going through. Take Ixtlahuaca for instance. I couldn't roll my tongue around that I–x–t–l to save me. We asked for Toluca instead.†

Our gasoline was running low. Before we got into Toluca we had to stop occasionally and rock the car vigorously so it would fill the carburetor. The big fifty-five gallon drum still had a few gallons in it, but it wouldn't feed on a slight pitch. We asked, "*Donde esta camino para Mejico?*" for the thousandth and last time.

---

* It's April 7, their fifth day in Mexico and the fifteenth of their trip. The brothers are up in the mountains!

† Ixtlahuaca de Rayón is just a few miles west of the Mexico City, actually a little closer than Toluca, which today is the fifth-largest city in Mexico. Toluca sits at the foot of the Nevado de Toluca, which, at more than 15,000 snow-covered feet, towers over the city, itself a mere 8,750 feet high.

Toluca and pavement! No extravaganza of mountain scenery or desert vista looked as sweet to our eyes as this asphalt ribbon leading off to the east and to Mexico City. After 700 miles of irregular parabolas, it was good, very good, to pull over to port and settle down to a comfortable forty—and look out for the ox teams! I understood there has been no immigration from the north into Mexico since the ancient Toltecs swept down and captured the country in the seventh century, and after traveling this overland route I can well understand the reason why.[*] There may be detours around the mountain ranges, but we certainly didn't find them. We climbed everything in sight, and now we were attacking the last barrier, the highest of them all, but, thanks to God and the Mexican highway engineers, on a magic carpet of asphalt which carried us swiftly upward, always in high gear, to the west portal of the Valley of Mexico.

I said it carried us swiftly upward. That is not quite true. The road was all right, but that confounded gasoline would stop feeding and the engine would sputter and die unless we kept the right wheels half in the ditch so the crown of the road would give the law of gravity a chance. We ventured out in the center just once—to pass a bus load of shouting Aztecs. When we had pulled up even and were about to pass— pop! sputter! and we were left behind while the natives whooped with delight. The car behind nearly crashed as we veered for the ditch, so after that we stayed over while I got out at times and hopped up and down on the running board to force in another cupful of gas.

I would like to tell how the Valley of Mexico lay spread out before us as we crossed the summit. Popcatépetl and Iztaccíhautl, the twin mountain guardians, and Gods of the Aztecs, reared their snowy heads from the plain far off to the southwest.[†] And so, also, would I like to tell of the eternal city of the New World, forming a grand mosaic at our very feet. But, alas, I cannot tell you these things for although they were all there—just as I have described them—the plague that has visited the modern Mexico City hid them from us and all we could see was a dust storm rising high above the valley and making indistinguishable all but the closest mountains. Perhaps that barely visible mass in the distance was old Popo, it *ought* to be, for that was where he should stand, but it could as easily have been a cloud, so hazy was the air.[‡]

---

[*] Except for the people who came to call themselves the Aztecs.

[†] Popcatépetl ("Smoking Mountain") and Iztaccíhautl ("White Woman") are two of three highest mountains in Mexico, at 17,802 and 17,159 feet, respectively. Like the Nevado de Toluca, they are perpetually snow-covered.

[‡] These days it's an impenetrable smog. Popcatépetl is often referred to as old Popo.

We had anticipated this moment for weeks and now to look into the Valley of Mexico and see nothing but dust, dust, dust, was maddening. I cursed—not silently—the engineers who had so efficiently drained the valley floor that the former lakes were now nothing more than breeding grounds for dust storms. But on with the March of Progress. We decided to go down and have a look at the city close up.

"Ease off that brake, Brother, we don't need gasoline now. The inexorable law of gravitation will soon have us knocking at the city gates."

Chapter VI

# In Mexico City without a Road

Sixteen days—to the hour—after leaving New York, we started down the Avenida Juárez, the Fifth Avenue of Mexico City. In ten days' driving time—five to Laredo and five more to Mexico City—our speedometer showed us that we were 3,126 miles south of Manhattan. The traffic cop gave us the *adalante* [go ahead] sign and at the toot of his little whistle we were off to find a hotel—and a road to Guatemala. The former was easy. At the Regis I asked for a bath with a room attached, if possible.* The clerk raised his eyebrows and eyed us suspiciously, with a truly American hotel clerk manner, as I hastily explained that we had just driven in from Texas and needed refreshing and reclothing badly. He relaxed a little and permitted us to sign the register. I am sure he regretted it, when, with the aid of two bellboys, we started carrying our assortment of suitcases, duffel bags, bed rolls, et cetera, through the dignified lobby to the elevator. We had decided to repack our things and leave all but the essentials in storage here. It was a little too much to expect our car to hold up indefinitely under such a staggering load.

Bit by bit and layer by layer the accumulated dust succumbed to soap and water and by evening we were presentable again. After checking our sack of silver with the hotel cashier, we wandered forth to inspect the city. Down to the incomparable Sanborn's for dinner.† This fine restaurant and department store combined is certainly a bit of Fifth Avenue transplanted.

* On the corner of Balderas and Avenida Juárez in the city's historic center, the Regis was a luxury hotel in every sense of the word. It was destroyed by the earthquake of 1985, which killed everyone in it, with only the mural by Diego Rivera surviving the subsequent fire. Immediately adjacent to the Alameda, the site is currently occupied by the Plaza of Solidarity, built to commemorate the victims.

† This is the Sanborns in the Casa de los Azulejos, which was declared a national monument the year after the brothers ate there. You can still eat there: Sanborns has grown into a chain owned by Carlos Slim.

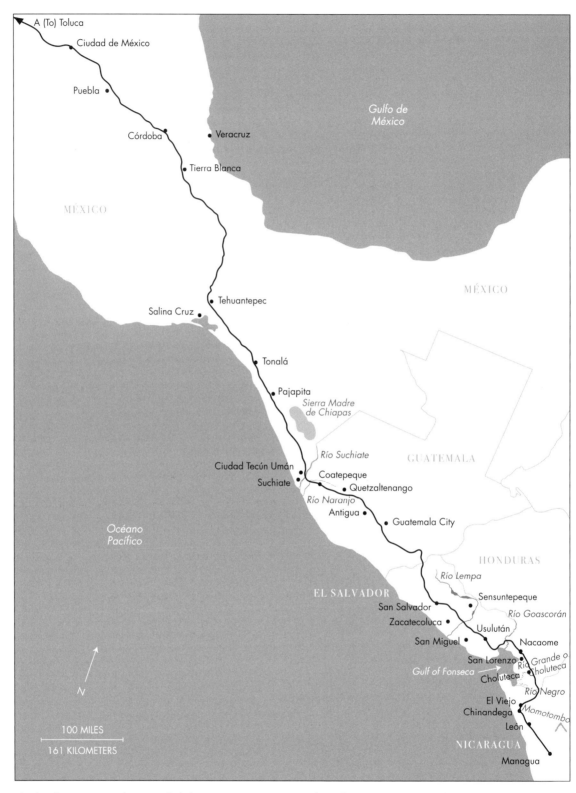

The brothers' journey from Ciudad de México to Managua, where thier epic journey ends.
Map by Morgan Pfaelzer. © 2020 Center for the Study of Place.

Too cold to sit, too tired to stroll, we slipped between crisp sheets on a real, honest-to-goodness mattress and forgot the woes of the world in untroubled slumber.

At the Mexican Bureau of Roads [the] next morning we were standing our ground but with sagging confidence.* An energetic little Mexican told us for the third time, and a little impatiently, "But, señores, I tell you there *is* no road to Guatemala! Although we are working at this time on the road to Oaxaca, I doubt very much if you could get that far. The uncompleted section is in the mountains, and there is only a mule trail at present. I returned only last week from a trip of inspection in that section and I know what I am talking about."

"From Oaxaca south there is nothing—not even a trail. It is impossible to drive to Guatemala."

His positiveness rather got my goat. With more spirit than the situation warranted I said, "Well, we are going to drive to Guatemala if we have to drive over railroad ties all the way. Can you give me an itinerary of the route from here to Córdoba? I understand there is a road that far. From there we'll take the railroad right of way and go as far as we can. And by the way, how about that trip that Italian count made from the Argentine?"†

"Bah! That man is the biggest faker that ever lived. He drove in here from Veracruz and told everyone that he had driven all the way from Guatemala. We found out later that he came overland, all right, but on top of a flat car.‡ Yes, I can give you an itinerary to Córdoba. The road is not very good, but if you drove from Laredo you will have no trouble with it. I'll have my secretary prepare the itinerary this afternoon and send it over to your hotel."

"Thank you very much. Good bye. Next time you hear of us we'll be in Guatemala."

"*Adíos* [Good-bye]! Good luck. I hope you make it."

And he might have added, "You'll need it."

The sun shone down on Mexico but not on us. It was two discouraged *gringos* who walked back to the hotel, discussing ways and means to reach Guatemala. The prospect of five hundred miles over the unballasted ties of the Ferrocarrilles

* It is April 8, the sixteenth day of the brothers' trip.

† As mentioned earlier, in 1928 and 1929 José Mario Barone was supposed to have driven a 1922 Studebaker from Río de Janeiro to New York City, ferrying it over water where necessary. But he also shipped it on trains.

‡ Questioned about his experiences in Central America and Mexico, Barone is reported to have said, "It is best to see very little and say not so much." (The source for the quote is unknown.)

Nationales de México looked rather hopeless. If the company would grant us permission to run along their [its] tracks—which was doubtful—it was hardly possible that the car would stand the gaff.

Up in our room we lay down on the beds to enjoy a *siesta* [nap]. I was about to drowse off when Joe jumped to his feet and announced, "Say, we are acting like a couple of pikers! We're not quitters, are we?"

"No," I said, "we're not quitters."

"Well, then, let's go down and see the superintendent of this railroad and get permission to run on his tracks."

"Let's go," said I.

So we went down to 22 Bolivar Street and asked to see the General Superintendent of the railroad. They asked us, of course, what we wanted, but we told them it was very important business, and we must explain it to the superintendent personally. After a while we were ushered into the office of the smiling, good-natured Señor Franco, and we explained to him our mission. To our surprise, he saw nothing wrong with this unusual request—we half expected to be refused pointblank—and promised to take it up with the President and General Manager, Señor Cardenas.* He was out at the time—in conference with the President of the Republic—would we wait? Certainly, we would wait. Señor Cárdenas and the President of Mexico must have had some knotty problems to solve, for they were in conference for two days—and we were in waiting for the same length of time. In the meantime Señor Franco entertained us with stories about the old days of railroading in Mexico when a freight car of soldiers went with every train and wrecking passenger coaches was the favorite pastime of the bandits and revolutionaries.

"You know, people write down here almost every day to ask if it is safe to take the train down from St. Louis," he said sadly. "We do our best to counteract the bad impression that Americans have of Mexican railroads, but it will be a long time before they realize that our railroads are really just as safe as theirs."

Señor Franco was elected President of the America Association of Railroad Superintendents when they held their convention in Mexico City last year. He is going to Minneapolis in the fall to preside over the next convention and is putting all his spare time into brushing up his English.

---

* Lázaro Cárdenas (1895–1970) was a general in the Constitutionalist Army during the Mexican Revolution of 1910–1920 and a stateman who served as President of Mexico from 1934 to 1940. Leo Trotsky (1879–1940) described Cárdenas's government as the only honest government in the world, and today Cárdenas is recalled as a visionary and effective progressive.

"I learned my first English while working with the American railroaders, years ago up in Chihuahua." He laughed. "I guess my vocabulary in those days was more profane than profound. When I first studied English under a teacher he said the first thing I had to do was to forget everything I had already learned and start fresh—with no railroaders around."

During the second day of waiting the president of an American railroad in Mexico came in. He was a big, bluff American and as he whacked the slight Franco on the back in good, old Rotary fashion and asked for transportation for his private car to Veracruz, I could not help contrasting the Mexican and American form of greeting. The latter, I am afraid, suffers by comparison.

The conference finally ended as all conferences must, and we were told that the president was ready to see us.

We followed Mr. Franco into his office, and after he had presented our case at length, it came my turn to expound it. From the way Señor Presidente was shaking his head I could see that he considered it a bit of foolishness hardly worth while interrupting the schedules of a great railroad for. I presented every argument I could think of and tried to infer, without actually incriminating myself by any direct statement, that this trip was backed by practically everyone of importance in the United States and Washington and was actually a good will expedition to help unite the countries along the Pan-American Highway. I pointed out that by pioneering over this route we would stimulate a great deal of interest in the early completion of the highway. In an offhand manner I mentioned that the magazine article I was writing would be read by thousands of people—not bothering to explain that they, the articles, were as yet still unwritten.

The last argument was a good lead. Yes, certainly, he would be pleased to grant *permisos* to the magazine writer to drive over the railroad. Why hadn't he mentioned it before? It was one thing to allow two irresponsible young men to play havoc with railroad schedules by wandering down the tracks to Guatemala but quite another to conduct a writer on a tour of the Ferrocarriles Nationales de México. He would telegraph the superintendents that we were coming and order them to conduct us safely through their respective divisions. One thing, though, did we have flanged wheels to run on the rails with? No, we did not. That was unfortunate, for he could not allow us to run on the ties. Our pace would be too slow and would too greatly interfere with train movements. Joe rose to the occasion at the unexpected turn of affairs.

"While we do not have flanged wheels especially for rails, these wheels of ours are well adapted to be altered to fit the track, and we have already made plans to fix them."[*]

* Again, this reflects Joe Jr.'s ability with cars.

The president and general manger shook his head doubtfully but said that if we were sure we could go on the rails, the permission would be ours. We assured him that that was the case, so he bowed us out with the assurance that the superintendents would be notified immediately.

Back on the street we ran O'Henry—our pet name for the car—out on the street car tracks and after an inspection decided it could be made to run on rails, just how was not clear, but that was another detail to be attended to when the time came.

Right now the thing to do was to get to Córdoba. We packed in a hurry, and after consigning one set of engineering books, three suits of clothes, and about two hundred pounds of other unessentials to storage, we were ready to leave.

"Why not try a little promoting on the gas deal?" suggested Joe. "If we can find a gasoline company which hasn't been hit up by the Belgian army in that Studebaker, they might shoot for a little publicity."

We tried one of the two largest companies. They agreed to go fifty-fifty with us. If we reached Guatemala City—which event the manager seemed a little doubtful about—they might do even better by us. So we crammed in two hundred litres at ten centavos each, which was half price, and climbed the pass near Ixtaccíhuatl. From there we got our first glimpse of Popocatépetl. During the three days we were in Mexico City it had been continuously obscured by dust clouds, and even now the summit was hidden by a cloud, but it was not lacking in majesty for all that. We had a good view of the closer Ixtaccíhuatl, the sleeping woman of Aztec mythology. As the story goes, one of their ancient kings in a fit of rage at his wife had her transformed into stone and laid her up here beside old Popo. There she lies now, sleeping peacefully, her recumbent figure with snowy breasts an object lesson to all Mexican wives who might be tempted.

We dropped down from the ten-thousand-foot summit into Puebla, than which no place has more churches.* Each hill—and there are many—on the outskirts of the town, was topped with a cathedral. As we stopped to look at this strange place where the churches actually outnumbered the inhabitants, all began to ring their bells. From valley to hill and back again echoed the clanging, as each vied with the others to toll the loudest and longest. The sun was dipping behind old Popo, its last golden rays throwing into high relief the seven churches within our view. As we looked, it dropped from sight, the echoes of the clamorous bells died away, and dusk and quiet

---

* The brothers dropped down from the summit of the pass, 7,000 feet below the mountain's summit and so from the state of Mexico to the state of Puebla, the capital of which is also Puebla. Puebla has long been noted for the number and beauty of its churches and for its tiles. It's also the fourth-largest city in the country.

descended upon us and the seven temples of God.* There was not a soul in sight to break the even tenor of immobility which pervaded the scene. It was almost incongruous to prod our dead motor into noisy action and rattle down the cactus-lined road into Puebla.

"Don't travel at night over these roads," said the men of whom we asked directions for Córdoba.

"Why not?"

"Banditos!" he answered, accompanying the word by a delicate gesture of drawing his forefinger across his throat.

"*Nada*" [nothing], said Joe. "How do you get out of town?"

"Turn right at two blocks and cross the bridge. Then straight ahead on the main road. But I warn you. Only last week . . ."

What happened last week was lost in the whirr of the starter.

"Maybe he's right. You know we heard about this Veracruz road in Mexico City," I ventured.

"Maybe he is right. But the chances are he has a friend with a 'very fine hotel' which he wanted to recommend to us."

"These Mexican bandits *are* overrated," I admitted. "We might as well hide this money some place, though, in case of trouble. Good chance to count it, too. I haven't checked up since the first day in Mexico City." So we counted up. Our resources totaled $72 American bills and $27.20 Mexican—about $85 all told. We reflected sadly that the three days in Mexico City had put a deep dent in our purses and resolved to tighten up considerably in Guatemala City. The bills we tucked away in the can of cold patching in the tool box and distributed the $27.20 between us.

True to form we soon lost the way and rolled up in our blankets in a clean bit of sand. We learned—as all novice out-door men do—that sand is not as soft as it looks.

Orizaba came up with the dawn, 18,314 feet of perfectly formed, snow-capped, volcano.† Humboldt, the German explorer who left little to be said about scenery in this part of the world, describes it as the finest peak in North America, and as I lay there drinking it in, I wondered if he hadn't understated it.‡ I don't want to see

---

* The reference here is Biblical and not to the Great Pyramid of Cholula (*Tiachihualteptl*), a huge Aztec complex four miles west of Puebla. Excavation of Cholula did not commence until 1931. Today, it's the largest known archeological site of a pyramid/temple in the world.

† With the three days spent in Mexico City, this makes it day eighteen, April 11. Pico de Orizaba (*Citlaltépetl*) is the highest peak in Mexico and third-highest in North America. Its last eruption was in 1846.

‡ Alexander von Humbolt (1769–1859) traveled extensively in Latin America between 1799 and 1804, exploring and describing its lands and geophysical properties for the first time from a scientific perspective.

a mountain more beautiful than Orizaba, it would put me under a spell from which I might not recover. Then the sun peeked around its side to warm us to activity. To have seen the sun set behind Popocatépetl and rise over Orizaba was beauty enough for any twelve hours. Like lizards we crawled forth to make fresh assault on "*el camino para Córdoba*" (the road to Córdoba).

At noon we tipped over a summit, like a roller coaster topping its highest point, and started down from the high plateau we had been on since leaving Monterrey.* And, like the roller coaster, in a few swoops and breath-taking drops we fell off the crisp, cactus-covered plateau into the warm lap of the flaming, florid tropics. The road was paved—with huge boulders! They were neither flat nor uniform in size. Low gear was too fast!

This was the day before Easter. The road was crowded with natives on the way to the town, Orizaba.† Hundreds of barefooted Christians trudged along the rocky road beside the family burros, loaded with food to provide sustenance for the Holy Week in town. How can industry amount to much when it can be deserted so easily. The whole population was on the move and, as we neared Orizaba, the procession swelled to such proportions that it well-nigh blocked other traffic from the road.

Gad! That was a strange parade, crawling down from that rocky trail, which had seen in its time the grand entry of Maximilian and heard the tramp of conquerors' feet from Cortez to General Scott.‡ And now the simple folk stream over its rocky surface to do homage to the Virgin Mary, Jesus Christ, and the God above. 'Tis in their very blood to do so. No man too poor, no woman too tired with toil or too weak from child-birth to press forward to do honor to the 1897th anniversary of the resurrection of Him who died that they might live, and rejoice, and seek no more. What sarcastic soul could say that more is necessary? Is not faith alone sufficient? No shoes? Did He have shoes? The Spaniards brought the *Bible*—and took the gold. A fair exchange, no doubt, but perhaps it was the wrong *Bible*. Were it the Methodist *Bible*, now . . .

At Orizaba the streets were thronged with the holiday crowd. All those who were not squatted on the ground bartering oranges, bananas, or avocados were try-ing to get aboard the little street car that ran from the outskirts into town.

---

* The brothers also left the state of Puebla for that of Veracruz.

† Orizaba, a city of around 128,000 people (2019) in the state of Veracruz, was an important town at the time of the Spanish Conquest. Today, it is known for its colonial buildings and active arts scene.

‡ Maximilian (1832–1867), the younger brother of Franz Joseph I, of Austria, was imposed as the emperor on Mexico by Napoleon III of France, which invaded Mexico in 1861. In 1867, president-in-exile Benito Juárez (1806–1872) defeated Maximilian, who was subsequently executed by a firing squad.

The old Imperial Road between Mexico [City] and Vera Cruz. The road Cortez followed. Maximilian rode in great pomp over this road and U.S. General Scott led 10,000 soldiers in his march to the Mexican capital along this same rough route. Near Orizaba. Apr. 12, 1930.

Pico de Orizaba should be in the background. Sharp spears in the foreground are Cacti, often called Mexican swords. Sat. Apr. 12, 1930.

Orizaba lies approximately half-way down the slope, suspended, as it were, between the temperate zone and the tropics.* The hills about are covered with a dense green foliage as unlike the barren plateau as anything near could be, but the air is still fresh and not oppressive. While the towns are still built solid with adobe houses, occasional huts alongside the road are of bamboo built on stilts with thatched roofs. Each pot-bellied child old enough to toddle carries a machete as do the adults.

Beyond Orizaba we dropped steadily but not so quickly, and soon we were in Córdoba, where the task of changing the wheels to go on the rails was to take place. That had caused us no little concern, and we had talked of little else the last few days. But there we were at last, and action would have to take place of discussion. At the railroad station the stationmaster told us that he had received the orders. When did we wish to start? Would we be ready by two o'clock tomorrow afternoon? Yes, we thought so. All right. Orders would be telegraphed ahead, so that at two tomorrow we would leave as a special train bound for Suchiate on the Guatemalan border, 1,041 kilometers [646.8 miles] south. *!Esta bueno* [It's good]*!* Two o'clock was the zero hour. Then to get ready.

It took us about two hours, with our imperfect Spanish and no interpreter to get this conversation over, and as it was dark when we finished, we drove the car up on the station platform and slept beside it, under the glare of the station lights. During the evening various groups of natives gathered around to inspect two gringos sleeping in public, but the watchman dispersed them after they had had a reasonable chance to inspect us.

At dawn we were up.† There was Orizaba in the clear morning air, even more majestic than it had been the previous morning. Then we were only some eleven thousand feet below its summit. Now it towered nearly sixteen thousand feet above us, a beautiful pink in the morning light. But no time for the scenery, as our train was to leave at two o'clock, and it had to be made into one, first. The closer we got to the job the tougher it looked. Now, with the car astraddle the rails on a side track it looked quite hopeless. It was just about four inches too narrow, to begin with. And if we could block the wheels out to the proper width, the rims were not built right to fit over the rails. Then the big idea popped! Why not wire two wheels together as tightly as possible on the right side, leaving the tires on, then with the tires off the wheels on the left side those rims would fit down over the rail. The extra tires on the one side would give us the necessary width, and the flanges of the rim on the other

* Orizaba's altitude is 4,000 feet.

† This is the brothers' twentieth dawn on the road, April 13.

side would hold us on. Yes, why not? It looked like a beautiful idea. The only drawback was that the car would be tipped slightly, the tires raising the right-hand side about five inches higher than the left.

"But hold on here a minute," said Joe. "That takes six wheels, and we have only five."

"I thought of that, and the answer is self-evident. We'll have to get another wheel. Leave that to me. You start pulling off tires, and I'll get one." The idea was my brainchild, and I didn't intend that it suffer a prenatal death for lack of one Ford wheel.

I scoured the town for the Ford dealer and finally found him about to sit down to his Easter breakfast. Good luck again. He spoke English and wore a Rotary pin. In the interests of service I persuaded him to open shop long enough to sell me a wheel, although this was the most sacrosanct of Mexican holidays.* He did better than that: He not only deserted his breakfast to go down to the agency, but he found two used wheels which he presented to me with the compliments of the Rotary International—long may it live!

All that morning, while the rest of Córdoba attended church and all afternoon while they went en masse to a bullfight, we wired and pumped and jacked on that car. By four o'clock we were just about done in from slaving in the hot sun—and listening to the crowd roar at the bullfight a block away—but the last tire had been pumped up, and Joe pronounced her ready to ramble. While he backed onto the main line I started out to get our running orders from the dispatcher.

He wasn't to be found in the station and after a fruitless trip to his *casa* [house] I learned that he had got tired waiting for us and had gone off to the bullfight. Now this was a devil of a note. Here we were, ready to start and the dispatcher had gone to the bullfight. I returned to tell Joe but found he was having troubles of his own and was in no condition to be told anything. The car was derailed by a switch and he sitting on a rail, ruefully looking at it. When I hove into sight he asked what the blankety-blank hell was I going to suggest now, and had I ever considered what would happen, with flanges on the outside as well as on the inside of the rail, when we ran across a switch. It didn't take much perception to see what *had* happened. As the outer flange, or edge of the rim rather, hit the diverging rail it raised it up and derailed the whole outfit.

"Well," said I, "what'll we do. Go back to Mexico City and wait till they build a road?"

* At the time, the Rotary's motto was, "He profits most who serves the best." Rotary, founded in 1905, is an international and secular service organization of businessmen—until 1985, when women were admitted—and professional leaders.

"Shut up. This is no time for sarcasm. Anyway, I got an idea. It might work, and if it doesn't, it will at least be equal to this brainstorm of yours. Get that heap back on the rails while I get some boards."

I was about to suggest that he had fully agreed with me that morning, but he was off on a trot in the direction of a new house that was building across the tracks. With the help of the crew that had gathered to watch our departure, I managed to get the car back on the rails. They were having a good time at our expense and thought our troubles were the best joke ever.

Joe returned, with three narrow boards about the width of the rail head and laid them on top of the rail across the switch.

"We've got to hurry," he said. "A bird over there tried to stop me from taking these, and when I insisted, he started off to call the police. Get in and try it."

It worked! We gathered up the boards and drove up to the station. The dispatcher had returned from the bullfight and was waiting for us with the orders. He pulled out his watch and marked on the orders *dos horas* [two hours] and *treinta y cinco minutos tarde* [thirty-five minutes late] and frowned fiercely at us, as if to say we had better be on time after this if we wanted to run on his railroad.

Joe checked his watch and after having ascertained that there were no trains running north and only one to follow us an hour later we signed the book—A. Lyon, Conductor, and J. Lyon, Ingeniero—and rolled majestically away. Most of the crowd that had been at the bullfight had heard of the crazy *gringos* who were traveling in an automobile by rail, and they were down to give us a send-off. As we slipped into high and started clicking down the rails, a mighty cheer went up, and we started off for Guatemala with the good wishes of Córdoba ringing in our ears.

I don't know how it happened. It might have been that a rail a little wider than the rest refused to fit the rim. Or maybe I pulled the steering wheel over when I reached out to shake hands with Joe. But happen it did. One kilometer [.62 mile] out our special train left the rails and with a wild lunge nosed off into the ditch. We were unhurt, but when I looked back at the trestle we had just crossed I felt some weak. I guess Joe had the same thought, for he glanced at the trestle, too, and shut his eyes, and if I am not mistaken his face didn't look as brown as it had a minute before.

"That," said the old optimist, with little optimism left in his voice now, "is that. Where do go from here, Señor Arturo? Back to the land of the free?"

"And the home of the brave, I guess. But let us get off the track before that freight highballs into us to finish the job."

Back in Córdoba that night we learned of a road which *had* been negotiated by automobiles as far as Tierra Blanca, seventy-two miles south. The division railroad shops were located there, so it occurred to us that in the shops we might be able to fix up some flanged wheels that would stay on the rails. It was a thin prospect, but as the only way out we chose to try it.

Personally, I don't believe any car had ever made that trip to Tierra Blanca, reports to the contrary notwithstanding.[*]

For twelve long hours we unleashed everything we had under the hood and added to it at times with one manpower more as we crossed rivers without bridges and jungles without tracks. More than once we had to back up and take a running leap at boulders which wouldn't go under the car. We jumped them all successfully, though at times I thought surely the engine and axles would be junk iron when we got across. The worst it did was to batter the engine pan and knock the plug out of the rear axle once. I stopped the flow of oil while Joe retrieved the plug.

Joe crawled out from under, after one examination, to suggest, "That crankcase must be roomy inside from the way it looks."

"Why?"

"It if weren't, there wouldn't be room for the connecting rods to go around, it's mashed so badly."

But tough steel will stand a lot of knocks, so we did eventually reach Tierra Blanca.

Tierra Blanca? Tierra Caliente would be more fitting a name! Some village, this. Twelve thousand people and two automobiles.[†] And now there are three! We had to take fifty per cent of them on faith, though, for in the four days we were there I saw only two automobiles, ours and one other. And I must say from the looks of it, it appeared as though it had made several trips to Córdoba.

I didn't know just how far the instructions that had been wired ahead went, but I hoped that they covered everything. Our Spanish was far too weak to cover this complicated situation, so after a futile half-hour with the superintendent we set out to find an interpreter. The one man in town who spoke English was missing so we awaited his return. Toward evening he appeared from somewhere, and we bought him two bottles of beer and led him by the arm, lest he escape, over to the superintendent's office. That worthy had gone home for the day, however, so now we had an interpreter but no one to talk to. We bought the interpreter two more beers and made him promise to come back in the morning. Thus passed one day in Tierra Blanca.

---

[*] This would be April 14, the twenty-first day of the brothers' trip.

[†] It still only had around 53,000 inhabitants in 2019. It is the municipal seat and is located in the Papaloapin River Valley at an elevation of 200 feet.

Above: What follows a Mexican revolution. We learned that this R.R. had been inoperative only three years. In that time the jungle had almost swallowed it. Rails rusted. Near Tierra Blanca. April 14, 1930.

Opposite top: South of Cordoba. We were using the R. R. tracks for a road when the car jumped the track.

Opposite bottom: Between Cordoba and Tierra Blanca, or first taste of the tropics. This is not a road, just burro trails. It was blocked by a fallen tree so the natives hacked out a new path with machetes. Apr. 14, 1930.

This game of hide-and-seek didn't appeal to us too much so we pounced on friend interpreter before he was much awake in the morning and led him toward the railroad offices.* As luck would have it, we had to pass a *cantina* [canteen] on the way.

"It is very hot, no, *señor?*"

"Yes, it is very hot," I could feel it coming.

"The *cerveza* [beer] is very good, no, *señor?*"

"Yes, the beer is O.K. But listen here, you bum, we have business to attend to. After we see *el señor superintendente*, then comes the beer."

"I do not like for the *señor* to call me a bum. I am not a bum. But first we must have *una cervaza*. Then I shall talk for you all day if you wish." So into the *cantina* we went, and one beer was three, but that was O.K. and we hurried our laggard's steps across to the office.

Great guns! The bird had flown again.

"El Superintendente has gone to Veracruz, not to return until this evening. So sorry. But surely *mañana* [tomorrow] he will be present. It is the weekly inspection trip. Could the *señores* return tomorrow at 9 a.m.?"

The *señores* said, yes, they would return and dejectedly retired with the victim. Suppose, I thought in a panicky moment, our interpreter should decide to go fishing for a week or two. That would leave us in a fine pickle indeed. That gentleman seemed to have no intention of deserting his beer-buying hosts, though. However, at noon he remembered that he had some work to do on his brother's farm which was three leagues away. For two *pesos* he could send an *hombre* out to substitute for him. Could we "lend" him two pesos? As, *muchas gracias*, now he could stay in town and help us. Half an hour later he shambled into the hotel and shamelessly threw one of his newly acquired *pesos* on the bar and asked us to have a beer, on him this time.

And so passed the second day in Tierra Blanca. I rather enjoyed the respite from continuous traveling and slept in spite of the flies rather comfortably in a chair on the shady side of the hotel; but Joe, all business, had found a ruler divided into centimeters in the railroad junk yard and was very busy running back and forth measuring flanged railroad rims and the wheels on the car. After about two hours, during which he woke me up three times to ask whether a meter was thirty-nine and forty-seven-hundredths inches or three and forty-seven hundredths inches or three and forty-seven-hundredths feet, he announced that he had found railroad rims or, as they are called, tires, which would just fit on over the car wheels and would, if bolted on, make a perfect rig for the rails. That was good news, and I came to and together we verified it. All we needed now was the permission to go ahead.

* This is April 15, the brothers' twenty-second day on the road.

April 18, 1930. Ready at last with all four steel flanged "tires" bolted in place on our wheels, and on the rails! Joe looks a bit grimey [sic] after sleeping several nights in the Round House. Edward Lopez, master mechanic, stands next to Joe and Joaquin, the straw boss with a wrench in his hand, did most of the work. The man underneath is probably tightening the clamp that locks the front wheels straight ahead.

Two things happen every day in Tierra Blanca, that is, of course, besides the sun rising and setting, which really makes four all told. The other two events are the arrival of the morning trains and the arrival of the evening trains. Looking up and down the street half an hour before train time, one sees a somnolent scene as devoid of activity as a Mexican in a hammock at *siesta* time. As the hour approaches, the activities begin and soon cries of, "*limonada* [lemonade], *limonada*," echo up the street, the vanguard of the horde that is to appear on the scene, each with a pail and a glass to tempt the traveler's thirst. Soon the street is alive with people; old women with baskets of *dulces* [sweets], young women with baskets of fruits, men with cigars and cigarettes, girls with watermelons—one train from Córdoba and one on the main line from Veracruz or Santa Lucrecia—they swarm around and in and out of the coaches peddling their wares and having a huge good time doing it. When the morning trains leave the town drowses off again still the evening trains awaken it again. So we drowsed and roused with them to rush over to the station twice a day.

We cornered the evasive superintendent on the third morning and put our proposition up to him.* His orders had read to escort us over his division and to tender us any assistance necessary, but he was doubtful if that included the use of the shops. We assured him that was most certainly what *was* included, but he played safe and wired to Mexico City for authority to proceed. It seemed that some law or labor-union manifesto prohibited persons who were not employees from working in the shops or using the tools. That meant that the work would have to be done by the railroad mechanics.

The telegram was answered with orders to proceed, so we drove back through the maze of switches and tracks into the roundhouse and showed the shop foreman what we wanted. He knew a few words of English, which made matters somewhat easier, and before long we had four mechanics at work lugging railroad rims around and drilling them for the clamps. They hadn't looked heavy to us, but we found out they weighed four hundred twenty-five pounds apiece, the four of them being almost as heavy as the car itself. But no matter, so much more for stability and what's weight if it's below the springs? I'll venture to say, though, that that job set a record in the proportion of "unsprung" weight to "sprung" weight, it being about equal, if not heavier, below the springs.

* Which would be the brothers' twenty-third day, April 16.

Official Order for "Train Number 13", Dated April 18, 1930, 10:41 A.M. We are advised that Train No. 201 is on time and Train No. 223 is 1 hour and 30 minutes late.

In the meantime we moved our cots over into a corner of the roundhouse and slept at the job. The soot was terrific. After two days our sheets had become the same dingy color of everything else around a railroad and our clothes, too, were about the shade of a locomotive boiler. There were other disadvantages, too: The hostlers had a habit of blowing the whistles when they brought the locomotives in, probably to see us jump. And if you think we didn't, just try sleeping in a roundhouse some time and have a whistle screech right over you when you are sound asleep! But it could have been worse. The smoke kept the mosquitoes away, and I prefer a lot of the former to a few of the latter.

How slowly they worked. It took a consultation of all the mechanics on the job and half the foremen in the shop to decide where to bore a bolt hole. But the second day the last hole was bored, the last clamp was made, and we put her on the rails.[*] She looked every inch a special train, too!

Now to pay for the labor—that would be the only charge, the superintendent said.

"*Cuánto vale para labor, señor* [How much for the work, sir]?"

"*Un ciento veinta y cinco pesos en todo.*"

One hundred-twenty-five pesos! And the mechanic's pay was around six pesos per day. Well, no use to argue about the overhead, but what a crimp that would put in our bank roll.

I flew the distress signal, and Joe excused us to talk it over. A careful check revealed that the exchequer balanced at $70 American and $4.55 Mexican. There was no exchange differential in this part of the world, so by subtracting $62.50 from $70 it was self-evident that we would have $8.50 left plus four and a half pesos. That was not much to contemplate a trip to Panama with, and I tell you we thought a long time before handing over the hundred-twenty-five pesos. But, after all, you are never broke until the money runs out, so "Here you are, Mr. *Superintendente*, and *muchas gracias* for the fine job. When do we leave?"

He said as soon as we signed the book we could go.

"*Esta Bueno. Vamos* [It's good. Let's go]."

Our escort was buckling on his pistol in the dispatcher's office and declared that he was ready, so we signed up again. Our orders were to proceed to Santa Lucrecia, 236 kilometers [146.6 miles] south, and at that place get new train orders, [and] in the meanwhile to keep a weather eye open for the afternoon passenger train and get on a siding when it was due. The dispatcher gave us a book showing the time of all trains, and we were set. The orders set us down as special train No. 13. I called this to Joe's attention.

---

* That is, on April 18, the brothers' twenty-fifth day.

"Hell's bells, now is no time to get superstitious. The unluckiest number I have heard of for a long time is hundred-twenty-five pesos. Compared to that thirteen is downright lucky. How's the steam?"

"Warpin' the crown head," said I.

"And the air?"

"Hundred and ten in the shade."

"O.K.," and he sounded the horn five times to call in the "flag." The "flag," in the person of Señor Aguilar, came on the run and at 11:10 a.m., Mexican standard time we started. There was no bullfight this time to draw a crowd to us, but all the shop force turned out to admire their handiwork and bid us goodbye. Oh, yes, the interpreter was there, too. The sorrow he expressed at our hasty departure was no doubt real—it promised to be a long drought before the next job of interpreting should come his way.

The smoothest highway we found in Mexico. This jungle we found between Tierra Blanca and Sta. Lucrecia is as dense as the Congo jungle according to authorities. Apr. 18, 1930.

Chapter VII

# Special Train Number Thirteen

The clickety-click of steel on steel was a pleasant sound indeed. As Henry A proved his ability to stay on the rails, Joe gradually opened her up until we were skimming along at forty-five mph [miles per hour], and the old bus started humming her song, which I hadn't heard since we dropped off the pavement up near the Río Grande.

"Let her out," I called from my perch on the after-deck where I had gone to view the scenery.

He pushed it gradually up to fifty. It held there for a while, but after a few moments the front wheels started to "shimmy" so violently that we were almost wrecked. Eight-hundred-fifty-nine pounds of wabbling steel at fifty miles-an-hour was no joke. Señor Alvarado thought we were doomed, for as Joe brought it to a stop he was out on the running board ready to leap to safety. That satisfied our desire for excessive speed. After tightening the clamp which locked the steering gear straight ahead, we continued. In places the irregularity of the rails cut us down to thirty, but for the most part we drove between thirty-five and forty.

This part of Mexico is known as the *tierra caliente*—hot lands—and is for the most part virgin jungle with an occasional banana or sugar plantation.[*] A few miles out from Tierra Blanca there is reputed to be a settlement of Mormons from the States, but we saw no fair-skinned followers of Joseph Smith.[†] Among the crowd at one of the stations were two titian-haired, brown-skinned native girls, though, who bore witness to literal interpretation of Smith's command to "propagate and multiply."

---

[*] "Virgin jungle" is a bit hot for a place that has been inhabited for thousands of years, but vegetation does grow in the tropics.

[†] Joseph Smith (1805–1844) was the founder of Mormonism and the Latter-day Saint movement in America. He published the *Book of Mormon* in 1830 at age twenty-four.

A few iguanas, which looked like diminutive crocodiles, were sunning themselves on the rails over the numerous bridges. They would raise their heads as we approached but would not dive over the side until we were almost upon them. Aside from the iguanas, there was no sign of animal life with which the jungle is supposed, in popular fancy at least to teem. We looked in vain for monkeys, crocodiles, and North American tigers, which our guidebook says are found here in abundance. But if the animal life was scarce, the vegetable kingdom is certainly overcrowded. Ten feet or less from the tracks is the solid jungle wall, with most everything that grows or creeps or climbs. Picture if you will, a branch railroad line abandoned only three years, overgrown and all but obliterated by the fertile tropical growth.

We lost our escort when the afternoon train back to Tierra Blanca passed. Then we alone were in control. If no unscheduled freight trains showed up, we had clear sailing. I took my turn at the wheel, which simply consisted of setting the hand throttle and keeping an occasional eye on the track for obstructions or cattle. We had one scare. A small boulder was lying up against the rail and not until too late did I see it. I threw on the brakes, but steel on steel slides too easily and we hit with a crash. Luckily enough, it didn't derail us. The disappearing figure of a small *muchacho* told us who was responsible for this practical joke. Superintendent Aguilar had told us to watch out for just this sort of thing. The natives, he said, think it is great sport to derail a locomotive, and it frequently happens that they succeed. The engineers are very cautious, however, and are continually stopping to remove boys and boulders from the track. I was another engineer who developed a streak of caution.

But this was ideal motoring—no steering, no braking, in fact nothing to do except to move the hand throttle a notch or two as we go up [hill] and downhill. So we cruised along over the smoothest road in Mexico, as carefree as the country we were in, and totally unconcerned over the fact that the eight dollars in the "kitty" wouldn't buy us a ticket to anywhere if we got stranded.

An American oil company representative saw us come in at Santa Lucrecia.[*] He was aghast at our ignorance of Spanish and took us under his wing to talk to the superintendent. That affable fellow all but presented us with the railroad and said that our wishes were his commands, as per instructions from Mexico City. We expressed a wish only for a quiet side track where we could set up our tent and make

---

* In 1932, its citizens renamed Santa Lucrecia as Jesús Carranza. It had around 26,000 inhabitants in 2019. It must have been tiny in 1930. Jesús Carranza is near the border of the state of Oaxaca into which the brothers will soon run.

camp. He hurried off to move a string of boxcars out of the way and switched us off to a side track where we set up our tent. We expressed doubts as to the safety of our stuff, as we were right in the center of town and most of the native population was assembled around to look at the first automobile to visit Santa Lucrecia.

"*Un momento*," and he hurried off again to return in ten minutes with an armed guard to protect our outfit and keep any stray locomotives from bumping the car.

With our outfit in such good hands, we returned to the railroad dining room to sit down to the best that Santa Lucrecia afforded as the guest of the American. That good Samaritan was chuck full of health suggestions for the tropics.

"Don't ever drink any of this water without boiling it," he said, pouring himself a glassful and downing it immediately. We sipped the beer he had thoughtfully provided for us.

And a little later, "You'll get dysentery sure if you eat any uncooked vegetables or fruit in this country," and he finished his sliced tomato without batting an eye.

After an admonishment to refrain from strong alcoholic beverages in the tropics, he led the way to the bar for a few whiskey-and-sodas before we parted. As we rose to go he finished the lecture on tropical hygiene.

"Now don't forget, six grains of quinine a day or you'll go home in a box."

When we got outside Joe exclaimed, "Tie that, if you can! I'll bet he's been telling that stuff to the folks back home for so long he can't get out of the habit. But for all the comedy he certainly has a big heart. Thanks to him, we're still eight dollars ahead of the wolf—or I guess you'd say down here—ahead of Señor Lobo!"

"Yeah, and if our good friend knows what quinine looks like I miss my guess."

About midnight I awoke to find our tent all but floating. The rainy season was still a few weeks away, but this little pre-season performance gave us a hint of what was to come. I guess it rains hard in many spots of the world. I myself have seen a single cloud in a Western sky descend and wash away most of the topsoil in a few minutes. But never have I seen it come down like it did that night in Santa Lucrecia. Before I could get the flap over the door down, everything in the tent was soaked. Our Kodak was floating around on the floor and the bedding was dripping. A waterproof tent does little good if you leave the flap up. We hung the Kodak and the gun up to the "umbrella" spikes and wrapped up in the wet sheets and slept. Yes, sir, we slept, although it was just like sleeping in a bathtub with the taps running.

"Nice little freshet we had last night!" sang out the optimist in the morning when we went for breakfast.* "Of course, it doesn't really rain here until May."

* This is day twenty-six, April 19.

"Please cease," I begged. "We are too wet to hear about the terrible drought that has descended on Southern Mexico. But join us in breakfast, won't you?"

"I will, only, of course, if you will allow me to pay for it. I haven't much chance to entertain Americans down here, so please don't try to infringe on the privilege. What do you say to an eye-opener?"

We opined that an eye-opener would be O.K. but protested rather feebly, I am afraid, that breakfast should be on us.

"No, couldn't think of it. You're my guests this morning, and I only wish you could stay longer. Well, here comes Señor Encinas to conduct you to Matías Romero. He's a fine old Mexican. Too bad you don't speak Spanish. He could tell you some good yarns about the old revolutionary days. I understand he is barred forever from the U.S.A. A matter of dynamiting a few passenger trains up near El Paso, I think."

"*Buenos días, señor.* You old cutthroat, have a little drink with us."

"He wants to know if you slept well."

"Sure," we grinned. "Tell him we never slept better and thanks for the armed patrol."

This was repeated in Spanish, and Señor Encinas bowed and smiled.

"He wants to know what time it would please you to leave."

"Eight o'clock is all right for us."

At breakfast the discussion turned to the pot-bellied native children and the cause of such abnormal proportions.

"That is caused by hookworm," our host said. "The infection comes from the ground through the feet. They all have it as they all go barefoot."

I couldn't help glancing at his feet, but he disappointed me this time. They were encased in a shining pair of oxfords.

At eight o'clock sharp we clocked out on the second day's run.

The fat Señor Encinas took up a good half of the seat room, so I stayed out on deck most of the time. It wasn't long before the aspect of the country changed, considerably.* We climbed out of the rank jungle into an open, hilly country where the road wound in and out of numerous canyons. The changed nature of the country could hardly be attributed to the altitude, as the maximum elevation of the railroad on the Isthmus of Tehauntepec is only 730 feet. It is more probably due to the absence of the moisture-laden winds from the Gulf of Mexico and the presence of the dry breezes from the Pacific. The air was remarkably fresh and clear and no mists or haze obscured the blue vistas of the mountains of the Pacific coast.

* At this point, the brothers have entered the state of Oaxaca.

Special Train No. 13 On time at Matias Romero. Two Division Superintendents transferring control. Heavy rains damaged our film last night.

While we were stopped at a small station picking up orders, the air mail plane flew over with a roar. The inhabitants hardly looked up at this commonplace visitor but were more interested in the strange vehicle on the rails.

The fat and jovial Señor Encinas was not at all reluctant to tell us about exploits in the revolution. His answer to our question of why he could not visit the Estados Unidos [United States] he answered by a big grin and a slicing gesture across the throat. Evidently that meant a price on his head. He explained why in great detail, but most of it was unintelligible to us. He evidently enjoyed the recounting of his adventures, though, so we made no attempt to stop the flow of Spanish and nodded and smiled at the proper intervals.

We then came to Rincon Antonio, the beginning of the Pan American Division, and a new escort.* Señor Encinas transferred our running orders to Señor Manuel Acosta, the live-wire assistant superintendent of the division, and we left immediately.

We crossed the continental divide a short distance out from Rincon Antonio and dropped quickly down toward the Pacific. The country is strangely like the coastal country of Southern California. Not quite barren, the trees are small and the under-brush scattering. It had rained there, too, the night before, and when we reached [the coast] the temperature was ideal. We got along famously with our new conductor, even though our conversation was badly handicapped with no common language. He was an up-and-coming Mexican with all the pep in the world. His brother was training for a flyer in the States.

San Jerónimo is the junction where we started south on the Pan American division down the isthmus.† The main line continues on to Tehuantepec, twenty-nine kilometers [eighteen miles] west, the largest city of the isthmus, and ends at Salina Cruz, twenty-nine kilometers further on, the Pacific port.‡ Before the Panama Canal was finished, this railroad carried the bulk of the inter-ocean traffic, and Puerto México on the Gulf and Salina Cruz on the Pacific were the two largest ports in

---

* This was known as Rincón Ferrocarrilero Antonio, but, in 1930, shortly after the brothers were there, it changed its name to Matías Romero after Matías Romero Avendaño (1837–1898), a Oaxacan politician and diplomat important in the war against the French and Maximillian. Clearly, both names were already in use in 1930.

† Formally known as Villa de San Jerónimo Doctor but today called Ciudad Ixtepec, the town was once an important rail center.

‡ At this point, the brothers have been on the Isthmus of Tehuantepec for a while. Here, the Sierra Madre of Oaxaca, which may be said to begin with Pico de Orizaba, flattens out, North America comes to an end, and Central America begins. Soon the Sierra Madre de Chiapas, which continues on into Guatemala, El Salvador, and Honduras, picks up, though the brothers are going to work their way down along the narrow coastal plain next to the Pacific.

Latin North America.* But the boom died seven years after its birth, with the completion of the Panama Canal in 1914, and now one mixed train a day handles all the traffic. That day it was increased 100 per cent by special train No. 13.

We turned around on the "Y" which marks the junction point and backed up half a mile into San Jerónimo for noontime refreshments. The patron saint, Mexican Hospitality, saved the day again for impoverished gringos and Señor Acosta politely but positively refused to let us spend a single peso for food, as indeed he refused all the way to the Guatemalan border. Our conscience got the better of us, however, and I did manage to sneak away and buy a few bottles of iced beer for the long desert ride ahead.

There in San Jerónimo we saw a few of the famed Tehuantepec Indian ladies who, reputation has it, scorn the attentions of men and wear twenty-dollar gold pieces around their necks for ornaments.† Another interesting custom attributed to these brown Amazons was a peculiarity of dress which "flows loose at the waist and shows a strip of skin there, as well as every curve of the figure."‡ But in San Jerónimo local custom evidently forbade such display of the person, for we saw no waists revealed, nor did we see any twenty-dollar gold piece necklaces. However, the women are of striking appearance, tall in stature, and with remarkably handsome faces, as different from the other Mexican Indians as it is possible to imagine, although supposedly of the same race.§

For miles we crossed what is in truth a desert, this time at sea level, but not hot, thanks to the Pacific breeze. Twenty miles south of San Jerónimo we caught a glimpse of the Pacific. We stopped and had a look at this, the first salt water we had seen since leaving New York.

It was not long before a thin trail of smoke in the distance announced that we were overtaking the daily passenger train. Soon we were pacing it a few hundred yards or so behind, and the train crew and all the passengers crowded on the back platform to see this roadster with a New York license zipping along the rails. At the first station Señor Acosta consulted with the conductor, and the train pulled onto a

---

* U.S. President Theodore Roosevelt (1858–1919) oversaw the realization of a longstanding goal of the U.S.: a trans-isthmus canal to link the two oceans. Begun in 1904, it was completed in 1914, 401 years after Panama was first crossed by Vasco Núñez de Balboa (1475–1519), the Spanish explorer and conquistador.

† Much has been written about the "matriarchal society" of Tehuantepec, much of it fantasy.

‡ Today, it's unlikely the brothers would use the phrase "brown Amazons" to describe these people of local Indian descent, whom they obviously respect.

§ Hard to know what Arthur means by "race," for Mexico is filled with an enormous variety of indigenous peoples, speaking more than sixty different languages and having very different histories. Those living in Tehuantepec are Zapotecs, and these are the first the boys have seen.

siding while we passed it on the main line. No side track for Señor Acosta, this special train with through orders had the right of way over mere passenger trains.

Tonalá terminated the day's run, and we turned in a card of 190 miles for the best day we had had since leaving Texas.[*] And, incidentally, we broke the passenger train record between San Jerónimo and Tonalá. Our sidetrack was on a narrow grade, and we had to pitch the tent across the rails. We went to sleep with a prayer that no wandering locomotive would slice us in two as we slept. About midnight the glare of a headlight and the roar of an approaching train aroused me. I let out a yell and jumped for the door in time to see it pass by on the main line ten feet away.

We reached Suchiate, on the Guatemalan border, at four the next afternoon.[†] By dark we had Henry A. back on rubber, special train No. 13 was just a happy memory, and Córdoba was 509 miles behind. More vital statistics were: Distance from New York, 3,839 miles; distance from Laredo, Texas, 1,604 miles. We were twenty-[seven] days out of New York and had crossed Mexico in seventeen days. And we were now face to face with Guatemala with $3.50 in the treasury and about twelve gallons of gas in the tank, and feeling pretty cocky about it at that.

We pushed the last pound of air into the tires and sat down to talk over the situation. But no time for conference now. Came the enthusiastic Acosta with plans for a farewell part to the *gringos*.

"Bless your hospitable nature, old fellow, but we are tired *hombres* and need a lot of rest for the battle with the Guatemalan border officials tomorrow."

"No, *señor*, we must celebrate! It is your last night in Mexico. Come with me."

So down [we went] to the Chinese restaurant for dinner.[‡] Awaiting us there was the railroad agent in Suchiate and with him was the Negro engineer of the passenger train from Tonalá. The latter greeted us.

"Well, you all is them *gringos* what passed me up this afternoon in that little cockroach, ain't you?"

---

[*] At this point, the brothers have been in the state of Chiapas for thirty-some miles, running along a narrow coastal plain between the Sierra Madre de Chiapas and the Pacific.

[†] On April 20, day twenty-seven. The border here was only fixed in 1882, at which point a *hacienda* [a large estate, farm, or ranch] known as Los Cerros matured into a village, originally either known as Suchiate or Ignacio Mariscal. In 1925, the *municipio* of Suchiate, equivalent to a U.S. county, was created, and the village was formalized as such. In 1952, its name was changed to Ciudad Hidalgo. So, today, the brothers would be in Hidalgo, in the municipio of Suchiate.

[‡] Yes, Chinese! Coffee growing was strongly promoted by the government of Porfirio Díaz in the Socunosco region; that is, on this strip of coast and up the slopes of the Sierra Madre de Chiapas. This attracted a significant contingent of Germans and Chinese, who began arriving in the area around 1900. Since then, Chinese food, especially Cantonese, has been an important part of the scene.

"Sure are them, boss, where you all from?"

"San Luis, I mean Saint Louis. Been down here seventeen years and almost forgot all de American I know. But I'm the only pusson in this here town what speaks American and Spanish, too."

"Well, well, that's fine. You can interpret for us then. You tell Mr. Acosta there that we want to thank him for the fine trip we had with him and tell him that he is a gentleman and a scholar and a very good judge of whiskey, too."

"Ha, ha, ha, Ah don't know's I can interpret that there scholar business, but ah'll try."

So we dined. The wine flowed freely—oh, too freely. We toasted La Republica de México, Los Estados Unidos, each other, and everything of importance betwixt and between the Río Grande and the Río Suchiate. Old Tom, the engineer, did the interpreting with great gusto, if a little carelessly. And what a racial mixture we were! The Chinese cook, who ran around talking excitedly in a tongue that might have been Spanish, had an Indian wife. The offspring of this union were peeking out of the shadows at us, slant-eyed and brown-skinned. Tom was black as night, Acosta was a dark-complexioned Spaniard, and we were blond Nordic, or had been a few weeks earlier at least.

Dinner finished, Acosta suggested that there were two things we might do: visit the ladies, as he put it, or play a game of chess in the *cantina* across the street. He strongly recommended the former, but if that didn't appeal to us he was perfectly willing to uphold the honor of Mexico in a chess game. Remembering the event of our introduction to Mexico in Nuevo Laredo, we decided that the painted ladies of Suchiate had a little less than no appeal at all, so chess it was.

I drew the black and before I had really decided whether to counter the Queen's gambit with a two Knight return or . . . I was two pawns and a bishop behind, and the crowd was roaring for the kill. Old Tom was too far gone to be of much service as an interpreter. He talked Spanish to us and English to the Mexicanos and refused to be corrected, roaring at intervals, "*Viva México!*" or "*Viva* Saint Louis!" The bloodthirsty devils didn't have to wait long for the inevitable checkmate, and the Stars and Stripes were soon lowered in ignoble defeat. That was a weird setting to play a chess game, there in a thatched Suchiate *cantina*, with swinging gasoline light above, and dirt floor below, and all of the rabble of that border down on the sidelines, cheering for Mexico!

I guess we got through just in time as it was, for Joe and Tom were off down the street toward the railroad station, and when we caught up with them they were laying plans for a nocturnal run in the locomotive. Joe explained that they got tired waiting for me to get checkmated, and Tom had volunteered to teach him how to run a loco-motive. They were planning a little run up the main line, which, as Tom explained was "p'fectly safe 'cause it is the only train between here and Tonalá—that's a day's run up No'th." They were quick to see, though, that it was hardly right to go running around at night wasting the company's fuel and wearing out their locomotive.

## Chapter VIII

# Some Low Gear Work in Guatemala

**D**id you ever try to cross a Central American border without benefit of Spanish or money, with the only bilinguist in the neighborhood on the northbound train halfway to Tapachula? No? Well, then, you just haven't had your share of life's vicissitudes, and you had better pray to God that the necessity for such a crossing never arises to blight your life, ruin your disposition, and cause you to consider in turn the advisability of homicide, suicide, or armed rebellion against the customs authorities of an otherwise honorable nation.

First, they refused to allow us to export our rifle, the self-same rifle that our bonding company pledged themselves to see re-exported within sixty days.* Well, the law says it can't be exported, and it also says that is must be exported. This was Monday, and I guess the Monday law is no export—that was that. The custom official graciously offered to solve this dilemma by offering us fifty *pesos* for the gun, which we accept so quickly that he tries to scale it down to, and we finally had to accept forty-five or give it to him. So we felt pretty cocky with money in our jeans, fifty-one *pesos* in fact, but not for long. Buying the gun was just a little trick of theirs to make us feel good and not complain to the government.

To export the car we had to give him back twenty *pesos*. The car, too, was under bond, but, as I think I stated, this was Monday and exports are very difficult on Monday.

When the Mexican racketeers finished they turned us over to the Guatemalan gang next door. After a preliminary skirmish in which they ascertained how much we

---

* This is the next day, April 21, the brothers' twenty-eighth.

had they took half of it and passed us along to the photographer for a final extortion for passport photographs, and if properly born and could prove it, and your intentions toward the Guatemalan government were honorable, we were all set to leave the country. Of course, we were carrying American passports, and they are all that is necessary, if properly visaed, to enter Guatemala. But not in Suchiate. No, sir! How would the photographer and the consul make a living if they didn't sell a passport now and then?

We started down the street toward the river, resolved to get on our way as quickly as possible—but no—not yet.* There came a soldier out of a cantina on the run. "No passa! No passa!" and from the gestures with his gun, we understood.

Not to be tricked by a lousy Mexican soldier, we went back and tried it again—this time we started down a side street. We made it a little further and were just congratulating ourselves on outwitting the [Guatemalan] Army when our hero, the guard, boomed out of another *cantina*, and from his threatening actions it was plain to see that the safest thing to do was to retire quickly and ask no questions. I spun around and headed back but not before he had jumped on the running-board and placed us under arrest. We mollified him a bit with an invitation to join us in a beer and managed to wring out the information that there was no going down to the river during the *siesta* hour as the border guards there were all to lunch.

At 2:00 o'clock, after the siesta, we went down without molestation and found out that the bridge which connects Guatemala and Mexico was for foot passengers only. The only chance to get our car across seemed to be to lash two of the small cargo boats together and make a ferry out of them. We approached the boss, a half-naked native who was wading around waist deep in the water, with this in mind. Yes, for five *pesos* he would transfer us across, but we must wait until the hundred or more cases of gasoline stacked up on the bank were transferred. You see, the method of international transportation there runs like this: The cargo comes into Suchiate on the standard gauge railway from the north; at the station, about half a mile from the river, it is unloaded; then, within the next day or two, I suppose, unless they happen to be holidays, which is more than likely, the stuff is hauled to the riverbank in oxcarts, ferried or rather pushed across the river (which at no place is more than four feet deep), then reloaded into oxcarts and hauled the half mile to the narrow gauge railroad station in Guatemala, all ready within the surprisingly short time of one week to continue on its

---

* This is the Río Suchiate, which forms the southwestern border between Mexico and Guatemala. It rises on the slopes of the Tocaná volcano in the Sierra Madre de Chiapas, known in Guatemala as *el Sierra Madre de Guatemala*.

way.* There's no hurry or confusion about it—if it doesn't move today, tomorrow or the day after will do as well. So we lay down in the shade of the thatched customs shack to watch this smooth[ly] functioning, if tortuously routed, international transportation system at work, to wait for our turn in the scheme of things. On good authority we learned that the Mexican government had offered to build a full-sized bridge at this point, bearing all the costs, but that the Guatemalan government had refused to allow it because of the fear of an invasion across it. Picture a four-foot stream of water a hundred yards across stopping an invasion!

On the other bank, the Guatemalan Army was having a little pistol practice. A group of barefoot soldiers in blue denim were blazing away at a target tacked to a tree. After every volley the Mexican soldiers on our side would yell across uncomplimentary remarks about their marksmanship, and they in turn jeered back. This hooting and yelling awoke the officer snoring in the shack, and he stalked out to put a stop to such unsoldierly conduct but not until he had added a few jibes of his own, directed, I suppose, at the Guatemalan *comandante* [commander].

Our turn finally came, so after lashing two boats together and laying planking across them we drove aboard and embarked for Guatemala. The officer in charge had walked across to see us load our car. Now he walked back and was waiting for us on the bank and gravely examined our passports and other documents before allowing us to land. Our crew set up a clamor for money. They said the five *pesos* were only for the boat hire, the four pushers demanded fifty *centavos* each. Well, what was a little more robbery? We were so used to it by then that we paid with hardly a murmur.

The official went with us to the town—Ayutla—which was on the Guatemalan side, for the remaining formalities.† First, we were officially admitted at the emigration station. We had to show vaccination certificates. Mine [had] refused to "take," and all I had was a certificate of inoculation. It had stamped across the face of it "This is NOT a Certificate of Successful Vaccination," but they stamped it with the seal and we crossed town to the customs inspection station to unpack everything for examination. Next we went to the police headquarters and reported for permission to stay in the country. There was a little mix-up there. After carefully examining our papers they elicited the information that we had crossed Mexico in seventeen days in an automobile. That was palpably an impossibility, so we must have stolen or forged

---

* These days, there's a combined road and railroad bridge here but no functioning railroad on the Guatemalan side.

† Ayutla is now just the name of the *municipio*. The town is situated on Río Suchiate and was renamed Ciudad Tecún Umán in 1960. In 2019, it had around 12,000 inhabitants.

the passports. After a vexatious half-hour with the aid of the hotel proprietor next door, who spoke some English, we convinced them that we had done that without access to black magic or stolen passports, and we were entered in the book as suspicious characters to be watched in the future. Anyone who crosses Mexico in a car "*para* sport," as we explained our reasons, is certainly to be watched.

The hotel man must have his glass of beer for pay. When I asked for the bill and was answered "*quince pesos*" my long-suffering soul rose up in rebellion, and I indignantly (and I am afraid raucously) refused to pay any such outrageous sum—in fact, I'd be damned if I'd pay anything at all. Joe and I rose as one, and when on the point of making a break for the street, the hotel man (he was laughing uproariously) asked us to please be seated and take a lesson in Guatemalan currency. Fifteen *pesos*, he explained, was twenty-five American cents or fifty Mexican [*centavos*]. The old peso used to be equivalent to the Mexican *peso*, but the government printing presses started running overtime and it dropped like a German mark until at that time it was stabilized at 60 to the quetzal, which was equal to an American dollar.* The new currency was divided into *centavos*, hundredths of a dollar, but the people hadn't gone in much for the new-fangled currency and mostly all prices were quoted in pesos. Well, that *was* a relief. We changed all the currency we had left, something over eight *pesos* Mexican, into 252 *pesos* Guatemalan, and with money bulging from every pocket we started out for Guatemala City.

There is no road from Ayutla, but we had developed a fine scorn for that luxury anyway, so we found our way to the railroad station, and before the startled eyes of the station-men we hopped a-straddle of the narrow-gauge tracks and bounded away down the ties. One of them ran after us, crying "*No pasa* [No way]! *No pasa*! *Alto* [Stop]!" but as he had no gun and looked quite harmless, we kept on. With true Latin lassitude, he gave it up after a few yards, and we went ahead unmolested. Unmolested, that is, but damned if we weren't badly shaken. Out of town the ballast between the ties disappeared altogether. Thirty feet and then stop; thirty feet and stop again.

If we persisted further than that the car would get synchronized to the bumps until it well might have leaped out of its skin. Once, actually, it bounded so high that it cleared the rails and started down the embankment. Joe all but tore the steering wheel from its post in an effort to hang on. It soon got dark, and we managed to get stuck a couple of times with all four wheels down between inconveniently spaced

* On October 10, 2019, one Mexican *peso* equaled 0.051 U.S. dollar and $1.00 U.S. equaled 19.45 Mexican *pesos*.

ties. Three hours of this and we decided to camp. We pulled off at a cross-road and begged camping space at an hacienda nearby. I thought we had covered at least four miles, but after a check-up on the speedometer Joe announced that we were one-and-six-tenths miles out of Ayutla. An average of about one-half mile per hour!

The *hacienda*'s owner, a young Guatemalan who was having his own troubles with the low price of sugar, came along and announced that we would be his guests, certainly, for tonight and for as much longer as we cared to stay. "Come to the house, *señores*, and I shall have beds prepared for you."

"No," we demurred. "It is better that we sleep in our tent as we are certainly too travel-stained to stay in the *señor's casa*"—and that we did.

In the morning we bustled around early, shaved and cleaned up a bit for a more respectable appearance at breakfast, to which we would certainly be invited.[*] But the breakfast hour came and passed and the señor never showed up, so we packed and went along.

"I guess," said Joe, "we still have things to learn about Guatemalan etiquette. Man, I was certainly primed for a hearty breakfast after no dinner last night! But evidently we insulted the *don* by not sleeping under his roof. Well, just watch me the next time an invitation is extended!"

"The thing to do, evidently, is to grab him by both hands and [ask], "How is the *señora* and *muchacho*," and "Walk in and start ordering the servants around" I agreed. "No more of this coy reluctance. They're not used to it."

The going was a little better by daylight. Most of the time we could run with only two wheels on the ties and sometimes we could get off altogether and drive in the comparatively smooth ditch. We had breakfast in Pajapita, for the sum of forty [Guatemalan] *pesos*.[†] After crossing the river at the edge of town on a railroad bridge fully a quarter of a mile long, we dropped off the ties on to a road of sorts, which had the reputation of being continuous, at least to the capital.[‡] We hadn't much more than got clear of the rails before the engine of the Mexicano Limited (or whatever they call the train to Ayutla) hove into view and went screeching across the bridge whistling at the pedestrians who clung perilously to the girders as it passed. What

---

* On the brothers' twenty-ninth day, April 22.

† Like Ayutla, Pajapita is in the department of San Marcos. Founded in 1920 as an important railway location, around 8,000 people lived there in 2019. The construction of new highways has diminished the role of rails here.

‡ This was the Río Naranjo. Like the Río Suchiate, it rises in the Sierra Madre. Today, its white water flowing through narrow canyons is popular with rafters.

would have happened to us had we met on the bridge can better be imagined than described. We paused to devour a watermelon, swinging our feet over the edge of the bridge, and taking in the sights along the river. Up and down as far as we could see were little laundry parties and swimming parties. The women wore a single cotton cloth from the hips down, as they pounded clothes with flat rocks. The men and, of course, the children wore nothing at all and splashed gaily around while mama did the laundry. A bull cart splashed noisily across as the driver took advantage of the wetting for the weekly bath, or maybe it was the annual one. At any rate his clothes hung on the staked sides of the cart while he made comical starts and stops. First, he would drop behind to give himself a good rubbing, then dash hurriedly up to his team to prod them along.

The way led us up out of the red clay of the lowland to the granite sand of the upland country. Almost imperceptibly we shook off the sticky humid atmosphere of the tropics and by noon we were well on our way to the Temperate Zone and altitude. At Coatepeque we were up 1,600 feet.* Then we left the railroad and started climbing in earnest, up endless ridges which broke around the side of a mountain occasionally giving us a glimpse of the coffee farms which dotted the hillsides. Intensively cultivated, they follow the hills up to the top or at least to a point so steep that the soil is gone. This is the best coffee land in the world. Guatemalan high-country coffee; that is, coffee grown above 3,500 feet, commands a premium in any market.†

Climbing precariously up ridges and around peaks we had magnificent vistas spread out beneath us, of coffee farms on edge, banana farms in the flats, and everything covered with the freshest, brightest green imaginable.

Hundreds of natives were on the road that day, bearing heavy loads of pottery or coffee or any other commodity which required transporting. They are vastly different from the lowland Indians a few miles back. Their dress is peculiar. The main feature, a heavy black and red striped wool cape, covers almost the whole body. Here, as contrasted with the Mexican high country, the natives dress to suit the elevation, and as we go higher they bundle up more in their woolens.‡

* Coatepeque is a small city (2019 population around 42,000) in the department of Quetzaltenango. The brothers left the department of San Marcos just after Pajapita.

† Guatemalan coffee remains a favorite of many connoisseurs, annually competing for ranking among the world's top-three coffee-growing countries.

‡ The indigenous people here are Mam, a Mayan population. Our guys didn't get here across the highlands of Chiapas, where they would have found the Mam, Tzotzil, and Tzeltzal equally wearing wool.

At Quetzaltenango we leveled off at 7,000 feet.* This mountain city is very cool indeed. Before we left we unearthed our overcoats from the bottom of the duffle bag where they had reposed since beyond Mexico City.

Quetzaltenango is the terminus of the now-electrified railway which runs to the Pacific Coast, connecting also with the main east and west road which runs from Guatemala City to Ayutla.† As the second city in Guatemala and the center of an extremely rich coffee section, it is an important city commercially and is by all means the most attractive place to the eye south of Mexico City.‡

We met one American there, a construction engineer. He showed us how to get out of town and we climbed on up to Totonicapán where the road took right up the side of a mountain, and in the setting sun we pitched up through a drizzle to the summit of the Guatemalan Sierra Madre.§ The going was bad, and we slipped and slid about through the darkness, perched time and again on the edge of a seemingly bottomless ravine. The trees were now coniferous pines and firs. Each time we topped a rise and started down again we thought surely we had reached the summit, but each time we climbed again until we were finally in a blizzard almost 11,000 feet up in the air, and the visibility was just about zero—from the steaming tropical jungle to a snowstorm all in one day! You can't climb forever, even in the Guatemalan mountains, so some three hours after dark we did reach a bare, wind-swept ledge, which was the top, and started down. From here, so we had been told, eleven volcanoes are visible on a clear day. In the storm we were lucky to see the sides of the road, let alone eleven volcanoes.

We dropped even more precipitously than we had climbed, and in less than an hour were out from under the clouds and fog and sleet and were buzzing down one decline after another in search for a warm enough altitude to make camping less than a game of freeze-out.

After dropping into a deep ravine down a series of switchbacks and climbing tortuously back out of it on the other side, we reached a town. Sure enough, it was

---

* Quetzaltenango is actually at 7,600 feet and higher. As it was in 1930, it is still the second-largest city in Guatemala with around 250,000 inhabitants (2019), most of them Mam (who are Mayan). It is set against a backdrop of volcanoes and claims it has the oldest set of Spanish colonial buildings in the country.

† Again, this is the narrow-gauge railroad that no longer functions.

‡ The brothers seem to have forgotten Puebla, and they also missed Oaxaca in Oaxaca and San Cristobal in Chiapas.

§ Totonicapán, 8,200 feet elevation, is in the department of Totonicapán.

not on the road but was the dead end of a branch trail. We had missed the main road somewhere back in the fog. It was still too cold to camp comfortably, so we started a slow retreat back through the night.

Two men on horseback loomed out of the shadows.

"Where is the road for Guatemala?" One of them looked doubtfully at us for a minute, then said it was many leagues away and didn't we want to stay with him until morning. Yes, we most certainly did, and we followed him to his casa to set up our cots in his granary.

We were off at sun-up to retrace our way to the forks of the road.* How we could have missed it the night before was a mystery, for in order to go where we did we had made a right-angle turn off the main, graded highway onto an ungraded trail. But miss it we had.

The scenery this morning was glorious. Most of the eleven volcanoes were in sight from the road as we traveled along, the clouds had lifted, and a blazing sun was drying the road from the storm of the night before. Hundreds of men at work along the road gave evidence that Guatemala was forging ahead with her link of the Pan-American Highway. We zipped along this almost perfect mountain road at thirty and forty, with prospects of an early arrival at the capital. How far away that was no one seemed to know.† We asked innumerable times, and the answer was always, "*Muchas leguas* [Many leagues]." The actual distance was becoming an important matter to us, as our gasoline was running low. Albeit, we had rigged up a pressure valve to eliminate the gravity feed, it was a question whether we had enough fuel to make it.

Antigua is the old capital of Guatemala.‡ Here were the ruins of the old capital buildings which had been shaken down by an earthquake thirty years before. Guatemala had become tired of rebuilding after every temblor, so at that time they moved the seat of the government to its present location at Guatemala City.

We measured our gas there, and after a complicated calculation we estimated that we had about one gallon and a half left. The distance was stated to be ten leagues, about thirty miles, so we decided to chance it.

At twenty-five miles the outskirts of the city appeared, and we rolled into town on the last quart of gasoline—and, I might add, the last one hundred *pesos* we had left.

Top: Arthur and Joe in front of the Ford Agency in Guatamala [sic] City.

Bottom: This outfit pulled in front of our car at the Agency. Wonder if the owner is bargaining on a trade?

# Chapter IX

# Problems of Traffic, Coffee, and Finance

Guatemala City hardly came up to our idea of what a city of 125,000 inhabitants and the capital of a sovereign nation should be.* Its main business section is paved with ancient stone slabs, which are worn to a high degree of roughness—so rough in fact that automobiling over them is a little less than torture. The traffic is about evenly divided between oxcarts and automobiles—the former, with their rumbling, and the latter, with their squawking horns, creating a traffic din hardly surpassed under a New York elevated at midday. A barefooted crowd thronged the sidewalks, which, I hasten to add as a favorable point, are considerably wider than the Latin American average. The setting and climate, though, leave little to be desired. In the center of a volcano-lined valley nearly 5,000 feet above sea level, it is a delight to the eye and a tonic to the system.†

We finally drove up before the American Consulate. Our hungry request for mail was answered by five letters with which to pass the afternoon. But no check from Tierra Blanca fluttered out to pave the way for further travel. We drove over to the Ford agency to arrange for greasing and change of oil, which was all the car needed. As I pulled away from there to drive over to a hotel, which had been recommended

---

* These days Guatemala City is thriving with a 2019 population of around 1,000,000 (city) and 2,750,000 (metro area), the most populous city in Central America. Established as a capital city in 1775 by Spanish colonists on a former Mayan city, Guatemala City serves as the nation's cultural, economic, governmental, and transportation hub, attracting hundreds of thousands of rural migrants from interior lands and as the main entry point for foreign immigrants seeking to resettle here.

† The valley is called Valle de la Ermita (Hermitage Valley).

to us as fairly clean and reasonably cheap, one of those musical-noted horns sounded behind me. At the sound, a bus out in the middle of the street cut sharply into the curb and carried us via the left front fender with it. Two Packards rolled grandly by, and the bus driver, aided and abetted by a policeman, came back and started telling me things—plenty of them. I pled not guilty to much knowledge of Spanish, so the policeman told me the equivalent of "Tell it to the Judge!" and escorted me to the police station. Meantime, Joe dashed back to the agency and got an interpreter, but by the time they arrived I was all booked up. The charge is for not clearing the way upon the approach of the presidential car! I pleaded ignorance of the custom and promised to do a nose dive for the curb at the sound of the presidential horn in the future. That was greeted with a stony stare and a request for my driver's license. I didn't have one, but I borrowed Joe's New York City driver's license and handed it over. As the police captain didn't think it strange that Joe should be carrying my license, I explained how very difficult it was to obtain the license in New York, how very severe the tests were, and so forth. That won the day, I guess, for he released me with the admonition to always remember to get out of the way for the president.

We rested on our laurels—and not much else—for the time being. As the first to drive a car from the States to Guatemala, we acquired a sort of local fame. The time of one month, exactly, for the trip I hereby announce as the first established record from New York to Guatemala City. One of the local papers gave us a write-up with some pictures, and another gave us a line in the society column. So with our reputation on such a firm foundation, we began to devise ways and means for continuing the journey. The refund check for $32.50 from Tierra Blanca was conspicuous by its continued absence, but each day we trotted up to the American Consulate hoping against hope that it would arrive in time to pay our hotel bill at least, which was mounting at the rate of $5 per day.

Guatemala was in the throes of the coffee depression.[*] The national revenues, derived almost exclusively from the import duties, had fallen off over fifty per cent. In pairs and groups the panic-stricken coffee growers could be seen every evening in the local cafes and bars bewailing the low prices of coffee. For some inexplicable reason, the depression was almost universally attributed to the high tariff policy of the United States, and loud were the ejaculations against it.

The people drank coffee, talked coffee, and read about coffee. The news that an American utility company with large Latin American holdings had given a banquet in New York to urge the four o'clock coffee hour was front-page, headline stuff. The

---

[*] This was a consequence of the general economic depression affecting the world in 1930.

news from the London disarmament conference, if printed at all, was apt to be tucked away on the inside between the whiskey advertisements and the death notices. This banquet was certainly the event of the hour as far as Guatemalans were concerned. It kept its place on the front page for days. We were able to read all about it in minute detail—who was present, what was said, what a milestone it marked in the introduction of the four o'clock coffee hour to the United States, etc., etc. Weeks later I could pick up a paper from most any part of Central America and there would be a picture of the event—front paged and headlined again, as if it were hot off the cables. In fact, I got quite well acquainted with the gentlemen present and would like to assure them that a banquet like that once a month would be sufficient to keep most everything else out of the Central American prints—except, of course, the doings of one Sandino, the Gandhi (I am quoting *El Diario de San Salvador)* of Central America.

And now I began to see what a golden opportunity we had overlooked in not capitalizing on the interest in the coffee situation. As the self-appointed representatives of the "Four O'clock Coffee Club" of the United States, Unincorporated, we could have Central America at our feet and undoubtedly have had a reception accorded visiting potentates, a nineteen-gun salute, and all the trimmings. I mentioned it to Joe, and he spent the rest of the day wandering gloomily around, cursing our lack of foresight, and wondering if it wouldn't be a good idea to go back and start over as good-will coffee emissaries. I offer the idea for what it is worth. I predict that anyone who goes to Guatemala with a plan for the salvation of the coffee industry will be given the country—deficit and all—and get a reception that will make Lindbergh's look like a quiet Monday morning in comparison.[*] But opportunity had gone her coy way, and our budget was rapidly sinking into the unbalanced state of the Guatemalan government's. Our expectation and our debts balanced on the fifth day. On the sixth, we wrote off the expectations and faced the deficit, around $35, with about the same amount of confidence that Mr. Coolidge has in the export debenture plan.[†]

After talking over the situation with a fellow guest, we decided not to make a proposition to the hotel manager for an extension of credit, secured by a Kodak and two suitcases of clothes. A guest had departed the day before leaving a bill of some $200 and a trunkful of lead-silver ore from the mine he had been trying to sell, so the manager was not in a propositioning mood right then.

[*] Charles Lindbergh's ticker-tape parade in New York City on June 13, 1927 was the largest ever. He was equally feted in other American cities for his solo flight across the Atlantic.

[†] So this would be day thirty-six. Export debenture plans had been proposed as ways to deal with plummeting farm prices during the late 1920s. They were opposed by President Calvin Coolidge as socialist ploys.

Then we made a half-hearted attempt to stave off the crisis by selling the car. The only offer we got was $200—$50 down and the balance in six months. That was out of the question, so we decided to lay the case before a friend of ours who had been good enough to offer his services in case we needed them. Our concrete proposal was for him to cash a draft for us on a $50 nest egg we had left on deposit in the States. He rather surprised us by cashing the draft immediately and gladly, so we were free to leave for points south if we chose. And that's what we chose, that afternoon, in fact.

But we didn't put in all our time worrying about our finances. In fact we enjoyed life pretty thoroughly that week. For two days we did little more than sleep and gorge our starved stomachs on the quite satisfactory food the hotel put forth. The first breakfast was a little weak, but after our status as Americans became definitely fixed, they supplemented the fruit, coffee, and rolls with bacon and eggs and toast with a look, however, that implied one lost caste by not sticking to the continental breakfast.

The Plaza Central was a beautiful little park.* After the sun slanted down in the afternoon, it was a great place to sit and idly dream away the hours before the pageant of pretty girls in bright-colored finery, silk-stockinged, with dresses which showed no intention of hiding the knee. Styles in New York City and Paris might be sweeping the ground, but Guatemalan *señoritas* had no idea of covering up such attractive extremities. They were vitally interested, though. On being introduced to a Guatemalan lady, her first question would almost invariably be, "And are they wearing long dresses in *Nuevo York*?" At the answer in the affirmative, she would sigh and suggest hopefully that it would not last so long. I guess they take extremely short dresses as a sign of emancipation down there and also, more important, another helpful asset in the contest for the fickle male's attention which, with the devotion to and attendance at the church, completes the circle of her life's work.

Of course, flashing *señoritas* were not the only passersby at the plaza. Bare-footed native women, usually with a basket on their heads filled with an unknown something, were constantly passing back and forth. One reached the curb and stopped. With a slow, sweeping motion so as not to disturb the basket's balance, she turned her head around to see if a car or perhaps, an oxcart was approaching. Seeing the way clear, she swung slowly back to eyes-front and marched slowly but resolutely across the street, never flinching an iota as her feet struck the sizzlingly hot asphalt.

* This is *Plaza Mayor* (Central Park).

Then came a man carrying on his back, by a wide supporting band across the forehead, a large, ten-tube, double-triplexed, super-dyned cabinet radio.* Pure man-power may have its drawbacks, but for transporting a radio it is well-nigh perfect. Without a mar to its polished surface or a jar to its delicate tubes, he carried it swiftly by, on a dog trot, for delivery to some not-too-impoverished coffee planters. These people may have to cut down on the grocery bill, but they must have their music. The streets were actually alive with these trotting furniture vans, and the local phonograph record agencies are the busiest places in town.

Of an evening we would prowl around the night-life section of the town, occasionally putting in at the Palace Hotel bar to listen to the marimba band, which held sway in the ballroom adjoining.† These musicians got a surprising amount of rhythm out of their xylophone-like instruments in spite of the fact that modulation meant to them only louder—and louder. I felt like telling the leader that the music would be vastly sweeter if one had to listen for it occasionally instead of being driven into the furthest corner to escape its noisy volume. The marimba ranks as Guatemala's contribution to the world of music, and as such it has the place almost of a national institution.

The Palace Hotel, by the way, is known as the finest in Central America.‡ It is a quietly sedate place, except when the fruit companies' tours are in, when it is alive with restless, Kodaking Americans, finding time between their photographic assaults on the native capital to do a little "unamended" drinking in the spacious central lobby. It is a beautiful white structure and has the reassuring affidavit of an American engineering firm posted in the lobby to the effect that the building is earthquake-proof.

When viewed in the light that the only building takes place after earthquakes and between revolutions, the capital city is to be complimented on its progress at that. But the smoking volcanoes in the distance and the underground rumblings of dissatisfied politicians give promise of more disastrous crises in the future than the

---

* The band, known as a tumpline, allows the load to be supported by the spine rather than the shoulders. They're not worn across the forehead, though, but rather across the top of the head just back from the hairline, pulling straight down in alignment with the spine. As the bearer leans forward, the back supports the load.

† Such bands can consist of a marimba, several marimbas, or a marimba with trumpet, sax, drum, and so on. The newly independent Guatemalan state declared the marimba its national instrument in 1821, though the idea was brought to the New World from Africa during the sixteenth century. Classically, the marimba is a wooden percussion instrument, similar to a xylophone, but with resonators attached to each bar. They're extremely common from Oaxaca south through Central America.

‡ The brothers are likely referring to the Hotel Royal Palace, which opened in 1929.

present coffee-cup calamity. When you come right down to it, the whole trouble with Central America lies in the fact that the great body of the people is divided into two groups: government officials and dissatisfied politicians. The panacea, of course, would be to eliminate the latter. Of course, they try their best to do it, but the firing squads' rifles misfire, and they pop up again to cause more trouble. Talk about a Southern Democrat being a strong partisan—I am referring, of course, to the days before Al Smith and prohibition—why, compared to a Guatemalan Liberal, he is a loving little high-school politician campaigning for his friend running for class president.* The only act a Conservative down there can do, deserving of approbation from the Liberals, is the act of committing suicide. Even then the Liberals probably would claim he was only cheating the firing squad.

On one of my nocturnal prowls—Joe had gone to the all-talking, all-Spanish moving picture show—I bumped smack into an invitation to go places and do things with two of the young representatives of the United States of America who are working their way up to ambassadorships via the Foreign Service. They had evidently already been places and had things to drink other than coffee and Coca-Cola. One, in fact, was in that half-way between here and Heaven stage and was undecided whether to lie down on the sidewalk for a rest or sneak up behind the traffic cop in the middle of the street and steal his night stick. As he wrestled with this problem, two smartly dressed young men bore down upon us.

"Straighten up Fred, for God's sake," said the first would-be ambassador. "Here come the Britishers from the legation. You don't want them to get anything on you, do you?"

"I see no Bw'shers. Let me alone, will you. I don't want to stand in this doorway. Someone'll think I'm a burglar," with which he lurched forward to grab a lamp post but missed and plumped down on the running board of a parked car.

With typical Brit imperturbability, the Englishman stepped out of the way and with a casual, "Good Evening," went on smiling broadly.

The Guatemalan Country Club has a fine location overlooking the city. We drove out with an acquaintance on Sunday and met a couple dozen of the younger members. Almost without exception they had been to school in the States and spoke English fluently, besides swinging a mean niblick. The "pro" was a husky young American who came along one day with a bag of golf sticks and a couple of silver

---

* Al Smith (1873–1944) was a progressive firebrand who was notable, among other things, for his opposition to Prohibition and for losing the 1928 presidential race in a landslide to Herbert Hoover. He was also elected Governor of New York four times.

cups and was hired on the spot. I expect that this man's main job was teaching the nineteenth hole, for all I saw him do was changing the phonograph records and opening bottles.

Early in the week we went to the oil company, whose gas we were using, and explained the proposition that had been made to us in Mexico City. The manager had no instructions to give us a concession on our gas but promised to cable them asking our status.

At the oil company we found that, in answer to the cable, the head office had instructed them to take care of our gasoline requirements not to exceed forty gallons. And this time it was to be free! All we had to do was to sign a letter with the manager, already written out for us to save us the trouble, stating that we had used their gasoline in our "record breaking" drive from Mexico City, were more than satisfied with the performance of our car with it, and would continue to use it wherever it was available. I'll say we would continue using it, as long as it was available at that price! We might even be tempted to buy a few gallons if we ran low. Tempted would be all, however; in our financial state at that time, we could hardly have bought enough to get out of town, with gas selling at the price it was: forty cents per gallon.

And so it came to pass that we found ourselves the proud possessors of $3.12, forty gallons of gasoline, a fresh supply of canned milk, bacon and eggs, and an open road to San Salvador.*

* This is on April 29, the thirty-sixth day of the the brothers' trip.

## Chapter X

# We Attend a Band Concert—in Pajamas

Thirty-nine miles out of Guatemala City we had a puncture. That would not be important enough to remember were it not the first flat tire since leaving New York and only the second since the car left the factory. I got out my log and checked up on mileages. We had driven 4,516 miles on the trip to date. The total mileage on the speedometer was 15,581, which, as Joe pointed out, is a long way to travel to find two nails. This made us tire-conscious, as it were, and we examined all the rubber for possible bruises or cuts, but none were to be found. I became enthusiastic whenever I thought of the tires. Think of starting out from New York on a set of tires that would be considered nearly worn out and being able to drive to the capital of Guatemala without a flat one.

We were cruising through a night made almost light by the thousands, yes millions, of fireflies which swarmed along the roadside.* His sister who chased after him had made a sparkling crown for herself by entwining the light makers in her hair. I have heard that, in some places, the natives enclose a number of them in a screen and use it for a lantern. I thought it was a myth, but now I believe it possible.

We drove up a side road to find a comfortable campsite. The night was warm, luscious, intriguing, alive with sparkling beauty, perfectly silent except for the chugging of our motor as we climbed a little hill toward a large house where we sought permission to spend the night on the *hacienda*. As we drew up before it, a crowd of men, women, and children swarmed around us, overwhelming us with friendly salutations. The *haciendado* himself, a short muscular man in puttees and riding breeches

* The brothers are probably somewhere in the department of Santa Rosa now.

smiling a big pearly smile underneath a black mustachio, pushed forward to welcome us to La Sonrisa—which literally means The Smile. And what was our errand?

"We seek a place to camp, *señor*. Our destination is in Salvador and beyond, whither we are driving from *Nuevo York*. If it is not too much trouble, may we pitch our tent in your fields for the night and cook a little food?"

"Ah, you seek a place to camp? It is not necessary to camp. *Mi casa*," with a sweep of the head, "it is yours. And food shall be prepared if you are hungry."

"*Mil gracias, señor* [a thousand thanks, sir]. We shall accept your kindness."

As we sat on the veranda gazing out on the beautiful night, our host plied us with quiet questions.

"The Chrysler Building in *Nueva York*? It is very tall, no?"

"Yes, indeed, it is very tall. More than three hundred meters [984 feet]. And very beautiful, too?"

"The disaster from the stocks falling in prices? Very bad. No?"

"It was bad in many ways. The losses, though, were but little more than the gains of the year before so not so large as many outsiders imagined."

This point impressed him immensely, and he pressed us for more information. In common with most everyone with whom we talked on the subject, he believed that the United States had lost in stock deflation as much or more than we had gained in expansion since the war.[*]

To him, too, New York, the city of 1,000-foot skyscrapers, Wall Street, and stock market crashes, was the most interesting place in America. He would take a trip there with his family, now at school in Guatemala City, if coffee were not so cheap. His income, he assured us, was only one-third this year of what it had been two years ago.

We naturally drifted onto the topic of coffee, praising the fine quality of that which was served in our hotel in the capital. I explained that I had learned there how delicious coffee could be without sugar or cream. When he learned the name of the hotel, he clapped his hands with delight. That very hotel used only his coffee, grown and roasted right there. Would we like to try it now and see if it were not the same? We would.

His foreman, who spoke English, joined us, and our conversation flowed easier then. The coffee was served black, and was it good? We drank cups.

Yes, it was good, but the very quintessence of quality was only found in coffee just fresh out of the roasting oven. We should see for ourselves.

He called for his servants and bade them roast some coffee for his guests.

---

[*] It's important to remember that the Great Depression had barely begun.

"*Mañana?*" [Tomorrow], they queried.

"No, *inmediato*" [right now]!, he directed and sent them hustling off that we might taste the best that Guatemalan highlands could grow and experts prepare.

With a dash of rum first—for the malaria, he said—he treated us to the finest coffee, I am positive, that anyone, anywhere, has been privileged to drink. So we sat silently sipping, the exquisite aroma tantalizing our nostrils, sensuous, and positive. If our Latin friends are more sensitive to such than we, we are much the loser.

Keenly awake now and refreshed, we talked late into the night. Our conversation, perhaps, would not be interesting, but this coffee grower's plans, his hopes for his boys, his simple and charming hospitality, I shall remember a long, long time, and someday I hope again to be a guest at La Sonrisa—The Smile—and drink fresh roasted coffee on a high veranda against a background of black tropical night patterned with the incandescence of a million fluttering fireflies. Está bueno—It is good!

Those pesky inspections, as we rattled off toward the Salvadorean frontier, were somewhat of a nuisance.* I have said that we enjoyed those little encounters with the guardians of the peace in the form of wayside requests for name, number, and destination, and in a measure it was still true. But, as usual, they ran a good thing into the ground. At one village, for instance, we had to sign our way in, register with the *comandante* off on a side street of unmemorable name and unfindable location, and sign our way out. Check and triple check! If anyone ever drives from Guatemala City to the border without the army finding it out, he will have accomplished a feat of no mean proportions. As I recall it, they had fourteen separate reports on us over the distance. In one book we signed, we were astonished to find no less personages than President Hoover and King George, who were only a few hours ahead of us and, apparently, were traveling together. But, as I have said, it's all in fun. If the Guatemalan Army needs the exercise, far be it from me to complain.

As we climbed up through the hills, almost barren then by some trick of nature—probably lack of rainfall—and approached the border, I began to have an ominous feeling of trouble ahead.† We had recklessly squandered fifty-two cents along the way for a package of cigarettes and a dozen eggs, leaving a balance on hand of $2.40. If the Salvador customs authorities decided to lay an import tax on our spare gasoline or if there were any fees to be paid or bonding to be done, we should certainly be confined to the sovereign state of Guatemala.

---

* The brothers are on their thirty-seventh day, April 30.

† At this point, the brothers are in the department of Jutiapa, the only one in the country without any indigenous inhabitants.

Well, it wouldn't be long until we knew the answer. There was a little sign announcing the end of Guatemala. And beyond it, of all things, a fine, surfaced highway! But no customs officials. Beyond a ways, perhaps. Joe uncorked it along the upper fifties and we sailed along, getting surer every minute that either the guards had been asleep when we passed a shack by the roadside, which might have been a customs station or that there was none between these countries. Neither supposition was reasonable—and neither was true. As we slid into a little village the upraised hand of his majesty, the Law, flagged us down for inspection.[*]

Those boys were nothing if not thorough. They did everything but sample the toothpaste. We literally held our breath while they leisurely but exhaustively examined everything. Then, just as the examination was finished and we were starting to reload, a mustachioed lieutenant with a happy grin called his superior's attention to the gas tank in the rear.

"*Que está en tanko?*" that one demanded.

We admitted it was gasoline.

"It is forbidden to carry extra gasoline into Salvador to the extent of more than five gallons."

After a short argument during which we were in a fair way to lose, a happy thought occurred to me that this was not extra gasoline but in fact the main supply. I attempted to cinch the argument by opening the hood and showing him the gasoline connection from the tank. This was a new one on the customs. They brought out the book to look up a precedent, but none was available, so after a little discussion they waved us on. The immigration examination was cursory—we had had our passports visacd in Guatemala City—so we rolled into the land of El Salvador, safe and still solvent.

The highway continued wide and surfaced into Santa Ana, the second city of the Republic.[†]

The combination automobile and phonograph agency which was the distributor of our make of car was presided over by a young Salvadorean graduate of the University of California. He was there and way over. He fixed our tires for us, refused any pay, and when we left he dropped a package into the car, which he advised us to open

---

[*] The village was possibly Candelaria de la Frontera in the department of Santa Ana. The elevation here is about 3,000 feet, so the brothers are a lot lower than they have been.

[†] In 2019, Santa Ana was the third-largest city in El Salvador, after San Salvador and Soyapango, with a population around 177,000. When the boys were there, however, coffee was king and, as the center of the coffee-growing region, Santa Ana was the most prosperous in the country. The local Indians were still Mayan.

later. When we decided to push on, he called up his friend at the Sitio del Niño and made arrangements for us to stop with him that night.

Santa Ana is by reputation the most progressive and thriving city in Central America, outside of the capitals, and it is ahead of three out of five of them. They are preparing a program of paving that will encompass the whole city and leave it second in that respect only to San Salvador. But for all that, it looks for all the world like the rest of them: narrow streets, whitewashed walls, and barefooted Indians.

With improved highways behind us, we plugged along through the firefly-lighted dusk into Sitio del Niño, one of the largest coffee and sugar plantations in the country.[*]

The package was a carton of cigarettes. With a little good luck now we might be able to stretch our $2.60 across San Salvador.

In the dark it was hard to tell the difference between the lowly brown employees and the white overseers. But soon the badge of demarcation became evident. All the bosses carried little pearl-handled revolvers in sight on the hip. Right there in the center of the best-governed country between North and South America, it seemed a little odd that guns would be so openly and universally on display. It only went to show that down there stable government is much like an armed truce and that law and order are administered by the whites—or near-whites—and on the spot.[†]

An Englishman who helped us get located was a chattering, hollow-cheeked skeleton from malaria. I resolved to be more regular with my quinine. I had considered that disease to be more of an aggravation than a scourge, but that poor fellow was a living example of the reverse.

Skirting Mount San Salvador the road wound through a great lava flow which San Salvador had seen fit to splash over the countryside some thirteen years before.[‡] Whenever the land was bare, it was under cultivation, and green acres and white houses high up on the cone itself testified to the faith the coffee growers had that old San Salvador would not repeat.

---

[*] Improved highways but little else. Reading Arthur, you'd have no idea that, the following year, El Salvador would be subjected to a military coup following its first freely contested election, and that the abject poor had been organizing until being crushed in 1932 by the military in what is known as La Matanza, when between 10,000 and 40,000 were killed. But then we also slipped through Guatemala without him once mentioning the United Fruit Company that monopolized trade in tropical fruit (especially bananas) grown on expansive plantations in Central and South America.

[†] One must wonder how Arthur'd feel about the U.S. these days with its obsessive attitude toward guns.

[‡] This would be May 1, the brothers' thirty-eighth day. Mount San Salvador formed maybe 70,000 years ago; 30,000 years later, Boqueron formed within it. They're a gently sloping stratovolcano with a crater at the summit (6,211 feet elevation). The 1917 eruption was the most recent.

The black mass which had flowed all around us was a brittle cinder-like stuff, which crushed easily with an unpleasant grating sound not unlike a shovel being dragged across concrete.

And around the volcano, San Salvador, lay San Salvador, the capital of El Salvador, and I'll have you know, the best paved city in the world.* In fact, no other place could be better paved, for a year or two ago the government let a contract to an American paving firm for the paving of every square foot of the city's streets, and they stand today a solid sheet of unbroken asphalt.

Well, we hopped up onto the asphalt, and after a preliminary skirmish with the blue-denimed police force—for going the wrong way on a one-way street—we drove to the Ford garage and had a few minor repairs done, such as replacing the light globes and [having] the oil changed.

We were carrying a letter to Señor Manuel Lopez, Superintendent of the Zona Central de Carreteras Nacional, and were soon on our way to the San Salvador country club for luncheon with Lopez and Julio Majica, whose father-in-law was in the saddle as president of the republic.

Salvador was preparing for an election, and the country club was the rendezvous for presidential candidates.† We had time to meet a couple of them before luncheon. One was a little doctor looking not at all as though he could or would wage war for the office. Perhaps they don't in Salvador—they have had some successions to the presidency without bloodshed, which is near a record in Central America.‡

Coffee, it seemed, was at the base of the current hard times in San Salvador. Over cups of it we discussed its future. We talked roads, too. Señor Lopez was keenly interested in the progress of the Pan-American Highway, and we gave him a report of it firsthand from Texas to San Salvador.§ He tempered our enthusiasm for El Salvador's section of it by warning us that the worst was yet to come.

* The largest city in the country, with a metropolitan population in 2019 of around 2,290,000, it's in the department of San Salvador. The city was founded in 1525 by Pedro de Alvarado (ca. 1485–1541), a Spanish conquistador and governor of Guatemala known for his cruel treatment and mass murders of native populations.

† Again, these were to be the nation's first freely contested elections.

‡ Yes, presidents designated their successors.

§ Having, of course, seen nothing of the road south of Mexico City until they encountered it again in Guatemala. The highway runs down through Oaxaca and up into the Sierra Madre de Chiapas, through San Cristobal las Casas and Ciudad Cuauhtémoc, crossing into Guatemala at La Mesilla. The brothers ran into it outside of Antigua.

Beyond San Vicente, in fact, the road was more a line on the map than an actuality. With supreme confidence, considering the state of our finances, we waved it aside as a mere trifle and got from him what he considered the best route.

As the coffee and, I might add, excellent wine warmed the good fellowship between us, Señor Majica, deciding that such an expedition as ours should have the cooperation of the government, promised to wire ahead to the governor of the province of Cuscatlán, of which Cojutepeque is the capital, and request him to aid and abet our progress through that state.

Back to the garage to change into our traveling togs and receive the helpful information that the light globes and the oil were charged to advertising. That was a generous gesture, and we were, we confided to each other, in a fair way to cross the Republic of Salvador without so much as putting a gringo dollar in circulation.

Climbing out of the capital the road winds along a high ridge with Lake Ilopango, a strikingly beautiful sheet of water lapping up against the precipitous, heavily vegetated mountainsides on the right and a grand sweep of green hills and greener valleys stretching away to Honduras on our left.[*]

The air was cool, misty, damp, and a fresh rain-bearing wind was sweeping in across Lake Ilopango from the Pacific. We leaped and curled through the fingers of clouds into Cojutepeque to search out the governor's mansion.[†]

The governor himself, a fat, jovial man with a beaming smile and a monstrous watch chain across his ample middle, greeted us at the door and bade us enter. Yes, he knew of us by telegraph, the adventurous and brave *gringos* who had driven all the way down from *Nueva York* and would this night honor the city of Cojutepeque with their presence. With great gravity he assured us that he was highly honored and that we could have that which was at his command.

Our wants were simple, we told him. A place to camp, could that be found near? He looked doubtful, but when I suggested the city plaza he smiled and said we could use all or any part of it.

"But why not a hotel? Is it not more comfortable?"

We hastily assured him that our trip was, "*Para sport, señor*. We desire to camp out as often as possible."

---

[*] Lake Ilopango fills a volcanic crater, the last eruption of which is the probable cause of the most severe and protracted short-term episodes, in CE 535–536, of cooling in the Northern Hemisphere during the last 2,000 years.

[†] The capital of Cuscatlán, Cojutepeque (2019 population around 70,000) is known throughout El Salvador for the variety of sausages (*chorizos*) made here. It's also the jumping off point for Cerro de las Pavas, where an image of Our Lady of Fátima is an important pilgrimage site.

He led us to the plaza central where we prepared to stake down our tent. It began to rain slightly, and he abruptly decided that it was a reflection on the city that its guests be out in a storm, so he led the way to the hotel where he bade us stay and be comfortable. Resigned to our fate, we drove the car in the double front doors and wondered how in blazes we were going to pay for our room and keep.

The dawn came up like thunder in Cujutepeque that morning, all right.[*] As the sun peeked into our little room to herald the new-born day, the blare of a brass band, playing a martial air outside, bounced us out of bed to see what all the excitement was. We rushed for the door, pajama-clad, and there we were face to face with the local band booming out the national anthem of Salvador. With a startled glance up and down the street lest we be mistaken and not the recipient[s] of this high honor, we decided it *was* for us and snapped into a salute, while they finished playing the national air. As we bowed and applauded our appreciation, they swung into the "Star Spangled Banner"—all for two *gringos* standing there in pajamas in the morning sun, trying to look pleased and nonchalant. That respectful gesture over, they swarmed off down the street and left us in a rather dazed condition to face our matutinal duties.

"Bless me," exclaimed Joe, "if that isn't the first band that's been called out to give me a welcome. We'll have to reward the governor with some token of our appreciation."

So saying, he stripped out some pictures from the scrapbook, which we autographed for his honor.

After breakfast we inquired cautiously for the bill, but that, too, was on the governor, so we sought him out for a sincere "*Mil gracias, señor*," and with his good wishes in the name of the State of Cuscatlan we hastened on our way.

Our spirits rose with the flawless morning, and as we rolled down into San Vicente we rode the crest of a wave of exuberance which had started as the band played in Cojutepeque.[†] All that we had hoped for and anticipated in the flaming tropics was there: hospitality supreme, splendid climate, fair roads, and the sword of financial destitution still hanging—by a thread to be sure—but still hanging. And such scenery! Another perfect cone of a volcano was to the southeast, rearing its head up out of a green, luxuriant jungle, spaced and plotted into coffee farms almost to its misty summit.[‡] The road, a hard-worn, narrow strip through the prolific bush,

[*] Making this the beginning of the brothers' thirty-ninth day, May 2.

[†] San Vicente (2019 population around 42,000) is located along the Accihuapa River in the department of San Vicente.

[‡] This is San Vincente Volcano, also known as Chinchontepec, whose peak tops 7,000 feet. El Salvador is home to twenty-two volcanoes, six of which have erupted since 1880.

at intervals was bounded by cultivated land of bananas, cane, and coffee. Tumbled blue-green mountains, marching away to the north and—stop!—while we piled out to look, a silver-winged airplane, cutting the blue as it winged its way northwest with the Pan-American mail!

To remain on the crest of a wave is one of those things which is nearly impossible. We slipped over the crest with a splash in San Vicente. No one there had any other answer to our question about the road to San Miguel than "*imposible, imposible*," which translated literally, means "impossible, impossible."* With a wonder at just what condition would seem "impossible" to these usually optimistic people, we started out in the general direction of San Miguel. As we bumped along a road, rough, it is true, but still easily negotiable, our spirits rose a little. But that was a short-lived revival. Just before the trail dropped off into a boulder-strewn river bed, we passed a group of highway engineers on a new survey for the Pan-American Highway. With technical precision they answered our questions.

"Yes, the road is passable."

"Do many cars make the trip?"

"No. Only one has made it that we know of."

"When was that? How did he get through?"

"About six months ago. There were four of them in the party, and from what they said they had to pick and shovel and roll rocks four days to make it. They were pulled part of the way by oxcarts, too."

Well, well. The road *was* passable—with a pick and shovel crew along and a few oxen to pull occasionally.

I put the question: "Do you think we can make it?"

He looked us over a bit before answering: "Say you drove down here from he States?"

"Yes."

"Well, in that case you might get through—with the aid of a few pulls from oxcarts."

With those reassuring words we hopped off into the boulder-strewn river. Two hours later we emerged triumphantly on the opposite bank. An hour later we were back, heading north, after facing a similar crossing a mile south and being assured that there were no less than four of them between us and the Río Lempa, six miles away.† This second crossing was knee deep in mud, besides the boulder obstacles.

---

* In 2019, San Miguel was the fourth-largest city in the country, after San Salvador, Soyapango, and Santa Ana. The city had around 162,000 residents and the metro area nearly 600,000 residents.

† Like most of the Central American rivers flowing into the Pacific, the Lempa rises in the Sierra Madre, in Guatemala.

We dickered with a bull-team driver for a pull, but he refused successively a suit of clothes, an overcoat, two pairs of shoes, and, as a last resort, a Kodak. He suggested twenty *colones*, about five dollars, as the proper price, but, as we had only eight *colones*, we couldn't close a deal.

After a scrutiny of our maps, we came to the conclusion that the only alternative was the route through Zacatecoluca.* We were told it was a worse road, if that could be possible, but it ran approximately parallel to the railroad, and we were hard to stop once we got astraddle a narrow gauge!

We made the return crossing in less than an hour—we had rolled most of the movable boulders aside the first time.

"Oh, for the clearance of an oxcart!" sighed Joe. "We'd sleep in San Miguel tonight."

"Oh, for ten bucks!" I echoed. "We'd sleep in San Miguel *tomorrow* night!"

But we had neither the clearance of an oxcart nor ten bucks *oro* (gold) so we slept with the highway engineers instead—and San Miguel was still twenty leagues away.

After all, we could have spent a worse Saturday night. Those highway engineers were nothing if not hospitable, and their "camp" turned out to be the country home of a wealthy American in San Salvador. They were down at the bank to welcome us back and lead the way up to the estate which was on a little hill back from the road.

We parked the car beside the swimming pool in the yard. Yes, sir, a real honest-to-God tiled pool with a spring board and all and went around to inspect this unusual engineers' "camp." It was laid out with an eye to solid comfort, all right. Running water, shower baths, screened doors, and windows—they were little American touches that appealed to us. The huge living room across the front had such desirable features as a fireplace, a well-filled bookcase, and an abundance of overstuffed furniture, into which we sank to a sweet repose of rest.

Those boys were typical engineers, all right. All had been to school in the States and knew how to handle a Saturday night in the good old American fashion. The chief of party was a sober old fellow, but he evinced no desire to interfere with the festivities.

"Clap hands, here comes Charlie," they whooped, and here came Charlie or rather, Juan, a mustachioed old fellow forever holding a hand over an irrepressible grin, on a pattering, bare-footed trot to ask, "What do the *señores* want?"

In five minutes he was back with a large tray clinking with ice-filled glasses and a still broader grin. Old Juan was the pet of the engineers and well he might be, for he

* Zacatecoluca (2019 population around 76,000), in the department of La Paz, was the birthplace of José Simeon Cañas (1767–1838), who fought for and secured the emancipation of slaves in Central America by Spaniards in 1825. It's southwest of San Vicente.

well nigh wore out the tiled floor with his bare feet, sliding in and out with that huge tray. And I suspect that he did more than carry and mix, for he tried less and less to hide his spontaneous smile and occasionally bubbled over with laughter as the boys gibed him about his two wives and ten children. Several of the ten peeked in around the door, staring with big brown eyes at the "loco ingenieros" [crazy engineers] entertaining the "turistas" [tourists].

The dinner was a whale of a success. So were the after-dinner speeches. Joe sounded the keynote when he rose to announce that, while traveling incognito, we were in reality a committee of two to investigate progress on the Pan-American Highway. And that in our report we would have to say, "The Pan-American link through San Salvador, while still unfinished, is being pushed forward to an early completion and is in the hands of the most competent group of engineers south of the Río Grande."

Amid applause the erstwhile dignified chief of party rose to toast the visiting *Americanos* and with them great success in furthering the cause of Pan-Americanism. "And if you return next year, I assure you that you will find the highway completed from Guatemala to the Honduran border."

More applause and more speeches. Then we swam under the soft moonlight while Juan cranked the Victrola and played over and over, "In a Little Spanish Town" from the sidelines.[*]

So it went, from the crest to the trough, then back to the crest again. My dinghy had slopped over into a particularly deep trough when the breakfast bell rang in the morning, and, as it died away, Joe flopped my cot over on the cold tiles and promised me a swim in the nearby pool if I didn't hustle into some clothes and prepare to leave.[†]

"Shucks," he complained, "you promised me an hour ago you'd get right up if I'd let you alone. I've greased the car already, and here you are, still in bed."

I disclaimed any knowledge of being awake before, but, faced with such an energetic example, I contritely apologized for sleeping in and dressed hurriedly, after resolutely pushing myself under a cold shower to wash the traces of leep away.

The road from San Vicente down to Zacatecoluca was horrible. No need to go into details, but at five o'clock in the afternoon we had covered only twelve of the

* "In a Little Spanish Town" had been a hit for Paul Whiteman (1890–1967) in 1926, topping the U.S. charts for eight weeks.

† It was May 3, the brothers' fortieth day on the road.

seventeen miles; the oil pan had a hole in it where one of the many boulders we had hit had tried to go through and say hello to the connecting rods; the ratchet on our jack was stripped, making it useless; Joe had thrown his knee out of joint lifting on the car; and right then we were trying to get off a high center with the front wheels dangling in the air and one rear wheel resting on a suitcase, which had fallen off just before we stopped. It was wedged down in a rut so tightly that we couldn't extricate it nor could we move the car. Joe sat on the bank in a state of hopeless dejection while I made an abortive attempt to back. Dropping in the clutch I looked back in time to see parts of *Terry's Short Cut to Spanish*, a *Commercial Travelers' Guide to Latin America*, and various and sundry other articles, including my only clean shirt and Joe's safety razor, come zipping out of the suitcase and go splattering over the landscape. But she moved! Joe signaled wildly to keep coming, so amid a shower of clothes, torn books, and personal belongings I careened back to a flat spot in the road where the ruts were inches instead of feet deep. A checking of our scattered belongings revealed that that which hadn't been torn to shreds or broken was smeared with toothpaste and shaving cream, with one lovely exception—the Kodak was safe and sound, [and] although scarred up a bit, it still worked or would if we could afford to buy film for it.

After this physical inventory, we took another of the intangibles. The value as a going concern was just about nil. We weren't going—we had gone.

"Well, shall we go back?" I ventured.

"Never!" Joe exploded. "I wouldn't go back over that road for, for"—words failed him.

I couldn't think of anything either, which would come near to justifying a return trip.

"In that case we have two alternatives," I suggested. "We can try to go ahead or we can call it a trip. The first looks to me to be impossible. As to the second—that car isn't exactly an asset where it stands—but it would make a beautiful bonfire with all that gasoline in it. How about having a little sacrificial fire? We can stand on the sidelines and heave what's left of our possessions and hopes into it as it dies down and walk back into the night 'shedding a lonely tear' and all that sort of thing."

"The idea *has* merit," Joe mused. "Think of the effect. 'Two lonely gringos in south Salvador stand silently, sadly by as blasted hopes go slithering skyward in scarlet, scorching flame—'."

"And as the embers die down they crawl out into the cool, calm night to drink of sweet nepenthe in the teeming, torrid tropics—where we forget."

"That's a whale of a climax!" declared Joe. "But," with a queer look at me, "I'm not quite ready to go native and drink this nepenthe stuff—not yet. We might as well have another try at this place with the ungodly name Za-cat-tak-ah-something. Crawl under there and save what's left of the oil with a frying pan while I look this map over and try to figure out where that railroad is. If we could get over to it, we might make it yet."

The oil was still dripping, so I salvaged what was left by letting it drip in a pan, and together we tried to plot our position in relation to the railroad.

At this point an *hombre* rode up. The pearl-handled badge of authority was dangling on his hip.

"Good day, *señor*, how bad is the road to Zacatecoluca?" (It's really pronounced to rhyme with 'You-go-take-a-looka.')

"Very, very bad, *señores*."

"Is it worse than from here to San Vicente?"

"Much worse."

"Where is the railroad from here?"

"Over there, *señores*," he pointed off to the west, and, sure enough, there was a line of telegraph poles about a mile away across the fields.

The upshot of it was that we cut down the fence—the *señor* assured us it was his fence, and he could cut it if we wished—poured in a pint or so of oil we had saved, and with a roar and a jump climbed up out of the ditch, which was the road, and bumped across the fields to the railroad.

"Isn't this great?" said Joe. *Bumpity, bump, bumpity, bump.* "Know just what to expect." *Bumpity, bump.* "No high centers or boulders to wreck the axles." *Bumpity bump.*

Funny how a little stretch of Salvadorean oxcart trail will make one appreciate the ties again.

The oil was below the gauge entirely, the funds were exhausted (we had staked the seven *colones* on a few hands of poker with the engineers—as I said, they had been to school in the States), and we had a hole in the oil pan. So as we pulled up at the plaza central in Zacatecoluca, I can confidently say that two more desolate, road-weary, hungry, discouraged *gringos* had never rolled into that little city.[*] While we sat, exhausted in the car, too weary to climb out even, the rest of our oil dripping out onto Zacatecoluca's main street, the Sunday evening crowd in the plaza marched to the band, chatting, laughing, singing, as happily as only Latins can be.

---

[*] At 537 feet elevation, Zacatecoluca is as low as the brothers have spent a night in a while.

"Well, well," said Joe, slumping down into the luxury of sheer absolute inaction. "It is nice to know that there is some gaiety left in the world. If I don't have to move a single muscle for one solid hour, I may recuperate sufficiently to get out and barter with an innkeeper for a night's lodging and some supper. In the meantime, *don't* disturb me. If you feel like salvaging what's left of the oil, go to it. As far as I'm concerned, it can run out and be damned."

Chapter XI

# A Detour in the Interest of Commerce

"**M**an alive! Where you all goin'?"

He was a white-clad young man of olive complexion, sparkling brown eyes, with a soft Texas drawl. He had eyed us curiously from the crowd for several turns around the square, then apparently, picking out the New York 1930 license, he made a dash across the street. Then, before we could answer—

"You're not from New Yawk, are you?"

"We aren't from no other place, brother! And as to where we're goin', unless a miracle happens, we aren't going any place at all. We're already there."

"Well, my name's Hireji. And what's yours? Lyon? Well, I sure am glad to know you. Don't tell me you drove all the way from New Yawk? Is that so! And you're coming to Zacatecoluca? What for? Oh, you were going on to Panama, but you decided to stop in Zacatecoluca. Well, that's just fine. I'm sure glad to hear some English again. I'm the only person who speaks English in this town. Where you all stopping for the night?"

We confided that we hadn't decided which hotel at which to put up. In fact, we said, we had looked them over and just about decided to go back to the outskirts and set up our camp—"Cleaner, you know."

"There's no need fo' you to set up camp at all. I have a little shack up here—I'm all alone in it—and you fellows can just as well come and stay with me. Of cou'se, you know how it is down here. The plumbing and all that isn't quite what you're used to, but there *are* electric lights, so it's not so bad."

Can you beat it?! From the deep, blue depths again to the warm hospitality of young Doc Hireji—he got his D.D.S. in Houston the year before. So we bumped up the street to the "little shack" getting better acquainted every minute, swapping college yarns and one thing and another. If he laughed at our predicament—we soon confessed our absolute freedom from the taint of money—we could laugh as heartily at his. Down here with a full-fledged D.D.S. from Texas, which the Dental Board of Salvador refused to recognize. He had to confine himself to pulling ulcerated molars out of swollen-jawed peons—all for sweet charity.

The "little shack" turned out to be the largest and finest *casa* in town. The bleak, inhospitable exterior gave way to a spacious, luxurious interior done in the latest Latin manner. The patio garden was a work of art, with its rose bushes, two little palm trees, and a velvety carpet of lawn. Around the patio was a wide, tiled arcade, and around the arcade were grouped the rooms, high-ceilinged, airy, and cool. Our chamber was elevated a few steps above the arcade, with wide windows of massive hardwood—no glass is used, there is no winter cold to keep out—opening on the one side to the lovely patio and on the other toward the cathedral across the way.

"Just pitch your stuff in and pile it up anywhere," said Doc, "while I find some sheets for your beds. It's all the bedding you need down here."

He read our wonderment in our faces, at how a dentist pulling a few teeth for charity could manage with an establishment like this.

"This place is really my father's. He built it a year or so ago but never got around to move up here from the old place. So I have it all to myself, and," he grinned, "to *entertain my friends from the States in.*"

So one day followed another in Zacatecoluca until three had sped by and we had been fed and rested into a state of high ambition again.\* The Hirejis—mother, father, and sisters—were as charmingly hospitable as Doc himself. Their cook was excellent, and how we feasted on delicious Spanish dishes and tasted and tried the tropical fruits. Bananas and oranges, of course, and mangoes, avocados, and others. But on the third day Joe sneaked out and found a trusting soul to whom he pawned his watch for ten dollars, gold. Or maybe Joe was the trusting soul, for the watch was a $75 Hamilton, in good running order. But at any rate we had the ten dollars and the crankcase plugged up and five quarts of fresh oil—what did we care? Panama was to the south, the rainy season was holding off, and our car with her running boards pounded down where they belonged, and her tie-rod, lashed back in place, looked as capable and willing to go places as ever.

---

\* The third of those days was May 6, the brothers' forty-third day on the road.

"Aw, shucks," said Doc. "You're not going to run off already, are you? Why, you've only been here three days.* Stay a week or two weeks or a month. Brush up on your Spanish and take it easy for a while. Besides, how are you going to get to San Miguel? I have talked to the four drivers of the four automobiles in this town, and three of them said there is absolutely no chance to get across to San Miguel, and it is doubtful if an oxcart could get through."

"What did the fourth one say?"

"Oh, he's that monkey with that old Chevrolet. He said that anybody who could drive over that road from San Vicente could probably get to San Miguel. He didn't believe you had done it, but that fellow who helped you get across to the railroad came into town yesterday and told him about you being out there."

"Well, I'm glad our story is substantiated anyway. I wonder if that good *hombre* was wearing the red necktie I gave him as a little token of our gratitude for allowing us to cut his fence and drive though his field? And by the way, what's this I hear about there being another road to San Vicente? Don't tell me we went all through all that torture when there was a good road nearby?"

"It's a fact," Doc said, "there is a good road from here, quite a bit longer but perfectly good."

I groaned.

We were getting mighty restless, but that evening a new angle developed which bade fair to keep us in Zacatecoluca or nearabouts at least for some time to come. In the course of things we mentioned that a couple of years ago we had put in a diesel electric plant for a small Nevada town. Doc got enthusiastic right away.

"Boy, howdy!" he exclaimed. "There's a town not so far from here just crying for an electric plant! Let's figure this thing out and see if we can't perhaps put up a plant there and make a piece of money."

So we talked figures for a while. I had had pretty close tabs on costs and prices on the plant we had put up in Nevada, so the thing to do was to find out what electricity was selling for in Salvador. Doc got hold of the franchise and city contract for the Zacatecoluca plant and what we found was amazingly encouraging. Of course, everything was done on a flat-rate standard down there, no meters, just so much a light, but figuring it out on the peak-load basis and taking into consideration that there was no service except, as the contract read, "from sundown to sunup," the only

---

* So, assuming this is the morning of their fourth day, it's May 7 and the brothers' forty-fourth day of their trip.

conclusion we could draw was that this company was getting about forty cents a kilowatt hour and would continue to get it for thirty years, the life of the contract. That sounded almost too good to be true—a city of comparable size or electric consumption in the States would be paying around ten cents a kilowatt or even less. A few trips down to the power plant to watch the "peak" and "off" load readings on the meters and an investigation of the company's income—through a faithless ex-employee—served to convince us that they had indeed found the Midas touch which turned all to gold. A few minor rackets such as an ice monopoly at two cents per pound and the exclusive right to replace burned-out globes at three to four times their market value gave them a net income of some fifty per cent on the investment, which is not to be sneezed at, even in Central America. The closer we looked into it, the more interesting it became. As Joe said, "At forty cents a kilowatt hour and wages at fifty cents a day, you could turn out electricity by hand and make a profit."

A lawyer, the leading and most learned in town, was a good friend of Doc's, and he was more than willing to be a partner in the enterprise. He had watched the local company (owned by an American syndicate) pile up profits for years with envious eyes, and from the legal standpoint he swore he could tie up a city in a contract more generous to us and binding to them than even the local company's was. If there are any monopolies around, nothing like being on the inside holding stock.

Visionary as the plan sounded, it did look like one of those rare opportunities to get into a lucrative business on the proverbial shoestring. Doc, his father, and the judge would put up the money; we would build the plant, and the ownership and profits would be divided equally, a fifth apiece.

Let's go! The town in mind was Sensuntepeque, high up in the mountains near the Honduran border.* It's listed as having a population of 20,000, about the size of Zacatecoluca, but local opinion differed quite a bit from that figure: Some said it was half as big as Zacatecoluca; others said it was no more than a quarter as large. The judge and I were chosen to make the preliminary survey, count houses, if possible, and interview a friend of his who was city treasurer to see how strong the city would be likely to go on a street-lighting contract.

I caught the early morning train for San Vicente to meet the judge there.† Back over the trail, but this time so easily. At San Vincente I had the devil's own time

---

* Sensuntepeque is in the department of Cabañas, about 2,700 feet in the mountains. Founded in 1550 as a Pipil Indian village, its name means "400 hills," and some 44,000 people lived there in 2019. That it's barely fifty miles from San Salvador gives you an indication of how small the country is.

† Making this day forty-five, May 8.

locating the judge. A drunk who assured me he knew the way led me all over town but wound up in Cantina No. 4. A year or so ago the Salvador[ean] government passed a law requiring the *cantinas* to paint out their names and substitute numbers. The competition in flowery and high-sounding names had insulted the good taste and moral standards of the citizenry. So while under a thick coat of whitewash such astonishing signs as "The Cantina of our Holy Virgin" or "Cold Beers on Draught at the Rosary" were plainly visible, over them the prosaic "Cantina No. 1" or "Cantina No. 3" appeared in freshly painted signs. I cursed the fellow roundly for his deceptive tactics and set out again, shedding coat and vest under the furnace heat of the climbing sun.

When I did find the judge, the stage for Sensuntepeque had left, so he hired a car for $25 for the forty-mile trip, and we started the climb over the mountains with two barefooted youngsters, one as chauffeur and the other as footman. The chauffer was a good driver, but he had me in silent prayer most of the way, as he plunged recklessly across mountain gorges and around grades cut in the side of nearly perpendicular ledges. It was great sport for him. On sighting a mule-pack team plodding along, he stepped on the gas, scattering mules and muleteers all over the mountain side, harassing the competitors, I guess, of his father's stage line. The footman, a pudgy, cherubic youngster, would climb out on the run, scoop up a couple of mangoes from the roadside, and sprint back to the car to devour this luscious fruit.

We could see a great distance, from the promontories, as we climbed higher and higher. San Vicente lay at our feet, Zacatecoluca was around the spur of the volcano San Vicente, and in the distance was the silver thread of the Río Lempa we had tried so hard to reach, and miles beyond was the tip of a volcano at the foot of which lay San Miguel, according to the judge.

After several hours of jolting ride, during which the judge and I clicked heads several times to the perturbance of his usually unruffled dignity, we slithered up the last muddy hill and dropped into the city of Sensuntepeque.

The home of our future utilities system was an unprepossessing town on first sight. The extra-large plaza was in an unkempt condition, overgrown with weeds and untrimmed grass. Shops fronting on the square were not numerous nor were they particularly prosperous in appearance. But, for all that, the town had a clean and healthy look, enhanced, no doubt, by the rain of the night before and the fact that it was located on steep ground. Zacatecoluca, by way of contrast, is mostly flat, and the open sewers down the middle of its streets were veritable cesspools.

The houses were too many to count, but we did get a check on the number of square blocks. And, more to the point, we had a conference with some of the city officials, including the treasurer, who was an old classmate of the judge's. They assured us that the city would be able to raise the tax for street lights—they at that time had kerosene lanterns on most of the corners—to approximately double its present amount, giving up an assured monthly income of eight- or nine-hundred *colones* ($400 or $450). In fact, they were so filled with optimism at the prospects of securing the civic asset of electric lights that they offered to canvass the townspeople in an attempt to learn what potential consumption we could expect.

The spot on the cloth of our plan that I could see was the fact that the city officials before signing the contract must submit it to the scrutiny of the national authorities at San Salvador. I was doubtful that they would O.K. an agreement which specified such high rates as we were planning to charge: twenty per cent higher than in Zacatecoluca. The judge assured me, though, that it would be simple. He had position and prestige. A mere matter of applying political pressure and, he rubbed his palms suggestively as if to say, a little oil in the right spots.

Oh, we were a fine bunch of potential exploiters and grafters, all right! Here we were planning to rook the public with rates a fifth higher than those in Zacatecoluca, which were at least double any I had ever before heard of. The American Power Trust—at least that is what Senator Norris calls it—is a philanthropic institution compared to what we were planning to be.* But then, as Doc and the judge pointed out, in a country where three per cent per month is not an unusual rate of interest on good first mortgages, one has to discount the future danger of revolution, or other political interferences, to the extent of charging enough to get the original investment back in a year or two at the most.

Back in Zacatecoluca the next night, Joe and I went into a serious huddle.† I explained the situation at Sensuntepeque carefully. We checked over our figures closely and went out for a little stroll in the park to arrive at a final decision. Around and around we went. The cathedral bells tolled out an hour, two hours, three hours, and still we paced around and around. The moon came up and smiled down on us, the soft evening air waved the giant palms, a distant gramophone played not unpleasantly, and while the rest of the town slept, or perhaps made love in the shady byways, we cast the dice for our future, there in the plaza of Zacatecoluca.

---

* George W. Norris (1861–1944) was a progressive politician from Nebraska. He served five terms in the U.S. Senate from 1913 to 1943—the first four as a Republican and the last as an independent—and was the prime mover behind the Rural Electrification Act of 1936. Reflecting on his battle with the power trust, he characterized it as "the greatest monopolistic corporation that has been organized for private greed . . . It has bought and sold legislatures. It has interested itself in the election of public officials, from school directors to the President of the United States," and so on.

† This is day forty-six, May 9.

It was a hard proposition to turn down, and it was harder still to turn down our friends who were so enthusiastic in their plans and so generous in their treatment of us. The judge had taken a new lease on life in the last few days and was bubbling over with franchise plans and legal preliminaries for the conquest of Sensuntepeque. And the venture itself looked as roseate as ever. If ever a money-making opportunity presented itself, this looked to be it. But turn it down we did, flatly, positively and forever. On the hundredth or so round it began to dawn on us that money, as they say, is not everything and in Sensuntepeque it would amount to such a small fraction of everything as to be practically nothing at all. While we figured a year on the job should be sufficient to conclude our building operations, good sense decreed that we allow a margin of another year before we could step aside and still have something to show for our labor.

"And two years in Sensuntepeque, if you do keep your health, which is doubtful, is two years too long out of any white person's life," I kept insisting.

Joe wasn't so sure.

"Two years isn't long. Getting the dough, that's what counts. We'll rebound off that into coffee or bananas and in a few years we'll be saying thumbs up or thumbs down to presidential candidates. It's our chance to get in on a good racket before the world finds out about it."

And so it went, pro and con, while the moon arched above the palm trees and the last bit of life ebbed from Zacatecoluca's streets, leaving us quite alone as we sat, now on a park bench, trying to peer a way into the inscrutable future, weighing the odds and counting the chances. But the God who guides our destinies, who harbors for one brief instant the dice from our uncapped hand to face them as He likes, was with us too, as He always is. He whispered. Joe spoke.

"Wouldn't it be hell to have a little white-headed, brown-skinned brat climb up out of the filth and call you daddy? And boy, you can't tell what monotony will do! It's a tough dish under the best of conditions, in Sensuntepeque . . . brother, let's go to Panama!"

Chapter XII

# In the Territory of the United States Marines

The road toward the Río Lempa and San Miguel was as bad as it had been pictured.* Some two hours spent on it, during which we had covered about five miles, found us hiding behind a clump of trees, out of sight of the wayside railroad station while the morning train passed. We didn't know when the next one was due, but as soon as it cleared from sight we flung discretion to the winds and climbed astraddle the steel for a bumpy ride to Usulután, forty miles away.†

At the Río Lempa we swung onto a long bridge more than a quarter of a mile across. With a prayer for the undisputed right of way we sped across it. At the far side were the railroad shops of the division. This let us in for a maze of sidetracks and switches and a good group of spectators, but we waved at the spectators and leaped the switches, not pausing in San Marcos Lempa.‡

For the rest of the afternoon we stayed with the rails, dodging off into the brush twice while trains passed but wasting little time as we crawled along into Usulután. At a wayside soft-drink station we learned that ours was the first car over this route in the memory of the oldest inhabitant. One other had tried it, going north, but the driver had given up right here and shipped into Zacatecoluca by rail.

So much for enforced railroading. It occurred to me that we had spent most of our time on the rails, either with or without flanged wheels, since leaving Mexico

* This is May 10, the brothers' forty-seventh day since leaving Manhattan.

† Capital of the department of the same name, Usulután, in 2019, was the country's fifth-largest metro area with around 72,000 residents. It's a hot-and-humid place resting in a rich agricultural valley located close to the Pacific. Hurricane Mitch in 1998 and the 6.6Mw earthquake on 13 February 2001 badly damaged the city.

‡ Which is a very small town on the river.

City. And when one considers that bouncing along the ties was far easier than attempting to negotiate the roads, the condition of the latter can be realized.

After supper in Usulután and with the prospects of a fair road ahead of us, we bowled along through the night toward San Miguel. At every prosperous looking coffee finca, I suggested a stop to sample the local brand of hospitality, but with a fair road under our wheels Joe's desire for miles was insatiable, so miles it was, until sheer exhaustion brought us to a stop a short distance out of San Miguel.

The light of dawn was showing in the east when we got our cots unscrambled and prepared to take a little slumber.[*]

San Miguel was just recovering from a seven-day orgy, celebrating the 400th anniversary of its founding by Alvarado, the Spanish Conquistador, and incidentally the 400th anniversary of the introduction of Christianity by the same zealous Christian, soldier, and conqueror.[†] Four hundred years of Christianity—and no shoes! Along her ancient streets trotted the barefooted recipients of the blessings of Christianity much as they must have trotted for 400 years, undoubtedly aware that the meek will inherit the earth and patiently awaiting the inheritance. Lest the faithful lose hope and turn unbeliever and scoff, the steel for a great new cathedral to the glory of God is arising on a block facing the plaza. In a few years, if the stream of *centavos* pouring into the church's coffer is undiminished, the zealous will be rewarded with a bigger and better place to pray for redemption. "Trot on, burden bearers, give ye hard earned pennies without stint that the great God of white men and the brown men, too, may smile from his majestic heights on the good city of San Miguel. Hurry, hurry, hurry, lest the smoke which curls so gently up from San Miguel volcano over there so near turn into madcap flame and molten lava to smother another church and man alike in hot fury at the laggard penny-givers."

As San Miguel settled down to the fifth hundred year, little remained of the previous week of festival to greet the eye. A few tattered strips of bunting hung bedraggled from shop fronts, a few peons, not aware that the celebration was over, staggered by, but on the whole business was much as usual. The corner traffic policeman waved the oxcarts by, stopped us for our names, and smiled sympathetically at

---

[*] So beginning May 11, the brothers' forty-eighth day.

[†] Finally in San Miguel! The brothers were headed here from San Vicente, got beaten by the "road," retreated, and spent the night with the highway engineers, headed to Zacatecaluca, fooled around with the electricity plan, and now, nine days later, have finally reached it. And it's sixty miles from San Vicente to San Miguel! That they could have walked it in a couple of days makes the point that the trip's about driving the car there. Incidentally, the city was actually founded, in 1530, by Captain Luis Moscoso (1505–1551), Pedro de Alvarado (ca. 1485–1541) himself having been defeated and forced to retreat to Guatemala.

the luckless driver of one span of fractious bullocks who couldn't keep the animals off the sidewalk.

Outside the city, the highway engineers' office furnished us with an itinerary covering the route as far south as Chinandega, Nicaragua, at which point the road ended again.

Joe made good his threat to buy film if we had to go hungry.

"What," said he, "is the use of making a trip like this if you have nothing to show for it?"

No good rebuttal coming to mind, I had to permit the expenditure, although I preferred ham and eggs.

Climbing up through the hills beyond San Miguel, we out-flanked a truck loaded with a tremendous steel bridge girder. When they build highways in Salvador, they go the whole route, certainly, in good bridges and otherwise also doing a first-class job.

Our way lay through green hills, across sparkling mountain streams, as we drew near another frontier, the border of Honduras.

A suspicious bumping on one side turned out to be a broken main leaf in the rear spring. While I mumbled a few remarks about useless expenditures for Kodak film putting our expedition on the rocks—and it certainly would have been on the rocks had we been forced to buy a new spring leaf, for we had but $3.50 left—Joe went doggedly to work with baling wire and pliers. After an hour's labor in the boiling sun, he announced that everything was O.K., and he guaranteed the job.[*]

The country there was almost barren of trees, and as we crossed the Río Goascorán into Honduras, the road flattened out onto a sort of desert plateau.[†] The native Hondurans presented a striking contrast to the friendly, happy Salvadoreans. They stopped, unsmiling, as we passed, and a request for information about the road was answered usually by a noncommittal grunt or at best by an unfriendly, "*Si, esto camino*" (Yes, this is the way).

At Nacaome, the first town in Honduras, we searched out the village bakeshop and purchased a loaf of bread.[‡] We were about to drive on when a policeman stepped up and asked us to call in at the customs office for inspection. How fortunate he

---

[*] Again, Joe Jr.'s mechanical ability saves the day!

[†] The river rises in the La Sierra mountain ridge in Honduras and flows southward for seventy-five miles, forming the border with El Salvador.

[‡] Nacaome, with some 58,000 residents in 2019, is in the department of Valle. The brothers will barely spend a whole day in Honduras.

noticed us, otherwise we would have driven on not aware that there was such a formality in Honduras. As it was, the officer merely looked over our passports and sent us on. He asked us if we were carrying any contraband, and, of course, we answered in the negative. That was good enough for him, and he never so much as glanced in our car. It was a very hot day to examine baggage, and, besides, why be troublesome to *turistas*?

Salvador had been a cheap country to cross. We were within its borders exactly two weeks and had spent $8!

On to Panama!

A short distance from Nacaome we swung onto the highway which runs from Tegucigalpa, the capital, to San Lorenzo, on the Pacific. A few years ago this was the only highway in Central America, and even now it was the only one of any length. It was a temptation to run up to Tegucigalpa just for the sake of a good ride on a good road and to see what had been described to us as the most decrepit capital of a sovereign state in the world.* This highway was its sole connection with the outer world, except by airplane or mule trail. But we were hardly interested in run-down Spanish-American cities and were more interested in visiting with the U.S. Marines in Nicaragua, who we had been reliably informed were heroes, villains, soldiers-of-fortune, saviors of Nicaraguan liberty, and cold-blooded butchers of women and children. Any group of men, Americans at that, who could be all these things, were worthy of some study, we thought.

After a brief seventeen kilometers [10.5 miles] to San Lorenzo, we splashed out through the swampy land that borders the Gulf of Fonseca.† Through the stickiest, mosquito-infested night that fate ever visited on a luckless pair of tourists, we wallowed through mudhole after mudhole and skirted impassible others over well-nigh indistinguishable cart trails, which wandered in uncertain manner through the blackest of tropical forests. We settled into one muddy arm of the sea with a positiveness that seemed beyond dispute. As the ooze flowed over the wheels we crawled out and with bare hands clawed it away in a desperate attempt to get out of the mud and into some outpost of civilization for the night.

---

* Tegucigalpa, set in a central valley surrounded by mountains, is a large city with a 2019 metro population of around 1,200,000 people. Known for its well-preserved Spanish colonial architecture, it is nowhere near the record holder in the decrepit department.

† San Lorenzo (2019 population around 23,000) is a small city in the department of Valle. The Gulf of Fonseca has long been, and remains, a source of controversy among El Salvador, Honduras, and Nicaragua, all of which have coastlines along it. It's basically a mangrove swamp. At this point, the brothers are in the department of Choluteca.

I recalled that it was very near here that Walker, the king of the filibusters—that impossible American from Tennessee who had fought his way to the presidency of Nicaragua—had been intercepted by a detachment from a British warship as he made a final attempt to regain the power that Commodore Vanderbilt, with the aid of the Costa Rican army, had wrested from him.* I recalled also that the British had turned him over to the Honduran army, which promptly marched him out and stood him up against the wall before a firing squad, to meet the fate of all unsuccessful filibusters and revolutionaries in Central America.

Well, the ghost of General Walker or some other supernatural force rose up to give us a shove, for we slithered through the mud, and after a brief second of spinning wheels on the banks of the morass we lurched forward to firmer ground and prowled through the wilderness to the banks of the Choluteca River.†

We made camp that night with a young Jugo-Slavian wandering up from the Argentine. He was, he admitted, a globe-trotter, and I guess he was a darn good one, too, for he had traveled over all Europe and South America and was now confidently plugging away toward the Estados Unidos via the overland route. The Choluteca River was to be crossed by ferry—and the ferry fare is one dollar—but we left that for morning and damned the mosquitoes.

Morning came, as mornings do, and between bites of breakfast and sips of coffee we tried to dicker with the ferry keeper for transportation.‡ He refused to be corrupted by a flowered bathrobe, a blue sweater, and a sack of flour, however long he fingered the robe with covetous fingers. His boss, he said, was an American [who] kept a close count on the cars as they passed his place near the town of Choluteca, and woe be unto him if he failed to turn in the full amount of ferry fares. Even after a cup of coffee he refused to budge, so we faced the prospect of parting with a full third of our capital to cross the river. Then the owner himself, a thin, weather-beaten Yankee with a big six gun and a slight limp in one foot, came up in his motor truck.

---

* This is one of the most bizarre fragments of Nicaraguan history. William Walker (1824–1860), an American lawyer and adventurer, organized private military ventures in the area to establish his own English-speaking colonies. At the time, doing this was known as "filibustering." Walker did become President of Nicaragua in 1856, but he was defeated in 1857 by a whole coalition of Central American armies. Honduras executed him in 1860. Cornelius Vanderbilt's (1794–1877) interest was in building a canal across Nicaragua to connect the Atlantic and Pacific, and he'd been granted a concession to do so. He became enraged when two of his subordinates tried to have Walker seize the company from Vanderbilt during Walker's presidency, and he interceded against Walker.

† The river is only a few hundred miles long, but it can carry plenty of water. Its flooding during Hurricane Mitch in 1998 destroyed a good deal of Choluteca.

‡ This would be day forty-nine, May 12.

Ilustrovani Lisf "Sviyet"
(REVISTA ILUSTRADA "MUNDO")
Zagreb–Yugoeslavia

We spent the night under a palm thatched lean-to shelter with this young Yugoslavian waiting for daylight to be ferried across the Choluteca River. Next morning Joe found out that a large Iguana had spent the night on top of the palm thatch about a foot above his face.

"Where the hell you goin' in that thing?" he snapped.

"We were going to Panama, but I guess from the looks of things we'll do well to get to Managua."

"Well, you'll sure have hell gettin' to Managua all right. Centers are high and the rains settin' in. Better sell your car for what you can git an' go on without it."

"What do you think it will bring as is, good rubber, good engine, nothing wrong but a few scratches on the body?"

"Let's see," he looked it over casually. "Oh, about $350 or $400 gold. Wouldn't take less'n $350 for it if I was you. Might get $400."

"You mean $400 American?" we gasped. We had tentatively set a price of $200 on it when we considered selling it.

"Sure, cars are high down here. But, of course, there's not much of a market, so you have to take what you can git."

"By the way, how are the Marines down here? Many of them around?"

"Yes, quite a bunch of them down across the border. Don't buy any gas when you get into Nicaragua. Make the Marines give it to you. It's about all they are good for down here, messin' up the country for why nobody knows."

That was one American's opinion of the Marines in Nicaragua.

Then he turned to his ferryman, spoke a few words to him in Spanish, and told us to roll aboard and go across, and, he added, "There'll be no charge."

Saved again from immediate financial disaster!

Across the river we drove into the little town of Choluteca and launched forth on the last gap between us and Nicaragua.[*]

Fording the Río Negro, which was at a low stage then, we were at last in Nicaragua, the romantic, turbulent state of Central America, bathed in a bloody past and facing a doubtful future with the forces of the U.S. Marines maintaining by force of arms an inter-election truce between the Liberals and the Conservatives.[†] As we climbed the steep bank onto Nicaraguan soil I half expected to find a Marine outpost guarding this important route from the north and asking us what we had seen of Sandino on the way across. Nothing of the kind was in sight, however, and we passed along unmolested and greatly cheered by signs at the crossroads pointing the way to

---

[*] Choluteca (2019 population around 100,000) is generally considered the regional center of southern Honduras and is the only major Honduran city on the Pan-American Highway.

[†] The location of this border was long a subject of dispute, one resolved by the International Court of Justice in 1960. The location of the Río Negro is another question, since it tends to move around. Today, there's a bridge in the vicinity and customs and immigration facilities.

Circa May 14, 1930. Fording the Rio Negro, the border between Honduras and Nicaragua 118 miles north of Managua.

Joe stands by his trusty "Model A" at a signpost put up by the Marines which reads, Honduras—Nicaragua, ←Choluteca  Chinandega→ This is Sandino and Bandito country!

Chinandega, the first Nicaraguan city of any size on the route. These were the first road signs we had seen since leaving Texas, and, sure enough, we found out that they had been erected by the Marines, a touch of Americanism, which proved they had indeed found time for some constructive work between fights with the Sandinistas.*

At a large two-story house we stopped and hailed a gentleman on the upper porch to ask the distance into Chinandega. He answered our question in English but didn't bother to ask us where we were from or where we were going. That was the only sign of a border post we saw. [There were] no customs formalities on the Nicaraguan border.

Once at the Puente Real, a toll bridge across a mud slough, we were passed by a car with some native officials and a Marine captain aboard. He was most cordial in welcoming us to Nicaragua. Looking us over and seeing no sidearms, he ventured a query.

"Are you carrying no arms?"

"Not since Mexico. We had a rifle there, but it was detained at the border."

"Well, well, that's a good one. Do you realize that the country you have just come through is one of the worst bandit-infested regions in Nicaragua?"

We pleaded ignorance of that fact and said we had seen no bad *hombres*. Jokingly we added that we had supposed the Marines had them all run out by now.

"Hardly," he said sadly. "We send a patrol up through here once a week, but it is little more than a reminder that we're on the job. Not so easy to patrol a thousand or more square miles of jungle with forty men. But I'm glad you came through with no trouble. Have to notify headquarters that tourists from the States are beginning to drift down here. Maybe they'll send me up a few more men to handle the situation. *Adios*. Must run along to Chinandega. Look me up when you get in." So saying, he hopped into the car and breezed away.

"Thanks for the road signs," we shouted after him and started off [trying] to keep up, but the native driver knew how to straddle the dusty ruts better than we, and we were soon left to ourselves in the maze of trails, which, without the signs,

* Although the U.S. first had forces in Nicaragua in 1852, U.S. Marines occupied Nicaragua from 1912 to 1933. The Marines had been sent in to protect American interests, originally a trans-Isthmian canal. The initial concern was protecting a Nicaraguan canal route—a bill supporting a Nicaraguan canal was introduced in the U.S. Senate as late as 1902—but once the U.S. had decided to back the Panamanian route, the U.S. government's interest shifted to protecting the Panamanian canal and preventing the construction of one in Nicaragua. Insuring all this required a U.S. hegemony in the region, one the more easily maintained if "law and order" prevailed. The occupation ended as Augusto C. Sandino (1895–1934) led his guerrilla armies against the government of Nicaragua, against the Standard Fruit Company, and against the Yankee Marines sent there to prop it all up, but by then the occupation had become a serious drain on the U.S., then in the midst of the Depression. The occupation came to an end in 1933.

General Sandino harassed and evaded the U.S. Marines in Nicaragua with raids and guerilla tactics from 1927 to 1933 when they left. His followers are known as Sandinistas. In one Honduran villiage [sic] we were told that his Buick and our Model A Ford were two of very few automobiles seen there.

would have been hopeless, indeed. One of these got us quite confused, though. It pointed to Chinandega as being in the direction from which we had come. A little sleuthing, though, uncovered the fact that there was a hole on the opposite side of the road, which looked as if it had been once the resting place of the sign. Putting two and two together, we decided that the sign had fallen down, and some helpful native had set it up again on the wrong side. That assumption was evidently correct, for we soon arrived in El Viejo, a short way out of Chinandega, and in a few minutes more in Chinandega itself, trying to change our Salvadorean currency into that of Nicaragua, a detail we had overlooked, that we might buy some supper.* That brought to mind the fact that we had never had any of the currency of Honduras. In fact, we had crossed that country without spending a single *centavo*! Such tourists as we would hardly go far toward improving the so-called "invisible items" on its balance of trade. Our expenditures were just a little too invisible.

After a late supper we did finally manage to exchange our five *colones* at par for two and a half *pesos* Guatemalan, and then we called on the captain. He suggested that we put up for the night at the *guardia cuartal*—army barrack—and, before we left, presented us with half a carton of American cigarettes, which his *guardia* promptly stole form our duffle bag at the *cuartal*. The force of forty men he had mentioned, we found, were all native *guardia*. Only the commissioned officers were Americans. It was the policy of the government to train a native army and replace even the American officers [with] Nicaraguans as soon as possible.

That night we held a stern council of war regarding our future. It was not hard to see that something had to be done and that quickly. Our $1.75 would hardly last another day, the rainy season was on us, and the road to Managua was impassable. Of course, we could try to make it down the railroad as we had done before, but we were nothing if not weary of bumping along railroad ties, and, besides, it was doubtful whether our car would stand up forever under the terrific jolting to which that mode of travel subjected it.

The answer was plain. We had to sell the car, pocket the proceeds, and continue as best we could to Panama.

With that in mind we arose early and drove out to a creek at the edge of town to wash off the layers of grime, which had accumulated since we left New York.† We emulated the natives along the stream, took off all our clothes, and between

* In 2019, Chinandega (population of around 127,000), in the department of Chinandega, was Nicaragua's fourth-largest city. El Viejo's a town of some 84,000 (2019) near Chinandega.

† This is May 13, the brothers' fiftieth day.

splashings on the car we found time to soap off a few layers from ourselves. Up the stream from us was a good part of Chinandega doing the same.

The running boards on the car were becoming flexible from so much bending. It took little effort now to force them back into place, and unless one crawled underneath and saw the broken brackets, they looked quite all right. We found a can of polish under the seat, so we gave it a good rubbing and rolled back into town with a shining car looking little the worse for its long trip. In fact, the only noticeable blemish was a rear fender I had crumpled back in Brooklyn when I tried to squeeze between a street car and a peddler's wagon.

Then for a buyer. The captain lent us his interpreter, and with him we scouted all the merchants, doctors, lawyers, and everyone else in town who might possibly have enough cash money to make the purchase. Our first prospect was a doctor. He came out, gazed reflectively at the car, asked our price, and started around to examine the other side. As he came upon the bent fender he raised his hands, shook his head, and pointed at the bent fender. No, no, he wouldn't think of buying a car with a damaged fender. Why, it ruined the appearance! What would his friends think of him if he should ride around in a car with a ratty looking rear fender! No, it was impossible.

The next prospect was a prosperous merchant. We almost got him to go for a ride before he spotted the blemish. At sight of it he withdrew all negotiations and even refused to dicker when we dropped the price fifty dollars, so he might buy several new fenders with the difference. He was doubtful that it could be replaced without ruinous effect on the rest of the car.

And so it went, one potential customer after another admitted a willingness to buy were it not for a slightly bent rear fender. Not one cared to try out the engine or the riding qualities and looked with a detached air while we expounded on the fine tires and good pulling qualities. Damn that Brooklyn peddler's cart!

At length we got disgusted with such childish buyers. We lowered the price successively to $275 but nary a nibble.

"Hell's bells," said Joe, "we'll go on to Managua, get a new fender, raise the ante to $400, and club off the buyers."

Chinandega was once a thriving city, the fourth or fifth largest in the republic, but in 1927, four months after the Marines were withdrawn in that year, the Liberals got entrenched in the cathedral in one end of town and the conservatives held the other end.* Then, with true Latin political animus they started banging away at each other. When the smoke had cleared there were 2,000 fewer voters in Nicaragua,

---

* In 2019, it was still the fourth-largest city in the country.

and most of Chinandega was in ruins. Many smoke-stained, bullet-nicked walls still stood in the otherwise leveled blocks of what had been the business section of Chinandega to testify to the bitterness of Nicaraguan politics.[*] To an outsider it seems strange that the United States government could justify an interference into the internal affairs of a sovereign country, but a look at Chinandega should convince even a Heywood Broun that long-suffering non-combatants Nicaraguan have a right to protection in the name of humanity.[†] I wonder what he would say if the Republicans called out the army to subdue the voters with socialistic tendencies in the seventeenth New York congressional district?

Back at the *cuartal* we called up the railroad station about schedules, and, having been informed, regretfully, that there were no more trains that day, we drove out to the edge of town and, with the aplomb of much experience, started to Managua.

We were little more than started when a speeding gasoline car came singing along the rails to meet us. With an insouciance born of weariness we got off the track just far enough to allow the glassed-in inspection car to pass, and as soon as it did pass we started on again.

And then the rainy season, so long deferred, came at last. As we struggled to put up the curtains, a black sky coughed up water like old Jupiter Pluvius himself. In its battering intensity it threatened to wash us off the face of the earth. But it couldn't wash us far. In fact, with everything wet and slick, we couldn't get off the rails at all. I made a couple of ineffectual attempts to block the wheels so they would climb off and then returned to the car where we sat dejectedly, praying to God that some unscheduled freight train wouldn't come blundering along and smash us into oblivion. That risk was preferable, to standing in the rain, or at least it seemed so right then.

After what seemed hours of waiting, the rain stopped as suddenly as it had begun and drained quickly off the railroad grade. As soon as we had sufficient traction we crawled off through the glistening night toward somewhere, two unhappy *gringos*, broke, hungry, and wet, and just a little tired of touring in the topics.

Out of the mists the lights of a city sparkled ahead. Must be Chichigalpa, we thought.[‡] Before we found a cross street to get off on we found ourselves rolling

---

[*] In 1927, the Liberals, under Francisco Parajón Montealegre, attacked Chinandega in one of the war's most destructive assaults. Fighting raged from February 6 to 9, with 500 Conservatives against a substantially larger number of Liberals. Hundreds were killed, and much of the city was destroyed.

[†] Broun (1888–1939) was a rabble-rousing, New York journalist. Founder of the American Newspaper Guild, he was a social activist who championed the underdog. He was also a member of the Algonquin Round Table. Again, the Marines had been sent in to protect U.S. commercial interests.

[‡] Chichigalpa (2019 population around 35,000) is a small city in the department of Chinandega.

through the station, which was built across the tracks, forming sort of a train shed. The telegrapher rushed out to greet this new kind of train, but before he could recover himself sufficiently to ask us for our orders, we drove through the shed and turned off down Chichigalpa's main street.

There hadn't been an automobile in Chichigalpa for six months, so we created quite a stir as we splashed down the street. A wig-wagging flashlight brought us to a stop. The wagger, one Lieutenant Calvert, of the U.S. Marines, recently of 48th Street, New York City, whooped with delight when he found we were Americans and promptly gave us the town, lock, stock, and barrel.

The lieutenant was the only Marine in town and had under him a small garrison of native *guardia*. He was the *jeffe politico*, which means chief of police, and did he run that town! He had the mayor in jail the month before. That almost got him a court-martial, but the colonel backed him up. At any rate the reception was splendid, and the lieutenant was O.K.

In the morning as we were preparing to leave, a native *guardia* dragged in a homely little woman and a scared-looking *hombre* to plead their case before the *jeffe*.[*] After half an hour of distressingly temperamental pleading punctuated with torrents of tears from the woman, the lieutenant turned to us and said, "Can't quite figure out whether it's extortion or seduction. These two were sleeping partners last night, and she claims that he went under the mattress and lifted the sack with her winter's savings. He insists that she had stolen it from him early in the evening and that he was merely recovering his own. What the hell would you do in a case like that?"

"They both act guilty to me," I volunteered. "Why not make 'em split it?"

"That's a fine idea!," and he ordered his *guardia* to divide the spoils. "Now vamoose, both of you." And to me, "She's a hellcat anyway, been up before, three times in the past two months. Have another brandy?"

Justice was done in Chichigalpa.

"That's a fair sample of what I get every day in the week. They all lie, and there's never a reliable witness to tell the straight of it. Here's to justice."

We did manage to find a trace of a road for three miles before we had to take to the ties again. It was high noon in León when we drifted into that dusty metropolis.[†] Here we found a fine cathedral, an exquisite plaza, but nobody who

---

[*] This is the brothers' fifty-first day, May 14.

[†] León has long been the political and intellectual center of the country. It was founded in its current location in 1610 and is thick with Baroque buildings. Its university, founded in 1813, is the second oldest in Central America. In 2019, León's population was around 140,00 (city) and 210,000 (metro).

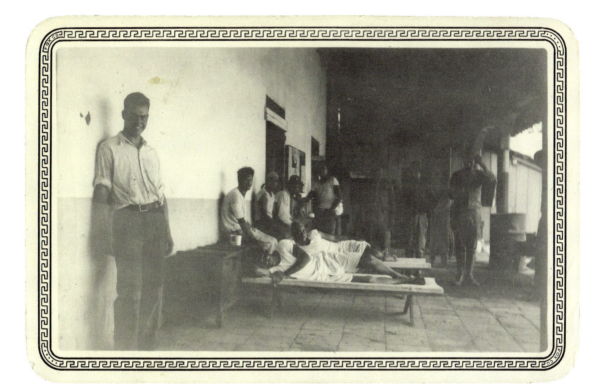

Above: Marine Camp. Guard House near where Joe was standing. The men in the guard house were looking out of the window and thought they would be in the picture. Those in the cots are sick.

Opposite: Lieutenant Walter M. Calvert, U.S. Marines in charge of a small garrison of Guardia National de Nicaragua at Chichigalpa, Nicaragua about 65 miles north of Managua.

Arthur looks over a method of transportation that may be more practical than ours in this part of Nicaragua. May 15, 1930.

evinced the slightest desire to purchase a Ford roadster "as is" and "no questions asked or answered."

León is the "Liberal" stronghold of Nicaragua.* Traditionally and actually they subscribe to that party almost to a man, and without Marine protection a "Conservative" would be almost as safe on the streets there as a fish peddler on Park Avenue. If they didn't shoot him on sight, they would probably lock him up in *veinteuno*— twenty-one—which is Leónese for the city bastille, until a Conservative president was "elected" and sent up the army to release the political prisoners. To understand the political situation in Nicaragua, if that be possible for an outsider, one should remember that a Leónese is always a Liberal. And a resident of Granada, the southern metropolis of the republic, is always a Conservative and that, until comparatively recent times, when the president was a Liberal, he designated León as the capital and moved the government bodily to that place from where the next Conservative president, after the revolution was over, would drag it back to Granada. And so the tug-of-war merrily went on until one day a president, hoping by such a strategic move to gain Liberal support, designated Managua, about half-way between the rival cities, as the capital. Now instead of the fruits of the victory being a capital along with the presidency, it is only the latter, but the battle still wages fiercely by the banks of Lake Managua and Lake Nicaragua, except, of course, when the Marines are in the saddle and maintain a semblance of peace between the sanguinary politicians. And take it from the Marines, it is only their presence that keeps the Liberals and Conservatives from cutting each other's throats.

As one lieutenant so succinctly expressed it: "We leave today, revolution flames up tomorrow. Day after tomorrow, both sides are yelling for intervention to stop the slaughter, and the day after that we're back again, just where we were in 1928 and have to start all over again, trying to educate these devils to the point where they can maintain law and order for themselves. So," he predicted confidently, "if they don't go plumb nuts up there in Washington, I guess we'll be here for some little time yet."

"And where does Sandino come in?" I asked, remembering the violent diatribes against the Marines and the lavish praise of "El León de Segovia" and the "Gandhi of Central America" so recently headlined in the Salvadorean papers.

"That blankety, blank, blank son of Satan is nothing more or less than a common thief, a murderer, a cutthroat of the lowest type. Even the Conservatives, who are 'out' just now, won't have anything to do with him, which gives you some idea of

---

* León and Granada were both founded in the sixteenth century, León by low-ranking Spanish foot soldiers and Granada by upper-class Spaniards. Their conflict has been continuous since then.

what he really is, as under most any circumstances they would welcome anyone who was fighting the administration."*

That was evidently true, for among all the people to whom we talked, both Conservatives and Liberals, very, very few had a good word for Sandino.† And among the Marines—well, they usually became incoherent when his name was mentioned, and often it took half a dozen beers to calm them sufficiently to voice their estimate of just what kind of a dirty blankety blank he was. He or his men had chopped up several Marines after capturing them, and the thoughts of those mutilated buddies brought a gleam to a Marine's eyes, which bespoke a hasty end to Mr. Sandino if he was ever indiscreet enough to get captured.

Five miles out of León, that which we feared happened. Our car, the sturdy little veteran of 16,000 tempestuous miles, cracked. The cracking was a broken axle. The result was a period of commuting back and forth to León by foot on my part while Joe stayed with the ship and unbolted all sorts of mechanical gear until the car, perched forlornly up on top of two hardwood logs, was stripped of most of its innards, which lay in dirty, greasy profusion over most of the railroad right of way.

On the third day the axle came from Managua, a friendly lieutenant of the Marines having phoned for it for me, and a trusting dealer having granted us credit.‡ In the meantime we lived the life of the natives of the land. In the front yard of a nearby native estate, consisting of a single bamboo room on a dirt floor with a thatched roof, we pitched our tent. The family was too poor to enjoy the ownership of livestock, so we didn't have to dispute the territory with pigs, dogs, and chickens, for which we were duly thankful. We entertained the two small children, a bright-eyed boy of ten and his little sister, while their mother crooned Spanish lullabies to the infant in arms and three times a day stirred up the pot of beans and the pot of rice to feed her *gringo* guests. When we left we presented our box of Woolworth's silverware and tin plates to her, which munificence so overjoyed her simple heart that she forthwith sent her husband out to procure a chicken for a parting banquet. But he was a long time in the procuring, and with our car repaired we were too impatient

---

* Sandino had been a Liberal general but turned against both sides when, in 1927, they became parties to the Espino Negro accord, permitting the Marines to stay in the country. Sandino read this as a betrayal of the nation and began his rebellion. In 2010, he was unanimously declared a national hero by Nicaragua's Congress. Sandino was plainly *fighting* the Marines, who, of course, didn't like him.

† Carleton Beals (1893–1979), the American journalist, had a different experience. Working for *The Nation*, Beals interviewed Sandino in the field and portrayed him as anything but a bandit in a series of influential articles. Sandino was plainly a hero to many, many Nicaraguans.

‡ This is the brothers' fifty-third day, May 16.

to wait, so Joe, with a great deal of dramatic Spanish, begged permission to leave our good Nicaraguan friends and go on our way.

After five miles of intermittent travel the intermissions being periods of waiting for the scheduled trains to pass, we saw the last mixed train go south and started down the ties behind it. For a few hundred yards all went well, then old man Bad Luck dropped around for another little call in the form of an unballasted roadbed. The old ballast had been dug out from between the ties, and, pending the arrival of new gravel, our roadbed was a series of impossible lows and highs. We were practically stuck between every set of ties, and after burning up a good deal of rubber crawling a bare fifty feet, we settled firmly to rest in one particularly deep depression. Our jack was a wreck. As we lifted and tugged to no particular avail, a meandering freight train, unscheduled and unheralded, hove into view ahead of us, gave a few shrill shrieks which plainly said, "Get out of the way and do it quickly," and started bearing down on us like a demon from hell. At the first whistle Joe jumped behind the wheel to make a last desperate effort to save what was left of our expedition, and I ran out in front of the car and started dancing around and waving my arms wildly. Joe gunned the motor and dropped in the clutch. The tires smoked, but [there was] no movement. He tried it again; this time the motor was bellowing a wide-opened roar. As the power hit the rear axle the car gave a slight lurch, then settled back as the gears gave way with a loud rasping sound, and the motor raced on unhindered. That looked like the end of things for fair. I yelled as I ducked aside from the locomotive which, with wheels sliding and sand spurting from the sandpipes, slid into the car. Instead of the crush we expected, the train ground to a stop after one gentle bump, which pushed the car back a few feet and there they rested, nose to nose, while the crew swarmed around us and, with a total lack of Latin courtesy, told us just what they thought of us in high-pitched Spanish. To add to their indignation we were struck with a desire to laugh, and as they shouted their "*carambas*" at us, we repressed our laughter and got out a rope with which to tow the car off the track. Seeing that we understood little of their invective, they gave up shouting at us and helped tie onto the car. The first two trials the engine backed off with majestic ease and snapped our ropes as if they were twine. The third time we lashed them together with everything we had, including the skid chains. They held, while the engine steamed backward and dragged the car out of the way.

As the train moved off the conductor stood on the caboose steps, shaking his fist at us and threatening, so Joe interpreted it anyway, to have the law on us for running, or trying to run down, the railroad tracks.

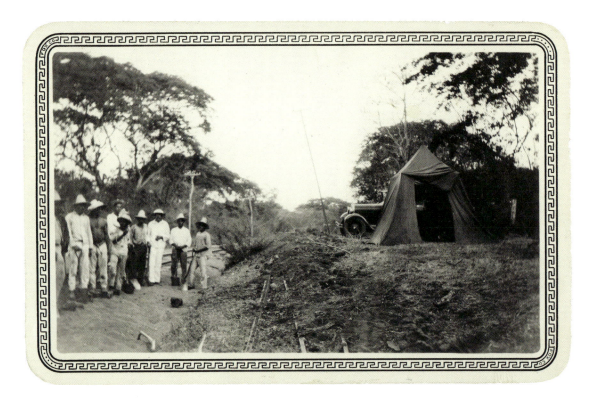

May 21, 1930—We camped on the right of way of The Ferrocarril Del Pacifico De Nicaragua waiting for the flatcar.

That left us in a pretty pickle. We lay down to sleep that night without any supper, wondering what the gods of chance would roll out for us on the morrow.

A little morning reconnaissance disclosed a section-house cook a quarter of a mile down the track who agreed to feed us as long as we were around in return for a well-worn sack suit, which was the only thing we had that appealed to him.* He put it on, vest and all, while he stirred up the beans and rice, which was the fare. That settled we prowled on further down the line where a work train was unloading a crew of section hands We explained our plight to the section boss, and he suggested we call up the president of the railroad in Managua and ask him to hook in a flat car in the afternoon train to Managua and load our car on that and haul it in. The only bad feature of that scheme was that all railroad freight had to be paid in advance. Well, we'd talk to the president of the road and see what he'd do. After a half hour we finally got a connection on the field phone, which the section foreman had tapped into the railroad telephone line.

"Hello, hello, Señor Portocarrero? *Habla Ingles, señor*" (Do you speak English, sir)?

"Yes, I speak English. Who is calling?"

"Lyon is my name. We, that is, my brother and I, are broken down along your railroad about ten miles south of León."

"Ah, yes, I have heard about you. One of our conductors wired in last night that there were two crazy Americans in a Ford stopped in the middle of the tracks up there. Well, what can I do for you? Do you want a flat car to stop and pick you up?"

"Exactly, *señor*, and we would like to extend our credit with the Ferrocarrilles Pacifico, if possible, and pay you when we arrive."

"Hmm. That is an unusual request. Tell me, how did you get to where you are?"

"We drove down from the United States."

"You mean to say you drove through Mexico, Guatemala, Salvador, and Honduras?"

"Yes sir, that's right, we drove all the way."

"Hmm. Well, for all I know, you are honest gentlemen. A car will be set into the afternoon train for you," he snapped. "Be ready to load as quickly as possible. When you get to Managua drop in and see me. Good bye."

With immense relief we hurried back and built up a platform of logs and dirt to load the car and thanked God for Señor Portocarrero.

At noontime we cashed in on the suit for more beans and rice and waited for the afternoon train. It was a work train, with a hundred or so section hands aboard, so

* This was May 17, the brothers' fifty-fourth day.

Part of the crew that man-handled our car onto the flat-car. Arthur is the one with the shoes, next to the car.

we literally lifted the car on, blocked the wheels, and settled down for a smooth ride of forty-two miles into Managua.

The long trail was ended. The Fates had spun their dice and here we were, riding down the shores of Lake Managua, high and dry on a flat car. To our left, the volcano Momotombo spouted a few wisps of smoke into a cloud-specked afternoon sky and a golden sun dropped over the coastal range to our right toward this Pacific.[*]

If you should ever happen along the Ferrocarriles del Pacifico sixty-eight kilometers [42.25 miles] north of Managua, you might see a 1930 New York license plate No. 9N1659 tacked onto a telegraph pole and under it an arrow with the notation, "New York 4,562 miles."

[*] Managua lies along the 400-square-mile lake's southern shore. The 4,000-foot peak of Momotombo lies above its northwestern shore. Here, the brothers are but fifteen miles from the Pacific Ocean.

Chapter XIII

# The Last Lap

From our little hotel, called El Primavera, which means "The Springtime" and was as far from anything resembling it as an adobe shack near the tracks, sans plumbing, sans cleanliness, sans edible food, plus a fighting cock tied to the corner of the bathhouse, which occupied the center of the open court, which crowed loudly and lustily at all possible and impossible times could be, we sallied forth in the morning to retrieve, if possible, our car from the railroad company.* It was now resting in the yards atop the flat car in Managua, it is true, but still not in our possession. Before we could get it out and have it repaired, it was necessary to pay the freight bill of $35.47, which was as absent as trees on the Sahara desert.

Well, we decided to see Mr. Portocarrera. He had allowed us to bring it in without payment in advance, maybe—perhaps—

"Good morning, Mr. Portocarrera. We have an automobile in your freight yards, which we shipped in from La Ceiba yesterday."

"Good morning, gentlemen. I am very pleased to meet you. Yes, I have seen your automobile. It does not look so bad for having been driven down here from the United States. Sit down and tell me about your trip. It must have been very interesting indeed."

We did. We told him many of the highlights, and he laughed heartily at many of our ludicrous experiences and predicaments.

"But, now, Mr. Portocarrero, we have another favor to ask, one that it grieves us very much to ask. We have told you about our trip, and I want to add that it was very expensive, so expensive, in fact, that our funds are exhausted. Since leaving León

* This is day fifty-five, May 18.

190

we have been broke, flat broke. Can you or will you allow us to take our car, get it repaired, and then sell it, paying our freight bill out of the proceeds of the sale?"

"Well, well! So you boys are broke? Why, certainly, I'll do that. I like your spirit. You look reasonably honest. You go down and get the car. I'll telephone ahead to the freight office to release it. When you sell your car, you will pay us the $35.47, is that right?"

"That's right, and *mil gracias, señor*. We shall certainly pay you the minute the car is sold. If we can't sell it, we'll return it to you."

"Well, I hope that won't be necessary. In the meantime the car is yours to do as you please with."

Light-hearted once more we took the auto up to the garage; the repair job would take two or three days, they said.

Over to the American consulate, of course. Cheers! A letter from home opened and two five-dollar bills flutter out. Greatly relieved and in immense high spirits, we started out to see Managua. Why not? We had ten dollars, forty-five hundred tough miles behind us, our car in process of being repaired, and nothing in the world to worry about except the high price of beer in Nicaragua!

"If the Army and the Navy ever look on Heaven's scenes, they will find the streets are guarded by United States Marines!" and the same thing can be said of Managua, Nicaragua. And if they ever look a little behind the scenes, they are as apt as not to find the United States Marine Corps propping up the governmental facade, drilling the native *guardia*, making love to the native women, drinking the native *aguardiente* and withal doing a fine, thorough job of it. If war be hell, intervention in Nicaragua can't quite be war.

There comes a roadster bulging with Marines. Hitting a wicked clip down Managua's narrow main street, they frighten a *cochero* (coachman) with his *coche* (car) up onto the sidewalk. He waves his whip after them and threatens vengeance. Further down the block a buxom brown lass leaps deftly for the sidewalk, scattering her head-basket full of buns from curb to curb as the Marine Corps went screeching by. "*Caramba* [Gee]*!*" says a dignified gentleman near us. "*Los Marinos son diablos*" (The Marines are devils).

The Hotel of the Springtime harbored a motley collection of guests. At dinner we all got together. Across from us was a Persian, enormous, fat, greasy, smiling. Next was an old German, sixty years old, at least; long-suffering from the squalor of third-class Latin American hotels, he complained bitterly but resignedly [about] the food, [about] the fighting cock crowing two feet from our table, and [about] Central America in general. The florid Irishman told us how to get by there: Drink at every bar in town, never pay but always sign for it, after a while of being in debt to everyone, they are very helpful. "Help you get a good job, sure. I owe this place $250, so see how swell they treat me?"

Lingering over our coffee, just Joe and I, debating whether to go out or turn in for the next installment of that long-deferred good sleep, we became aware of a gaunt, khaki-clad figure at the bar, drinking with evident relish several glasses of white or, rather, colorless, *aguardiente*, that standard drink of the native of Nicaragua. Perhaps I should have said that we became aware of each other, for he soon sauntered over to our table, clicked his heels together, gave a peculiar salute, and announced himself after this fashion:

"I am Major Rupert MacGloshum of the Royal Scottish Guards. Pardon my intrusion, but you seem to be of the same language as I, brothers under the skin and all that, so I beg the honor of buying you a drink. I have only this moment arrived in Managua from Rivas on the southern border, where I have uncovered a deposit of coal.˙ These samples," he motioned to several canvas sacks which lay on the floor, "are visible proof of its existence. Gentlemen, I have come to Managua to announce the discovery. You have the honor of being the first white men to learn of this stupendous discovery, a discovery which I say will reverberate through the Americas as the greatest mineral find of the century. What will you drink?"

"The same as you, major. Tell us more about this wonderful coal deposit," we answered.

We manfully swallowed several glasses of the major's drink, straight *aguardiente*, and listened while he unfolded his tale.

Harassed by jealous land owners and heckled, he intimated, by the emissaries of foreign powers which had wind of his find, the major had uncovered a tremendous coal field, the extent of which could only be guessed. In his prospecting holes he found coal, over several square miles of area.

"The only real coal fields south of the United States, a few miles from the site of the Nicaraguan canal, an event, gentlemen, of enormous economic possibilities. Further, an event which may embroil Great Britain and the United States in serious international complications. I, of course, am British. I shall immediately place this coal at the disposal of the British government. What can America do? Nothing, of course, but she will try. It is a shame for the English-speaking people to clash. But Britain is out to regain her commercial supremacy. Nothing," he banged the table,

* Rivas is on an isthmus of the same name between Lake Nicaragua and the Pacific. Its population in 2019 was around 30,000 (city) and 41,000 (metro), and its beaches are well known for their beauty and waves.

"nothing, I tell you, shall stand in the way! Hey, *mozo* (waiter)! *Tres mas aguardientes*!"

Joe almost brought the impending international crisis to a head. "Not for me. Hey, *mozo, dos mas aguardientes*. No more. I used to burn that stuff in my toy steam engine when I was a kid. Damned if I'm going to drink it now!"

The major was placated when Joe took beer. "Quite all right. Quite all right. S'long as you drink. After this one I'm going to announce my discovery to the world. Will you go with me?"

"Certainly, major, we are honored. Let's go!"

Lugging a few score pounds of the first coal ever mined south of the Rio Grande, the major's own words, we started out to announce this momentous discovery to an unsuspecting world, beginning with Managua. At Gambrinus, the first stop, the major collected a large and enthusiastic audience by simply ordering several drinks for the house.*

After three drinks, two second lieutenant Marines started to lead a cheer for "The Scotchman from Rivas, Major MacGloshum—the loosest Scotchman in captivity!" But he cut them short with a gesture. With a drink in one hand, a sack in the other, he leaped upon a chair and made his little speech. After a dramatic pause, he scattered the carboniferous contents of the sack the length of the bar room—the world knew there was coal in Nicaragua! Loud cheers! Joe was over in the corner plotting with a group at a table. As the major sat down and ordered more *aguardiente*, they swarmed around our table and boomed out, "The Campbells Are Coming."

By this time a German from Tapachula, Mexico, had joined us, at the major's request, and now they were in a bitter argument over who won the Battle of Jutland.† They were almost at blows when Frantz, the proprietor, came up with the coal his waiter had gathered up and, presenting it to the major with a bow, suggested that we go elsewhere and take it with us.

By midnight we had told half of Managua about the coal find of the century, the major had knocked down a coachman for asking for a tip, the Germans were singing, "Deutschland Uber Alles," the coal was all lost except two small lumps, and Joe and I were trying to persuade the major to go home lest these unappreciative Nicaraguan lock him up for assault and battery.‡

* Gambrinus is a mythological European hero, an icon of beer, brewing, and conviviality. His name has been given to a Czech beer and to beer halls throughout the world.

† Jutland was the largest naval battle of World War I, which both Britain and Germany claim to have won. It was the last major battle in world history fought primarily by battleships.

‡ These were the opening words of the first stanza of the German national anthem.

. . .

After reaching Managua we sold our car for $250. My brother returned home [to McDermitt, Nevada] via steamer to San Francisco. I continued on to Panama overland, walking, riding, sailing, etc., from which place I returned to New York by steamer.*

The trip from Managua down Lake Nicaragua and the San Juan River was made in company with some army engineers who were surveying the route for the proposed Nicaraguan Canal and was an extremely interesting part of the journey. From Greytown on the coast to Port Limon in Costa Rica I made my way on foot, by gasoline motorboat, by canoe, and by rail, ending up on the United Fruit Company's banana train into Port Limon. The boat was shipwrecked off the coast of Costa Rica, but the crew of two and the passenger were taken ashore by native fishermen in canoes, thereby making this letter to you possible. After spending a week or so working inland to the banana railroad I was quite ready upon reaching Limon to take passage to Panama on a United Fruit boat.

* And so, with this abrupt conclusion, Arthur ends his description of the brothers' trip. It seems likely that he originally intended to continue the description down to his departure from Panama, and the concluding paragraph bears this out.

Conclusion

# Celebrating America's Spirit of Adventure

*by Sally Denton*

I will build a motor car for the great multitude. It will be large enough for
the family, but small enough for the individual to run and care for. It will
be constructed of the best materials, by the best men to be hired, after the
simplest designs that modern engineering can devise. But it will be so low
in price that no man making a good salary will be unable to own one—
and enjoy with his family the blessing of hours of pleasure in God's great
open spaces.[*]

—HENRY FORD

Two intrepid Nevada "boys" were the first to cross transnational borders all the way
from New York City to the tip of Nicaragua. It was 1930, and automobiles built by the
Ford Motor Company were at their heyday of mass-production for the middle class.
Twenty-five-year-old Arthur Lyon documents the trip with a hand-written diary, nar-
rating his and his kid brother Joseph's adventure. Twenty-one-year-old Joe Jr. had just
arrived in New York City to visit his accountant brother while heading to the Massachusetts Institute of Technology, where he planned to enroll as an engineering student.
But the 1929 Black Tuesday crash of the New York Stock Market four months earlier
had thrown Arthur into a professional funk, and the arrival of his brother from the blue
skies of Nevada to the bleak, cold, and depressed city gave Arthur an idea.

[*] Henry Ford, as quoted in Roger Burlingame, *Henry Ford: A Great Life in Brief* (New York City, NY: Alfred
A. Knopf, 1954), 62.

"Brother Joe," Arthur writes, was "fresh to New York and burdened with nothing worse than good health, good nature and the reputation for being the fastest automobile driver in Humboldt County, Nevada." Arthur's notion began as a fantasy, but quickly took hold. "Joe . . . if you weren't planning M.I.T. next fall . . . I would venture to say we might crank up the Ford and let it lead us out of this dismal life. . . . We'll go further south than anybody ever went before in an automobile." When Arthur looked across the breakfast table at Joe whose "eyes had begun to sparkle with excitement, as eyes of twenty-one can sparkle," Arthur knew the plan was hatched.

So it was that, on March 23, 1930, they piled the rumble seat of Arthur's 1929 Model A Ford Roadster with five large suitcases, a duffel bag, cots, tent, camp equipment, soap, a bedroll, and a Kodak camera, and lit out on their fifty-four-day and 4,562-mile journey. The Roadster had replaced the eighteen-year-old Model T, and Arthur had bought it for $385. They had $324 between them, were weaponless, spoke little Spanish, and carried American passports and tourist papers, which their U.S. senator from Nevada, Tasker Oddie, provided them as a courtesy.*

Their amazing journey—at a time when Central America's Pan-American Highway was only recently envisioned and far from constructed—is part adventure story, part travelogue, and part photojournalism all wrapped up in Arthur's lively chronicle. He portrays encounters with "Tennessee hillbillies," the "utterly-commonplace of the so-called 'Bible Belt' of Arkansas," and on into Dallas—"And here, my friends, is a city," Arthur enthuses. " Just out of its swaddling clothes, it is rushing pell-mell into the manhood of skyscrapers and big business—with a vicious traffic problem thrown in for good measure. Handicapped with very narrow streets, a heritage of the Spanish era, she is bragging and boosting, and building herself into a modern city with all the accouterments."

Their excitement of moving toward the southern border—"boy, Howdy, we were leaving these United States behind us!"—is palpable. The two obviously share turns at the camera, capturing the wonderful romance of Old Mexico, the primitive streets of Guatemala, the jungles of Honduras, the rivers of Nicaragua, and on through rough "bandito" country to lush haciendas.

The Lyon brothers' journey conjures images of Mark Twain's *Adventures of Huckleberry Finn* (1885), Charles Lindbergh's *The Spirit of St. Louis* (1953), Jack Kerouac's *On the Road* (1957), and John Steinbeck's *Travels with Charley: In Search of America* (1962). In Arthur and Joe Jr.'s uniquely American quest, their epic Manhattan to Managua undertaking now takes its place in the panoply of exploration after the close of the frontier.

*See note § on the bottom of page 44.

An *Associated Press* dispatch of the brothers' amazing feat was picked up by *The Nevada State Journal* in Reno (see page 2). On June 2, 1930, the Reno paper reported that the brothers had camped out every night between March and June, "traveling unarmed and experiencing no trouble on the road." Their trusty little Roadster had made it to Managua intact, with its five original tires suffering only two punctures. They sold it for $250, and each returned separately to the U.S. by steamer, Joe Jr. to San Francisco and Arthur to New York City.

Arthur and Joe were born and bred with the pioneer nature, their forbears traveling to the Far West by covered wagons during the 1800s and settling first in the tiny Nevada town of National and then in the gold-mining camp of nearby McDermitt. They also came by their passion for transportation honestly, as grandfathers and uncles escorted wagon trains from Missouri to Oregon in the late 1880s and, in the early twentieth century, setting up a garage business that serviced bootleggers on Nevada's northern borders who were busily transporting booze to the dry states of Oregon, Idaho, and Washington. Lyon Super Service (see page 19) took advantage of the outfit's numerous cars and money to fix them. Then came Lyon Truck Lines (see page 19), conveying cargo in the post-World War I years.

After the Lyon brothers returned from their grand escapade of 1930, they spent their lives making their own contributions in transportation in Nevada and the West. By 1935, they ran the Idaho Nevada Stages and the Boise-Winnemucca Stages (see pages 24–25) by 1940. They handled every aspect of the business, from ticket sales to loading luggage, to driving the vehicles. Joe designed the Crown Super Coaches that hauled troops during World War II and, while serving in the Army, designed a tank retriever (see page 26) that would become the largest land vehicle for the American military.

This story resonates especially deeply with me, as one of my three sons recently set off on an exciting expedition nearly ninety years after the brothers launched theirs. Twenty-four-year-old Carson and a high-school buddy rode motorcycles from Santa Fe, New Mexico, to Ushuaia, Argentina, at the tip of South America. Nine months and 24,000 miles later, Carson returned to the U.S. a changed young man—evidence that the quintessentially American spirit of adventure embodied by the Lyon brothers—and the search for the last frontier—is very much alive and well in the twenty-first century.

A friendly little crap game at the forward deck of the S.S. Victoria on Lake Nicaragua. Army "Tans" vs. Nicaraguan "Browns". Army ahead by a "natural", Browns a "boxcar" behind.

# Appendix
## Arthur's Diary of His Continuing Travels to Panama
Reprinted with the permission of the Smithsonian Institution.


SUNDAY, MAY 25, 1930

Joe took the morning train to Corinto with $19, the amount we had left after selling the camp outfit. Some nibbles but no bites on Ford.


MONDAY, MAY 26

Downey decided to take Ford. No word from Joe. Decided he was O.K.


TUESDAY, MAY 27

Had a wire late afternoon from Joe. Tried all evening to send reply but wires were down. Dinner again with Downey; he advanced me $20 on car. Stevens and Ross invited me to stay at their home.


WEDNESDAY, MAY 28

Tried all day to get in touch with Joe. This climate makes one lazy. Received wire late afternoon from Joe asking for $20. Wired him $15 through Wallace. Met McWheny, at Legation, and O'Neil with West India Oil. O'Neil is from Quinto.


THURSDAY, MAY 29

Ross went to Granada. Lined me up for transportation down the San Juan River. See Lt. Caffey in Granada about it.


FRIDAY, MAY 30

Don Juan Leets is out of jail. Very interesting man. Offered to show me documents of startling nature regarding intrigues to get canal site. Met Fred Meyer, manager of Elite. Swiss from Bogota. Schlotfeldt gave me name of German to look up in Panama City, Randolf Schmacht.

### SATURDAY, MAY 31

Finally got the $250 cash for the Ford. After paying up, I have $160 left. Should leave here with $150.

### SUNDAY, JUNE 1

Up late, worked on notes and scrap book. Tried to see Bob Bernard at barracks but he had gone to Chinandega. Tried again to see Don Juan's papers, but he was not in. Spent my last evening at the Elite with Stevens, Keimbring, Don Juan and others.

### MONDAY, JUNE 2

Talked with Don Juan about C. A. situation. Showed me letters from Vail and Adams, Mexican firm, regarding canal site. Saw letter from Admiral Kimball to Madriz on April 9, 1910, praising his administration. Madriz was president from December, 1909, to August, 1910. Saw Don Juan's book "United States of Latin America." Juan Leets, L. Graham Company, Ltd., New Orleans. All very interesting material. Should work well in descriptive material on C. A. Sent $100 in bills to myself in Panama.

Left of 1:40 train for Granada to catch boat for San Carlos.

Looked up Lt. Caffey in Granada. He gave me letters to Lts. Nickols, San Carlos, Stanley, Ochoa (Camp Hoover), and Mulligan, Greytown. He assured me of trip down river in Army boat. Stayed in Granada at Alhambra. Had flashlight picture taken in Alhambra drinking beer.

### TUESDAY, JUNE 3

Embarked on S.S. Victoria for San Carlos. Presented letter from Ross to Lt. Talley. He is preparing article on Nicaragua for National Geographic. Knows Dr. Schowalter. Wants me to tell McDonald or James in U.S. Bureau of Roads that he is anxious to go North with party and make survey of Pan-American Highway.

Two privates came dashing down the pier as the boat was leaving, dived off in the water to swim out and catch it. Played 5 cent limit draw poker till 3:30 with Nicaraguan and two Army privates. Slept on cot on deck. "Just like one big family." Men, women, children. Passed San Jorge, 3 miles from Rivas, late in the afternoon. Captain did nice job docking boat in heavy swell and wind.

### WEDNESDAY, JUNE 4

Marine in Guardia and Army men on boat never speak. Realize more clearly the jealousy between services.

Docked in San Carlos about 9 o'clock. Saw Lt. Nickols and went over to Army headquarters to stay.

San Carlos, squalid little city with very historic background. It, like most other Nicaraguan cities, has been fought over for a hundred years or more. Not one wheeled vehicle in town. Sought hard tried to find one.

Heard about a private who had been too long in the jungle coming to town and after having a few drinks went to the local movie where Tom Mix was playing. When Tom reached for his gun, said private beat him to the draw and shot two holes in the screen. At date, he has two months more to do.

Talked with Mr. Kennedy, an American 78 years old who has been 45 years in Nicaragua. Interesting old chap, used to smuggle on the Caribbean down to Greytown and up the San Juan. Knew Richard H. Davis, Foster (a Gringo in Manana Land), and R. Halliburton. Said Davis was an ass, Foster was a gentleman, and Halliburton an old woman.

Used to drink with Davis in Managua. Said he wore a monocle and that all the "real guys," including himself, used to sneak out on him and leave him to drink alone.

Foster came through as a tramp but he realized he wasn't when he cashed a draft for $200.

Halliburton had his young brother with him, a sickly fellow. He told Kennedy they were going to take a canoe down the Amazon.

Kennedy showed me letter from American Boy and his answer.

Talked Army and Navy all evening with Lt. Nickols.

Boat touched at 6 a.m. at San Miguelito. Dragged in the mud last three miles to San Carlos.


THURSDAY, JUNE 5

Started down the river in Army launch with two pontons loaded with supplies for camps along the way. The San Juan River is gorgeous vistas of green and as placid as the well known mill stream. We made only six miles an hour or so with the heavy load. The river at its source and before its confluence with the San Carlos, about half way down, is two hundred yards or so wide. From there down it is about 300 yards wide.

We say one monkey in a tree on the bank.

There is very little color in the vegetation, just an unvaried but beautiful green.

After dinner at Camp Hoover (Ochoa), we went over to the Costa Rican side to visit with an officer, his wife, and two other women.

Saw a few sharks on the way down. They catch them frequently.

Down river in launch Menocal.

Passed the rapids and fortress of El Castillo around noon. Here, so tis said, is where Lord Nelson lost his eye when he was a junior officer in the British Navy.

Old dredges abandoned by canal company which started work in 1895.

Enlisted men returning to the job of surveying a canal route down the San Juan River.

Mess call in the tropics. Floating between river banks covered with beautiful tropical jungle growth. At 5 A.M. and 5 P.M. the monkeys barked back and forth to each other making a great racket.

Luncheon aboard Army convoy down the San Juan River. First from the left, in the act of swallowing a large piece of "Corned Bill" is the well known Typical Tropical Tramp, Arthur Lyon.

Unloading supplies from U.S. Army launch at Camp Hoover, San Juan River, Nicaragua.

Camp Hurley, Army camp 1 ½ miles from [sic] Greytown, Atlantic terminus of the proposed Nicaraguan canal.

Near the point where the San Juan River diverges, part emptying into the Atlantic at Greytown and part at Boca Del Colorado.

U.S. Army enlisted men catch up on their reading.

Mr. Wiltshire, Collector of Customs for the pot of Greytown, Nicaragua holding
a portrait drawing of President Moncada drawn by a 12 year old Nicaraguanese.

FRIDAY, JUNE 6

Up at five for an early start from Ochoa. We have two more pontons heavily loaded with drilling machinery which makes the going slow. Regular, symmetrical, natural hedges along river look like L. I. estates.

We went up the Deseado River, a small tributary near the mouth of the San Juan to an Army camp ten miles away. There, near the ruins of an old R.R. bridge built by the old Nicaraguan Canal Construction Co., subsidiary of Maritime Canal Construction Co., we left the two pontons of diamond drilling machinery and walked into Camp Hurley, 1 ½ miles from Greytown over the old R.R. grade.

These Army engineers certainly have their work cut out for them on this survey. Each traverse that they run means cutting a path thru the jungle and often as not wading thru a swamp. They are very cheerful about the whole thing tho and one hears very little grumbling, just a desire to go back to the States as soon as possible

Walked into Greytown to find out about a possible boat. Greytown used to be an important port when the San Juan was used as the port of entry for Managua. It had consuls of many countries and was perhaps the most important port on the east coast of C.A. Now it resembles a deserted mining camp. Tried unsuccessfully to democratize the Army, arguing with two young Lieutenants.

SATURDAY, JUNE 7

10 a.m. No boat yet. Worked on notes. Camp Hurley a nice stopping place at that. Picked up souvenir, stamp of Vanderbilt's old trans-Nicaraguan R.R.

Bought pair Army shoes.

Heard boat was coming in early Monday. Telegram, or rather radio, regarding same was rather obtuse.

SUNDAY, JUNE 8

Up at four o'clock to walk into Greytown. The Corporal of the guard awoke me and showed me over to the R.R. tracks. I noticed a light burning a short distance down the right of way. I asked what for? The guard said to keep the tigers away from the cattle. As it was pitch dark (the jungle came together over the tracks forming a sort of bower), I must confess I didn't tackle that mile-and-a-half walk into town with all the confidence in the world. I had heard the men around camp mention tigers before, but had thought nothing of it. I made a resolution during that walk to get a firearm of some sort at the first opportunity.

We rowed out to the bar and waited three hours in the rain. No boat. Back to camp and read the rest of day.

Walked into Greytown again and paid $5 for the privilege of walking most of the way to Colorado Bar. Went part way in a cayuca. Got plenty wet. Found there was small govt. boat leaving in morning for Parismina. Took picture of Mr. Wiltshire and wife. Also of drawing of Pres. Moncada drawn by 12 year old Nicaraguan boy.

Govt. boat was in bad shape. Not supposed to carry passengers. Capt. Said O.K. tho.

Distance Greytown to Colorado 16 miles.

These Jamaica negroes all talk with a typical English accent and use the English idioms. Sounds very strange to hear one say "I 'cawnt' help you, old 'chap.' Why man! My bloody boat is done in."

Found boat was worse than anticipated. 20 ft. launch 25 years old. Two cycle one cylinder motor same age. I had to wire the engine for the "engineer" and fix a pulley for the rudder rope before we could get away. Crossing the Colorado bar I regretted for a few minutes that I had started in such a shell. The going was better outside the bar, however, altho the engine coughed, wheezed, and stopped several times. Not exactly the kind of boat one wanted to be out in the Caribbean in.

The engine stopped dead finally. After two hours persuasion, during which I scanned the ocean with futile gaze searching for a sail, it started again but without much force.

We did manage to head into Tortuguero Bar, however. The Capt. wasn't so good, however, and instead of heading in straight the first breaker caught us sideways. We shipped about ten gal. of water and the coil and battery fell down the sump. With no power we had no control and how that shell did wallow! The spray was crashing in over the side and had the engine soaked. I did manage to get it rewired but as everything was shorted the damn thing ran backward. We put it in reverse to get some forward motion. The Capt. saw the position of the control and deserted his post to run back and put it forward.

At that moment a breaker larger than any before cracked us broadside, everything movable washed into the sump, and the fun was on!

We had managed to signal some native fishermen on shore. Two of them finally ran the breakers and reached us in cayuca. They took off the Capt's sister and small daughter and said they would be back for us. They never came. Too many sharks I guess.

I started to strip down to swim ashore but the Capt. said it was sure death from sharks. This looked like a hell of a place to die, down on the Costa Rican shore miles from anywhere, but I couldn't figure out any alternative. We were drifting away from shore and at the rate we were shipping water she couldn't stay up many minutes. It was useless to bail. For every bucketful you threw out about fifty gallons came in.

We had a small cayuca tied on behind but it was smashed almost to pieces from banging against the hull. I wanted the Capt. to take me ashore in it but (figure this one out) he was going to stay with his ship! I finally prevailed, however, so we started out in what was left of it. We capsized once and I expected to find myself in two pieces from a shark bite. This was my lucky day tho and we made it. He went back out and got the engineer. That poor fellow had a badly smashed finger but he was game to stay as long as the Capt. did.

We stood on shore and waited for the boat to go down but it righted itself after every breaker and kept afloat. Those breakers were sometimes ten ft. or more high.

Finally the sea calmed a little and I bribed one of those native fishermen for $5 to go out and get what was left of my luggage.

After a bit the tide turned and the S.S. America floated in near land and they all went out in their cayucas, tied on ropes and dragged it ashore.

I am sleeping tonight with these same native fishermen.

Am I blue! Everything I own soaked. Films, books, and clothes as good as ruined. But then it is a nice feeling to be on tierra firma at that. I am not as blue as I thot I was.

WEDNESDAY, JUNE 11

Up at two o'clock. Had a cup of coffee just at sun-up at a native shack, unpeopled of course, surrounded by the real old jungle.

Paddled 17 miles down the lagoon. From one spot within a period of five minutes I saw respectively a big monkey, a parrot, a tarpon, and a vicious looking snake.

At five o'clock the moneys began barking at each other in the tills alongside. They are the only timepieces out here in the jungle. At five a.m. and 5 p.m. they start barking and keep it up for perhaps 15 minutes.

Then I dragged, carried, and hauled my 75 lbs. of luggage a mile through the jungle to the beach. There I got a horse to carry my suitcase while I plodded 8 miles down the beach, with only a sack of clothes, to Parismina. The horse bucked my bag off into the ocean but the additional soaking didn't do it any further harm.

This was all before breakfast. I ate and had a drink of water, the first today, in Parismina, and hired a boatman to take me 9 miles up the river to a banana planta-tion owned by two Americans, Chas. E. Scott and Walter H. Scott.

I got food and a bed from them. They have a twin-engined launch 42 ft. long carved out of the trunk of a single tree. It certainly is a beautiful piece of craftsman-ship. The pilot house is raised up three ft. above the deck level.

We leave at four in the morning for a 25 mile trip up the river with a boatload of bananas. There I can get a fruit train Saturday morning for Limon.

THURSDAY, JUNE 12

Started up the Parismina River on launch with two boatloads of bananas in tow at 4 a.m. Volcanoes of central Costa Rica in view. Parismina looks for all the world like the San Juan River in Guatemala. Greeted at 5 o'clock with monkey chorus.

At a point 15 miles from Parismina we swung up the Reventazon River. 15 miles further and we were at Ana Farm. There the bananas were unloaded. A young native boy with two bunches of bananas on his shoulders, each weighing 60 or 70 lbs., would scoot up the steep bank as if it were the easiest thing he did.

I learned a few things about bananas. Each tree produces only one bunch. It is cut down when the bunch is cut and a new tree planted. This farm of Scotts' produces about 1300 bunches per week. Mostly the smaller, greener fruit for the English trade. From the time the banana is cut until it reaches the market, in U.S. or England, each operation is timed almost to the hour. The cutting and hauling to the R.R. here is done at the last possible moment. After the cutting is started they work day and night until the bananas are on the train bound for Limon. The banana train reaches Limon at the same time as the fruit boat when the cargo is immediately transferred and started to New York. Even the green fruit is very delicate and must be protected from the sun and all abrasion. The natives who handle the bunches are barefooted of course and if a bunch is dropped and bruised it must be discarded.

I am stopping tonight with Mr. Wright at Ana Farm. I finally got my belongings spread out to dry. They are a sorry looking lot. Maps, pictures, clothes, undeveloped films, Kodak et cetera have been soaked in sea water for 48 hours.

Scott asked me to look up Davis at the legation in Panama.

These negroes down here, mostly of Jamaican descent, are good cooks. The food is 100% better than that of the C.A. natives.

FRIDAY, JUNE 13

Finished drying out my things this morning. Not so bad after all. Ready to leave in the evening. Mr. Joseph Wright, my host, said the bill was $1.75 oro. His Jamaican wife came around when he was away and said to forget it. As I had only a $10 Nicaraguan bill which I could not get exchanged, I had promised to send the money from Panama.

10 p.m. and my train came in. I went down and watched them load the bananas. The way those black boys threw 800 bunches, Scott's shipment, on board was beautiful to see; big, shiny, ebony men, playing basketball with 70 lb. bunches.

I climbed into the first car and we roared thru the night with 6800 bunches aboard. It was Friday the 13th, we were on a 13-car train, and there were thirteen besides myself on this car. I wonder if they knew how lucky they were that I was aboard to make 14.

First stop La Junta; then across the Reventazon River to Siquirres; then 40 miles through the jungles and banana farms to Limon. It was a white moonlit night. Our cigarettes glowed in the darkness of the car while outside flowed by—the tropicos! I dozed off. Soon the cars jerked to a stop. We were in Limon, the greatest banana port in the world. To bed in a cheap rooming house.

SATURDAY, JUNE 14

Late breakfast. Lose $2.50 on exchange on $10 bill. Robbers. Down to see American consul, Mr. Malcady. Good egg. Had been fishing up at Tortuguero Lagoon; verified my story that sharks were thick. Said he had seen over 100 at the bar. We talked a lot. He lent me $8, deck fare (3rd class), to Panama and severed some red tape relieving me from paying a head tax to leave C.R., also getting them to waive the qualification that I have $200 in my possession (a requisite for deck passengers entering Panama).

Sailed at 5 o'clock on S.S. Calamares, United Fruit boat. Down among the machinery with the rest of the bums. I had a letter to the purser, however, from Mr. Malcady and he found me a cabin for the night. All thrilled over this—my first ocean trip. Not so exciting though. The Caribbean is as calm as a lake, in fact much smoother than Lake Managua.

Limon is a smart little port. Paved streets and a beautiful waterfront. It is by far the most attractive city of its size I have seen in C.A. The vista from the breakwater is heady. A small, palm covered isle lies half a mile or so away. Then Lady Caribbean beams at you and her dress is as blue as an artist can paint. Away in the distance a few mountains show deep blue above the horizon and over it all lies a typical tropical mantle of scattered clouds and embryo rainstorm—a rainstorm is always brewing over the Caribbean.

SUNDAY, JUNE 15

I was weary. Up just in time to get called up on deck to interview the immigration authorities. Lied blandly—said I had $175—they courteously enough didn't ask to see it. Sailing smoothly into Cristobal. Straining eyes for look at canal entrance. Hurried by custom inspection without even noticing it to catch train for Panama. Sent back at gate for inspection seals. Made Panama train two minutes to spare, rode second class with blacks and browns. Panama R.R. trains ramble. Beautiful ride with stately parade of ships making canal passage on right, Panama jungle on left. Into Panama City. Cab to Army and U Y.M.C.A. Fine clean quarters with little fuzzy-headed, Christian director leading the boys in community singing and other harmless pastimes.

MONDAY, JUNE 16

Took stock and inventory. Send two armloads of clothes to be washed. Settled down in my corduroy and tan shirt to reading Forster's "A Gringo in Manana Land," Franck's "Tramping Thru Mexico, Guatemala and Honduras" and Halliburton's "New Worlds to Conquer." Can't decide whether to go on or go back. My $100 was safely at consulate and one letter from Bert.

Gorging myself on ice cream. Panama rather unlovely as are all Latin American cities whose business almost exclusively is catering to the American tourists. Every other business is a bar. Colon and Ancon in the Zone by contrast are lovely places. Here the Americans have built a city, almost exclusively residential in character, with broad curving streets in which every vacant lot is veritable park with every conceivable kind of tropical tree and shrubbery.

Arrived in Panama City with $1.05.

TUESDAY, JUNE 17

Spent morning and afternoon still in seclusion waiting for clothes. In evening I trotted down to Star and Herald and gave them a little story on my trip. Tried out Kelly's Ritz about ten o'clock. Met manager. Gave me the low down on every celebrity who has been to Panama. Said they carried Byrd out every morning he was here. Evelyn Nesbit just finished a month's engagement.

WEDNESDAY, JUNE 18

Called on Mr. Thomas LaGuardia, head of Dept. of Highways for Panama at the Palacio National and presented my letter from Senator Oddie. He was most gracious and offered me a trip to Santiago as guest of the govt over the new highway. I accepted. To go on Friday. Still undecided whether to go over and call on Dr. Dickie on the Orinoco or to go back to New York.

THURSDAY, JUNE 19

Spent most of day in Library. Why the devil can't I figure out where to go from here. Have about $80, perhaps that is one reason. Now, if I had $100 there would be only one thing to do, go down the Orinoco of course. But I need a raincoat and a packsack and a gun. How can I buy them and still have enough to do it puzzles even my optimistic figuring. Well, I settle that manana.

Away at 8:00 with Mr. Arosemena (a distant relative of the President) for Santiago. He and I and $11,500 in currency was for the payroll. We drove north 9 miles along the canal then ferried across just above Pedro Miguel locks, just south of Culebra Cut. The road then led out through the hills west of the canal, winding around them in the most startling curves. At San Carlos, 65 miles out, we stopped for an early luncheon then drove 100 miles up a broad level, almost treeless plain to Santiago, 168 miles from Panama. There we delivered our precious cargo and there I met Dr. Calinto A. Fabrega "Medico-Ciragano," LaGuardia's father-in-law. He graduated from Columbia in '85, had an M.D. degree. We talked about Panama. He was here before and after the revolution. He said the revolutions and rebels before the U.S. took Panama under its wing kept them all broke. Now—and he pointed around eloquently—fat cattle, good farms, good horses. He was no anti-imperialist.

Sign on roadside building a short distance from Zone, "International Garage, Expert Mechanic, D.C. Wells Prop." What appeared to be Mr. Wells was sitting in his garage sipping contentedly on a glass of beer. A "Bamboo American" but a happy one.

Although my trip was most pleasant.

SATURDAY, JUNE 21

Back to New York! A decision once made is a pleasant thing to look back on. This one is no exception. No more beans and rice, no more ticks and red bugs, no more blistering walks in the sand. That's that. I guess I'll have to go down to Kelly's Ritz and squander a few more dollars just to be good and broke before I start. But after all I wish I had the $100. It's in my blood now. I'll stay in New York just long enough to get a stake.

SUNDAY, JUNE 22

Climbed Ancon Hill in the heat of the day. Nice view. Now I can get oriented. Before Ancon, Balboa and Panama were hopelessly muddled.

MONDAY, JUNE 23

Met Mitchell Hedges, well known "Hearst" explorer who, with Lady Brown, has returned from a trip in Mosquitio gathering archaeological specimens (I suppose) and more good yarns to purvey to the dear, and gullible public. His yarns sometimes have the ring of untrue exaggeration but who knows? Who else has been there to tell a different story? And another thing, Mr. Hedges has many, many letters after his name, is a member of societies without number, so has prestige to back up that which he says.

Taxied out to Miraflore Locks and was shown the "works" by Messrs.

The control room is a magical place. Do we wish that lock filled and that lock closed? Then, we turn these little handles and, as if by magic surely, ten million gallons of water flow to the designated lock, ten thousand tons of ship rises thirty feet, and seven hundred tons of lock swing silently into recess.

No! It isn't real! That's a toy ship on a millpond manned by ants and towed by tiny toy locomotives. She steams away toward a tiny rocky crevice called Culebra Cut and disappears, leaving only a thin wisp of smoke and a tiny wave expanding across our millpond.

Thus does Man's greatest single effort impress Man. It is all so simple, so easy. How could twenty thousand men sweat and toil for ten long years to bring into creation this magnificent toy which does a Herculean task so quietly and so efficiently that it is less impressive than a single steam shovel charging full tilt into Mother Earth.

The illusion of the miniature is still further enhanced by the control mechanism down the center of the control room. Here indeed is a glorified toy. Synchronized with the massive mechanism outside are tiny locks and chains going thru the same motions as their huge counterparts, the real locks and chains.

The United States government comes in for her share of criticism, some of it no doubt deserved, but where, I ask you, is an organization that could build the Panama Canal? Who could stamp out yellow fever and malaria and provide healthy homes for ten thousand American men and women in the tropics? Who could? At least who has?

My American Passport I have regarded as more or less of a necessary evil, something to be visaed, something to be presented when halted by a native guardia, a barefooted soldier or other outpost of law, order, and customs. I take it out and examine it again, this red-bound little volume of visas, health stamps, and official signatures in all degrees of illegibility and erasure. It has not the bright color nor fresh appearance it once had. It has been soaked in sea water, the pages are sweat-stained and the edges are crumpled. It is bent into a curve from being carried in a hip pocket, ready to be whipped out and shown to anyone who might challenge my right to pass. And I turn to page two, there it says among other things that the bearer, Arthur Lyon, is 5 ft. nine inches tall, has blond hair and blue eyes and *is an American citizen*. I am proud to be the bearer of this passport, I am proud to be an American citizen.

Little old red book, go back to that pocket and stay there. You only cost me ten dollars and your life is only two years but what is that you say? Arthur Lyon ——— is an American citizen!

Tried to rise at 5:30 to catch the Colon train at 7:00. Arose at 6:30 and caught the train at 7:10. Second class passage between two big black boys. The ride only lost one hour and 45 min. though. Second class $1.15, saving half.

Around Cristobal with a hopeless desire to book a $40 passage to New York. (Called on Ford incidentally.) There is no 5th class sailing from Colon so I buy $37.50 worth of transportation, which amount carries me to Havana, on the M.V. Santa Rita of the "Casa Grace."

I board her and suppress a reckless desire to give my "cargadore" the $1.85 which I have left. Instead I give him a dime and he gives me a scowl which we part the best of enemies and I seek out stateroom 50 which is on the "intermediate" deck. "Intermediate," that now is a word to conjure with. It means "between" does it not? A Christian and a gentleman would call it steerage—which it is. The only thing it's between is the devil and the deep blue sea.

My cabin mate is most agreeable young fellow, 23, a Bostonian, and from Boston Tech., by name Charles Mapes. He has been "puttin' on the Ritz" in Quito and what with a country home, rented for $100 a month, a butler "with a little brass buttoned sea jacket" and a big-hearted American manner. I guess he did it. And how! From what I gather he did everything it is possible to do in Quinto except "make" the President's daughter and it was just "one of life's little tragedies," due to the boat's sailing too soon, that that highly desirable event did not come to pass—thus cheating America out of another "peaceful conquest."

At any rate, Mapes and I hit it off together in great shape and have just about decided on a partnership to explore the Orinoco and the Amazon together. Either that or sail a schooner to the Galapagos or yet to cross the U.S. in a canoe with an outboard motor.

WEDNESDAY, JUNE 25

Just another day wasted away. I sleep and eat and sleep some more. Our cabin isn't so bad after all. Meant for four it is quite comfortable for two.

THURSDAY, JUNE 26

Mapes and I explore the ship. We decided to carry our mattresses up to the top deck aft and sleep under the stars tonight. He agrees to take my baggage on to New York in case I am unable to consummate my plan of stowing away from Havana. A few flying fishes and a U.F. steamer break the monotony.

4 p.m. All's well aboard. Mapes is snoozing quietly enough and I am writing these dumb notes.

Jenni Lyon as a contestant on CBS's *Survivor* in 2004. Photographer unknown.
Reproduced courtesy of CBS.

# Acknowledgments

I express my heartfelt thanks to my deceased Aunt Bertha Blattner Lyon, who was married to my Uncle Arthur, the true author of this book. For thirty years she remained a loyal friend and business partner of Arthur until his death. Bertha was known for her generosity and her support and encouragement of young people, including me. She honored me with the pleasant task of helping her make copies of the original 1985 manuscript as it existed a number of years ago, in spiral-bound form, at a Kinko's store in Reno, to send to friends and family. She also entrusted me with the original manuscript, the negatives of the photographs in the book, and the wonderful scrapbook full of photos, clippings, and official documents.

I want to thank my brothers, Dave and Gary Lyon, for their support, encouragement, and suggestions about publishing this book that means so much to our family. I also want to thank Dave's wife, Jackie, who provided historic details about some of the events depicted in my introduction to the book. I also thank my stepmother, Betty Mattheus, for making a significant financial contribution to the project. She played a key role in my early years in Virginia City, and her kindness and support are treasured memories.

My daughter, Jenni, appreciated the importance to me of having this book published, which was made clearer when we found, after her death from breast cancer in 2010, a "wish pillow" containing a note written by Jenni stating her wish that the book would be published and made into a movie with her in the female lead role. This wish, along with her indomitable spirit during her struggles with cancer, gives me the strength and courage to persist, and I plan to donate a portion of my proceeds from sales of the book to cancer awareness, research, and support in her name. I also want to thank my ex-wife, Jane, our daughter, Kim, son, Mark, and grandsons, Tyler and Mikel, for allowing me the time and space to pursue my dream of publication.

While I had little or no awareness of this book as a child, my memories of the main characters—uncles Arthur and Joe—are filled with examples of their kindness, generosity, and fascinating personalities. I'm honored to be sharing their story, which

Arthur Lyon, early 1940s, in front of the office of Boise-Winnemucca
Stages in Boise, Idaho. Photographer unknown.

exemplifies their lifelong friendship and partnership, with the rest of the world. And I am equally honored that my full name is Lawrence Joseph Lyon and that both uncles but especially Arthur called me LJ.

While I made some attempts to find a publisher for the book for a number of years, it was through a chance conversation with my good friend, Sally Denton, award-winning journalist and author, that the project began to take shape. I can't thank Sally enough for her advice and support along the way, including the gift of her afterword.

Sally's first suggestion was to ask her friend, Joanna Hurley, to act as my agent in finding a publisher. I'm eternally indebted to Joanna for finding a publisher, George F. Thompson, who immediately appreciated the book's worth and agreed to help develop and publish it. I'm also deeply indebted to Joanna, for her support and patience in guiding me through the process.

After some initial editing of the manuscript, George Thompson asked Denis Wood, the esteemed author, historian of cartography, and artist, to provide annotations to the original text. He and George then worked their magic. It has been a great honor to have Denis's expertise in adding to the cultural and geographical depth of the book.

I recently drove to Santa Fe with the priceless negatives of the photos in the book, the original manuscript, and the scrapbook full of photos, documents, and newspaper clippings from Arthur and Joe's journey and shared them with the designer of the book, David Skolkin, who is known for his skill in book designing. His enthusiasm in bringing this book to life was evident as we looked at all of the materials, and I'm thrilled to have him as part of the team. Thanks, also, to Mikki Soroczak, for her extensive editorial research and for preparing the manuscript, and to Morgan Pfaelzer, for preparing the three maps.

Finally, I want to thank George Thompson for agreeing to publish this book. The quality of books published by George, along with his reputation for developing and bringing to publication a wide array of important award-winning books about the road and American culture, from *The National Road* and *Route 66* to *The Great Valley Road of Virginia*, will surely establish Arthur and Joe's story as a testament to American ingenuity, persistence, and adventure. From the beginning George and I knew that this book is *sui generis*, but we also agreed it should be valued as much as a documentary history as a work for the armchair reader.

# About the Contributors

*Sally Denton*, born in Elko, Nevada, in 1953, is a third-generation Nevadan. She attended the University of Nevada-Reno before completing her B.A. at the University of Colorado in Boulder in 1974. Denton received a Lannan Literary Grant in 2000, Western Heritage Awards in 2002 and 2004, and a John Simon Guggenheim Memorial Foundation Fellowship in General Nonfiction in 2006. In 2008, she was inducted into the Nevada Writers Hall of Fame. Her career as an investigative reporter resulted in articles in *The Washington Post*, *Penthouse*, *The New York Times*, *Columbia Journalism Review*, and *American Heritage*. Her books include *The Bluegrass Conspiracy: An Inside Story of Power, Greed, Drugs, and Murder* (Doubleday, 1990); *The Money and the Power: The Making of Las Vegas and Its Hold on America* (Alfred A. Knopf, 2001), which was made into a documentary film broadcast on the History Channel; *American Massacre: The Tragedy at Mountain Meadows, September 1857* (Alfred A. Knopf, 2006); *Passion and Principle: John and Jessie Frémont, the Couple Whose Power, Politics, and Love Shaped Nineteenth-Century America* (Bloomsbury, 2007); *The Plots Against the President: FDR, a Nation in Crisis, and the Rise of the American Right* (Bloomsbury, 2012); and *The Profiteers: Bechtel and the Men Who Built the World* (Simon & Schuster, 2016). Denton resides in Santa Fe, New Mexico, and Boulder City, Nevada, and her Website is *www.sallydenton.com*.

*Denis Wood* was born and raised in Cleveland, Ohio, where he graduated from Western Reserve University with a B.A. in English. He received his M.A. and Ph.D. in geography from Clark University in Worcester, Massachusetts, where he subsequently taught high school. From 1973 until 1996, he taught environmental psychology and design at the College of Design at North Carolina State University, where he was Professor of Design and Landscape Architecture. Author of *The Power of Maps* (Guilford Press, 1992), he also curated the award-winning Cooper-Hewitt National Museum of Design exhibition of the same name (subsequently mounted at the Smithsonian Institution in Washington, D.C.). With Robert J. Beck, he co-authored *Home Rules* (The Johns Hopkins University Press, in association with the Center for American Places, 1994) about the transmission of culture that occurs in the process of "living a room." The book was designated one of the top 100 geography books of all time by the Royal Geographical Society. His other book publications include *Weaponizing Maps: Indigenous Peoples and Counterinsurgency in the Americas*, with Joe Bryan (Guilford Press, 2015), *Everything Sings: Maps for a Narrative Atlas* (Siglio Press, 2010; Second Edition, 2013), *Rethinking the Power of Maps* (Guilford Press, 2010), *The Natures of Maps: Cartographic Constructions of the Natural World*, with John Fels (University of Chicago Press, 2008); *Making Maps: A Visual Guide to Map Design for GIS*, with John Krygier (Guilford Press, 2005; Second Edition, 2011; Third Edition, 2016); *Five Billion Years of Global Change: A History of the Land* (Guilford Press, 2004); and *Seeing through Maps: The Power of Images to Shape Our World View*, with Ward L. Kaiser and Bob Abramms (ODT, 2001; Second Edition, 2005). Wood also exhibits his artwork and lectures widely. He has long resided in Raleigh, North Carolina.

## About the Editor

*Larry (Lawrence Joseph* or *LJ) Lyon* was born in 1947 in Reno, Nevada, and he grew up in Reno and Boulder City, Nevada. He completed his B.A. in psychology at the University of Nevada, Las Vegas, and his M.S. in experimental psychology and Ph.D. in clinical psychology, both at Washington State University. Since 1979, he has worked in the mental-health field in a variety of settings, including nineteen years in private practice in The Dalles, Oregon. Lyon currently works for the Veterans Health Administration in Las Vegas. He resides in Boulder City, Nevada.

## About the Book

*1930: Manhattan to Managua, North America's First Transnational Automobile Trip* was brought to publication in an edition of 1,000 hardcover copies. The text was set in Adobe Caslon, the paper is Hansol, 120 gsm weight, and the book was professionally printed and bound by PChan and Edwards in Korea.

Project Director and Publisher: George F. Thompson
Literary Agent and Editorial Advisor: Joanna Hurley
Editorial and Research Assistant: Mikki Soroczak
Manuscript Editor: Purna Makaram
Book Design and Production: David Skolkin

*Special Acknowledgements*: The publisher and Larry Lyon express special gratitude to Joanna Hurley, for all her efforts, and to those whose generosity made this book possible.

Published in 2020. First hardcover edition.
Printed in Korea on acid-free paper.

George F. Thompson Publishing, L.L.C.
217 Oak Ridge Circle
Staunton, VA 24401–3511, U.S.A.
www.gftbooks.com

28 27 26 25 24 23 22 21 20     1 2 3 4 5

The Library of Congress Preassigned Control Number is 2019948060.

ISBN: 978–1–938086–67–0